A New Book

A New Book of Dubliners

SHORT STORIES OF MODERN DUBLIN

edited by Ben Forkner,
with a preface by Benedict Kiely

A Methuen Paperback

A Methuen Paperback

First published in Great Britain 1988
by Methuen London
Michelin House, 81 Fulham Road, London SW3 6RB

This collection copyright © 1988 Ben Forkner
Preface copyright © 1988 Benedict Kiely
Introduction copyright © 1988 Ben Forkner

Photoset by Rowland Phototypesetting Ltd
Bury St Edmunds, Suffolk
Printed and bound in Great Britain by
Cox & Wyman Ltd, Reading, Berkshire

British Library Cataloguing in Publication Data

A New book of Dubliners.
1. Short stories in English. Irish
writers, 1900–. Special subjects. Dublin –
Anthologies
I. Forkner, Ben
823′.01′083241835[FS]

ISBN 0–413–18850–7

For Anthony and Liana
And for Nadine (and Knocknarea)

Contents

Acknowledgements

First and foremost, I wish to thank Ben Kiely and Frances for their many kindnesses all through the making of this collection. Ben's sparkling preface is a wonderful gift from a man who has been generous with wonders from the day he began writing. To Dublin itself, and to many kind Dubliners, I owe all manner of debts, and a crowd of fine memories. I first saw Dublin twenty-five years ago and, for me, one warm, slow-moving summer spent there in the 1960's has long been canonized among all the other good times Ireland has given me. Seen from the early morning boat from Holyhead, or from one of the hills near Dalkey, Dublin was a beautiful, shifting city by the sea: one moment close to the earth, half-hidden in shadow, dim and domestic as the bottom of a basket; a moment later taking to the air, a misty amphitheatre of steeples and chimney-pots under a revelling, operatic sky: a tidal city tasting of salt and governed everywhere by moving water, falling and flowing. It was a good city to walk in, and out of, and a good city to come back to, day or night. For all those Dubliners I should thank, a representative few will have to do: the two sisters, one very small, the older probably eight or so, who had stepped into cold water on a beach in Dun Laoghaire (when the little sister yelled out 'I'm frozen,' the older answered at once, 'You are not, you're only freezing.' I knew then, on my first day in Dublin, that I would have to watch everything I said); the soft-spoken milkman who slowed his horse every morning knowing how much I liked the sound of the hooves to last; the fatherly gardener I briefly worked for and who hired me simply to have someone to talk to (he told me right from the beginning, 'Keep the shears clipping, like a good barber, but for all our sakes don't touch the hedge.' Good advice that I've always tried to keep); the pub singer who sold me a car for five pounds and enabled me to get to Cork as quickly as I thought I needed to (he couldn't be blamed for having forgotten that he did not actually own the car. He saw that I was desperate, and out of his immense kindness did what he could to help me out); the unbewilderable Dublin policeman who took the train to Cork to hunt me down (he told me on the train ride back that all he wanted was the starting-key; the car itself, he confided kindly to me, was worth nothing, and was now officially abandoned in Cork. I had been in Dublin long enough not to insult him or me by asking him why he needed the key); the exuberant and adventurous group of medical students, all loyal in a brawl, who made me part of their gang and showed me Dublin, night after night, pub after pub (one unforgettable evening we gathered thirty other students and hiked into the hills. Around a bonfire these students recited poetry, sang songs, and performed scenes from Shakespeare until late the next morning). There are many more I should mention, but the page is short. Finally, each of the following has made an essential contribution to this book: Vivien Igoe and her mother Eileen Veale, David Marcus, Sean White, Frank Kernowski, Weldon and Barbara Thornton, Professor Jean Noël, Patrick Samway, Richard A. Stokes, my parents Mr and Mrs O. C. Peterson, my brother John, my son Benjamin, my colleagues and students at the University of Angers, Madame Ivonne Buchmann, and my editor at Methuen, Geoffrey Strachan. As for the dedication, it will have to stand, incompletely, for a feeling of gratitude, admiration, and love I will never be able to fully express.

'Ivy Day in the Committee Room' was first published by Jonathan Cape Ltd in *Dubliners* and is reprinted by permission of the Executors of the James Joyce Estate.

'The Tramp' was first published by Jonathan Cape Ltd in *The Short Stories of Liam O'Flaherty* and is reprinted by permission of the Estate of Liam O'Flaherty.

'Schoolfellows' from *Desire* is reprinted by permission of The Society of Authors on behalf of the copyright owner, Mrs Iris Wise.

'Dante and the Lobster' is reprinted by permission of John Calder (Publishers) Ltd.

'Old Friery' from *Tumbling in the Hay* is reprinted by permission of Sphere Books Ltd.

'Drink and Time in Dublin' is reprinted by permission of the Estate of the late Flann O'Brien.

'Ballintierna in the Morning' from *The Lion Tamer* is reprinted by permission of A. P. Watt Ltd on behalf of Bryan MacMahon.

'A Walk Through the Summer' from *The Trusting and the Maimed* is reprinted by permission of A. D. Peters & Co Ltd.

'A Change of Management' is reprinted by permission of A. D. Peters & Co Ltd.

'Charlie's Greek' by Sean O'Faolain is reprinted by permission of A. P. Watt Ltd on behalf of Sean O'Faolain. And by permission of Little, Brown and Company, from *The Heat of the Sun: Stories and Tales*; copyright © 1963, 1965, 1966.

'A Memory' is reprinted by permission of Constable Publishers.

'A Ball of Malt and Madame Butterfly' is reprinted by permission of A. P. Watt Ltd on behalf of Benedict Kiely. And by permission of David R. Godine, Publisher, from *The State of Ireland* by Benedict Kiely; copyright © 1980 by Benedict Kiely.

'Not Quite The Same' from *Yarns* is reprinted by permission of John Jordan.

'Bank Holiday' from *High Ground* is reprinted by permission of Faber and Faber Ltd.

Preface

Heaven knows and heaven, or Eamonn de Valera, be thanked, the appalling bombs of the Second World War did not fall on Dublin as they fell on cities from Coventry to Dresden to Stalingrad to Hiroshima. For even the most devoted admirer of what is left of Dublin Georgian architecture would have worried about the ability of many of the old houses to stand up to a tremor any greater than that caused by the passing of a double-decker bus. But there was one hot summer night in 1941 when, by a never fully explained chance of war, a few bombs fell on Dublin and on a part of it well-remembered by James Joyce; and it should have been my luck to be right in the middle, halfways between the German message that landed on Summerhill Parade and the much more calamitous one that descended on the North Strand Road.

When the guns opened up from Howth Head, or from the heads of the giant in *Finnegans Wake*, I, in a house in Ballybough, put my head out of the bedroom window to see what was going on, until the blinding flash from the North Strand persuaded me that that was not a spectator sport. Then my brother-in-law, Thomas Stanley, a true Dubliner and, even more so, a Dublinman, headed out to see what had happened and what we could do to help.

At the corner of North Richmond Street, off the North Circular Road, a man told us that in an upstairs room in his house, the windows being open to the warm night, the blast had lifted a chair from the floor and smashed it against the wall. Nothing else in the house had even been disturbed; and the man's aged father had slept through the whole hassle, gravitating bombs and levitating chair, and hadn't heard a sound.

Not the first wonder by any means to take place in North Richmond Street for that street had already been noted and mentioned by the man to whom, quite rightly, Ben Forkner devotes most of his introduction to this parade of Dubliners:

'North Richmond Street, being blind, was a quiet street except at the hour when the Christian Brothers' School set the boys free. An uninhabited house of two storeys stood at the blind end, detached from its neighbours in a square ground. The other houses of the street, conscious of decent lives within them, gazed at one another with brown imperturbable faces.'

Those brown imperturbable faces looked out at a boy who had headed out from that cul-de-sac in search of an Araby that was dead and desolate when he got there. Years before that they had looked out at a refined Quaker lady walking by to pay a visit to a Christian Brother who had once been a novelist, a poet and a playwright. He may, also, have had what seems to have been a gentle, platonic fluttering with the Quaker lady. But in a fit of flight from the world he had destroyed his manuscripts and taken to unalloyed religion. When he was told that the Quaker lady who was, also, blamelessly wedded, was in the parlour to pay him a call he gave the matter prayerful thought, sent her a message that he could not see her and went on being unalloyed.

That crisis of conscience of Gerald Griffin, the author of 'The Collegians', found no place in *Dubliners*, perhaps because Griffin was not a Dubliner, still less a Dublinman, nor, coming from Limerick, could ever be. But it is, at least, interesting that that moment in his life should have taken place in the same corner of Dublin in which the quest for love and Araby began, and ended in a boy's disillusion. Even in a cul-de-sac Dublin can be a complicated place.

That a courteous American scholar whose father was born in Peachtree Street, Atlanta, Georgia, and who himself is a professor in the orderly and beautiful city of Angers, in Balzacian France, should have the wish and the courage to walk in that intricacy of Dublin is something to wonder at and welcome. Joyce, as he points out, drew him and many another to Dublin. But he brought with him a wide knowledge of the literature of Ireland, past and present.

My first contact with him, well almost the first, was when he was assembling an anthology of modern Irish short stories for which Anthony Burgess wrote a preface, and said: 'You will keep this book and read parts of it again and again. . . . Each time you enter it you will be in the presence of Ireland.'

And just so: in the pages before you, Dublin is all around you.

It was by happy chance, and not by any planning that Ben Forkner had his selection made for the year in which the city is, it is said, celebrating a millennium. Which millennium? Today I overheard on the street: 'Is it a thousand years? Now I want to tell you this now. Ptolemy the Great, and he was as old as the Lord Himself, or older, said that Dublin was here when. . . .'

Perhaps before 1988 is over we may all have heard too much and too often of Molly Malone and of King Sitric, the Dane, who, I am assured, reposes, in a state of perfect preservation, under a car-park and quite close to the monstrous office-towers that developers, and the Corporation, raised as an affront to the citizens, to Anna Livia Plurabelle who would love to see green slopes rising up by her sleeping and symbolic side, and an insult, also, to Christchurch Cathedral and the ghosts of Strongbow, the Norman, and others.

For Molly of the lovely song and for King Sitric who made us what we are, I have, as we all should have, a deep affection. But it is always reassuring, while keeping the king and the quayside memory in mind, to walk out on the Dublin streets and mix and mingle with the ordinary people. As you do when you read these stories.

For myself I can vouch, and swear on any book you choose, that Austin McDonnell existed and that that was his name, and that he was my friend and that his widow liked my memory of him. Madame Butterfly also existed: whom I never had the pleasure of encountering. But that was not her name nor her physical appearance.

As much as does the publisher, and the anthologist, regret, so do I regret that space does not, at the moment, allow us more stories. But a good anthology must be accepted for what it contains, not for what the reader thinks he, or she, if he, or she, were making the anthology, might think that it should contain. So let me be the first to attack the anthologist for what is, and is not, here:

Gogarty, some might think, is an ancient monument.

But then, unlike poor old Nelson on his pillar and watching his world collapse, Gogarty still stands, and is still there, and who was more Dublin than he? Or knew as much or more about The Markets.

Nuns may no longer behave as George Moore thought they once did. Not so long ago, and here in Donnybrook, I saw two of them running, yes running, to catch a bus: and two nuns were seen to be wearing trousers while giving a lecture in the Royal Dublin Society building in Ballsbridge. But it was afterwards proved that one was a Filipina, and the other came from the United States where, as is well known, they know no better.

But then, from convents to Dublin Castle and dramas in muslin, and on to that masterpiece, 'Hail and Farewell', George Moore paid a lot of attention to Dublin and his ghost is still clearly visible in Hume Street, just fifteen minutes' healthy walking from where I write this.

All around me as I walk there are a hundred young writers clamouring for admission to this, or any other anthology. Thanks to Mannaman Mac Lir, our ancient genius, and to David Marcus, who has done so much to encourage young Irish writers, that is, in truth, the case.

With Patrick Samway, S.J., Forkner has done *Stories of the Modern South*, celebrating the copious writing in the American land he comes from, and also a vast and general anthology of the literature of the South. A tremendous book.

May we hope, someday, for a comparable Irish anthology. Meanwhile we have here a host of decent Dublin people, ready to talk to us, and even to listen to any language or any accent.

Benedict Kiely

Introduction

In one of the letters the hopeful young Joyce wrote from Trieste to the English publisher Grant Richards in 1905, in what turned out perversely to be a hopeless campaign to persuade Richards to honour the simple signed contract and publish *Dubliners*, Joyce explained that one of his aims in the stories was to 'present Dublin to the world'. Looking back as we can now, through almost an entire century of literature still dominated by Joyce's books, every single one of which is bound and bonded to the palpable, visible, vocal Dublin Joyce knew and remembered, his claim seems anything but brash. Not only has Joyce brought Dublin to the world, in *Dubliners*, *A Portrait of the Artist as a Young Man*, *Ulysses*, and *Finnegans Wake*, with these same books he has accomplished the finally more significant task of bringing the world to Dublin.

Once in Dublin, however, no world-reader of Joyce should wait long before searching out all the other masterpieces Dublin writers after Joyce have lavished on modern letters. The world-reader would have absolutely no excuse in ignoring modern Dublin drama, from Sean O'Casey and Denis Johnston, and on through Brendan Behan and Hugh Leonard, and should lose no time in getting hold of George Moore's dazzling Dublin memoir, *Hail and Farewell*, or Flann O'Brien's even more dazzling Dublin novel, *At-Swim-Two-Birds*. Both of these works are wonderfully preposterous, extravagant, crammed with cunning invention and, like much of the best Dublin writing, unable to accept anything short of complete independence. And as I hope this collection, *A New Book of Dubliners*, fully demonstrates, there should no longer be the slightest excuse for the world-reader to ignore what has now become, almost a century after the original *Dubliners*, a thriving tradition of modern Dublin short stories.

A New Book of Dubliners begins with the founder's 'Ivy Day in the Committee Room', surely one of the most Dublinesque of his stories, and tries to include the best of many stories that should, by now, be ranked right alongside the best of *Dubliners*. Stories of

George Moore, Liam O'Flaherty, Samuel Beckett, Sean O'Faolain, Mary Lavin, Benedict Kiely, and John McGahern are emphatically here, as they should be. These writers should be acclaimed everywhere modern literature counts for something. There are less well-known Dublin writers who deserve to be read, and acclaimed, and some, but by no means all, of their stories are here too. Thankfully, though the choice of stories deliberately stretches back through every generation of Dublin writers since *Dubliners*, well over half the writers included are still alive, and still writing. When we think of their work to come, and of the new generation that is even now, as Joyce once announced of himself, standing at the door, there is no doubt in my mind that long before another century is over *A New Book of Dubliners* will have to spread its covers and make some more room, or at the very least, move over on the shelf.

In writing of Joyce's fundamental role in bringing the world to Dublin, I mean to suggest, of course, more than the obvious sense of attracting literary pilgrims from all over the planet, though this strange magnetic power should not be made light of. It attests to what Joyce himself might have called fiction's special gift of complete human reality, presented to a world too often limited to the sub- or super-human. Joyce has room for these, of course, and for the outrageously common-place as well. But above all, Joyce's literary Dublin still describes a city that allows the entire human drama to work itself out, and surely one of the reasons the reader of Joyce feels himself physically drawn towards the real Dublin is the perhaps foolhardy desire to rediscover the city as human theatre. Foolhardy, because in all likelihood the reader's own city has long since replaced the public square and the public marketplace with mortuaries of reinforced concrete. And though he knows Dublin escaped the bombings of the Second World War, he cannot reasonably expect it to have escaped the wholesale vandalism of modern peacetime.

When Joyce began writing *Dubliners*, however, he did so with a living city still intact, and with the dawning discovery that, as far as human drama was concerned, Dublin was all he needed. The discovery took time to reveal all the far-reaching avenues it opened up, but as Joyce's life-long work advanced, and as he lived in one

European city after another – Trieste, Pola, Rome, Zurich, Paris – the drama of Dublin becomes more and more representative of the whole history of the human condition. It was already Irish, 'all too Irish', Joyce liked to say during the early years of his exile. And he would have said the same about its being 'all too English' and 'all too Roman' as well, making good use of the Nietzschean formula. To these fundamental identities, Joyce went on to add the Danish, the Greek, the Jewish and many more, and finally in *Finnegans Wake*, he crowns Dublin the teeming centre of the universe.

Even when he began writing the first stories of *Dubliners*, in the summer of 1904, Joyce must have sensed the plural nature of the Dublin character. After all, no matter how much he wanted to distance himself from all the negative forces *Dubliners* attacks, he knew too that he himself was a Dubliner, and would always remain one. His own character, if certainly singular, owed much of its singularity to the host of quarrelling selves it seemed to contain – thus, perhaps, Joyce's early decision to make a collection of Dublin portraits, and not the impossible solitary story of the definitive Dublin type.

He wrote his first story, 'The Sisters', at the invitation of George Russell, who paid for it and published it, in August, 1904, in his paper *The Irish Homestead*. Joyce immediately set out to do more of them – he projected ten in all – and had decided on the title right from the beginning. But though an enormous amount has been written about almost every step in Joyce's development, we seem to know little about the original impulse that led him to conceive of *Dubliners* as a whole.

Thanks to Richard Ellmann's richly informed biography, we do know that 1904, in a life of turbulent years, was the most turbulent year of his life. His mother was dead, his father's drunken fits at home led him from one temporary lodging to another, including a stay with his arch-friend Oliver Gogarty in the Martello Tower. He had no money, and was seen around town in the cast-off clothes of Gogarty, shifting roles as his mood and company – and the available costume – directed. In what became the most significant event of all, he met Nora Barnacle, and, as Ellmann points out, spent much of his time trying to convince her that he was not what he seemed to be. A fear of treacherous identities was to haunt him all his life. His falling in love with Nora filled him with enough resolve to leave Dublin, and by the end of the year he and Nora were in Trieste. In less than a year, he was to finish most of the stories, though, of course, *Dubliners* the book, damned by deception and broken agreements for almost a decade, was not published until 1914.

At the same time Joyce was writing *Dubliners* he was working on the long, never-finished novel *Stephen Hero*. He had begun the novel several months before he wrote 'The Sisters' and thus well before he had been struck by the idea of a collection of stories. Unlike *Stephen Hero*, the stories in *Dubliners* were written fairly quickly, with steady self-assurance, and this takes us back to the proposition that Joyce's vision of Dublin as dramatic stage somehow cooperates with the sudden confidence and purpose that guided his completion of *Dubliners*. Joyce had long been interested in drama and the history of theatre. His first major esthetic proclamation was the paper 'Drama and Life', which he read before the Literary and Historical Society at University College in 1900. The same year he became a university celebrity with the publication of his essay on Ibsen, 'Ibsen's New Drama', in one of the leading English journals of the day, the *Fortnightly Review*. But closer to home, and far more bound up with Joyce's own unsettled identity as a young Irish writer, he followed every new development in Yeats' crusade to establish the Irish Literary Theatre in a permanent home in Dublin.

He attended the performances from the beginning. When Yeats' *The Countess Cathleen* opened the theatre in May, 1899, Joyce singled himself out from the angry Dublin audience by applauding the play while his fellow university students hissed and hooted. When these same students wrote a petition protesting Yeats' unconventional vision of Cathleen's heroic sacrifice, Joyce staged a counter-protest of his own by publicly refusing to sign.

His attitude towards the theatre shifted two years later when Douglas Hyde's play in Irish, *Casadh an Tsugain*, and Yeats' and Moore's unfortunate collaboration, *Diarmuid and Grania*, were announced. Joyce objected to a preoccupation with the archaic, the far-away, the legendary, a turning away from the dramatic matter of the modern world and the language of modern life.

He interpreted these backward looks as symptoms of an excessive willingness to appeal to the 'popular devil' of public taste. He presented his objections in an essay he entitled 'The Day of the Rabblement'. If his tone was haughty, and if his remarks, in Dublin style, were meant to gall Yeats' well-known disregard for popularity, the essay as a whole is not dismissive. Obviously, Joyce continued to consider himself, if not a camp follower, clearly on Yeats' side in the struggle towards the new age of Irish culture. He recognized that Yeats had succeeded in transforming Dublin's artistic and intellectual life almost overnight. George Moore has given an amused account of receiving the emphatic telegram Edward Martyn sent him from Dublin where *The Countess Cathleen* was in rehearsal: 'The sceptre of intelligence has passed from London to Dublin.' It was an audacious, and to most observers, a mockable enterprise. Moore, true to character, had roundly mocked it on first hearing of the project. But before long even the mocking Moore was swept away by the irresistible force of Yeats' enthusiasm. By 1904, that miraculous year again, the year Synge's *Riders to the Sea* was performed, and the Abbey Theatre founded, Yeats' prophetic claims for a new Irish literature powerfully brought to life on a Dublin stage could now carry considerable conviction.

For Joyce, though, Yeats' accomplishment did not go far enough. He could see plainly that if Yeats – along with his co-dramatists Moore, Martyn, Russell, Lady Gregory, Colum and Synge – had realized the improbable feat of reviving Ireland in Dublin, Dublin itself stood alongside its own stage almost as a foreign town. Yeats would not have denied the charge. He never hid his dislike of Dublin, and his experiences with Dublin audiences and the Dublin middle classes over the years did nothing to change his mind. He would describe it in his poetry as a loud, spiteful, 'unmannerly town', an 'abounding gutter' ruled over by the shopkeeper and his 'greasy till'. Yeats, like his father, had a Dubliner's gift for the ripe contemptuous phrase.

Yeats' Dublin was the domain of the politician, the journalist, the merchant, the clerk, Trinity College, and the clownish West Briton, the Irishman who aped the English, and, like Edward Dowden, the Trinity professor, turned himself into an exaggeration of the Englishman not to be found anywhere in England itself. Yeats' ingredients for the new Irish soul all came from the Ireland outside Dublin, a combination of the folk and the heroic, the manor-house horseman and the peasant poet. For Joyce, a revival that would exclude the Irish capital could only be a half-revival. He could wholeheartedly agree that Dublin was decayed and corrupt, but he would go further and hold out that its corruptions were Irish too, and that at least half the duty of the Irish artist was the duty of completeness of vision. If Yeats would insist on forcing Ireland into an unwilling Dublin, Joyce would do all he could to force Dublin back into Yeats' unwilling Ireland.

To do so, he would begin with a diagnosis of the Dublin character, arguing that the first step of any revival, individual or collective, physical or spiritual, depends first of all on recognizing the nature of the decline. Health and sickness, wholeness and incompleteness: these are the polarities that appear most often in the Joyce letters that defend subject and method in *Dubliners*. He refers to Dublin as stricken with 'hemiplegia or paralysis' of the will, and writes that it is not his fault if his unflinching inspection results in a world over which floats a 'special odour of corruption'.

Joyce's 'medical' esthetic owes, of course, a great deal to his friendship with Gogarty and other Dublin students. Joyce himself for a short time thought about becoming a doctor, and allowed himself to drift into the role of a sort of part-time pre-medical student. He certainly heard every detail of the wild student pranks and jocularities in the classrooms, laboratories and hospital wards, and he shared, at least up to a point, Gogarty's taste for explaining everything – politics, romance and religion included – in terms of blunt, but poetically elaborate physical metaphors. Joyce's brother Stanislaus reported in his diary – 13 August 1904, the very day 'The Sisters' appeared in *The Irish Homestead* – that James himself liked to speculate on an actual pathological cause behind Dublin paralysis: 'He talks much of the syphilitic contagion in Europe, tracing practically everything to it.'

That same summer of 1904, in his highly satirical poem 'The Holy Office', Joyce wrote what came to be looked back on as his final farewell to the Irish revival. He had broken with Gogarty, and felt himself carefully snubbed by the leading lights of the literary movement. Unlike Gogarty, for example, who at any rate was far more at home in the Anglo-Irish social circles, Joyce was not invited with other young writers to the meetings of revivalist discussion at George Moore's house in Ely Place.

In 'The Holy Office' Joyce assumes the role of a literary doctor, as well as literary confessor, and calls himself 'Katharsis-Purgative', ready to attend to the neglected needs of the Irish body amid all the talk about its mystical soul. He argues that the group of writers orbiting around Yeats manage to deny as many realities as they claim to affirm; they are especially deficient in the proper respect for the physical world, and for the unpleasant here and now. In his story 'A Little Cloud', Joyce has his would-be Celtic poet, Little Chandler, prefer not to think about the 'grimy children' squatting 'like mice upon the thresholds'. Instead, Little Chandler picks 'his way deftly through all that minute vermin-like life'.

'Holy Office' thus brings together many of the ideas behind Joyce's sudden decision to begin a collection of Dublin stories, and announces too a growing sense of purpose in completing what he had begun. If Yeats and the other revivalists were not interested in a complete dose of realism on the Dublin stage, nor in acknowledging the Dubliner – impure and confused though his character may be – as a legitimate version of the modern Irishman, Joyce would combine all these rejections and give the reader dramatic portraits of the real Irishman in each disavowed Dubliner.

The reference to *Dubliners* as a collection of dramatic portraits is meant to be a little more than a convenient turn of phrase. It brings us back to the idea that Joyce's changed attitude towards a too-exclusive Irish theatre almost certainly inspired him to turn theatre itself to his own advantage. Up to the time of *Dubliners*, most of his imaginative prose had been written in the form of short half-page pieces he called his 'epiphanies'. Many of these were already embryonic forms of drama, brief snatches of suggestive dialogue, overheard slices of vocal Dublin life. The others were highly charged prose poems: lyrical, descriptive soliloquies without a context. By their very nature, both forms of epiphany seem to demand a further step in dramatic development.

I have heard it argued, or decreed, that the one-act play is a sort of theatrical twin of the short story – not, perhaps, in isolation, the sort of comparison that would inflame a discussion, one way or the other. But there can be no doubt that many of the stories in *Dubliners* give the impression of having been designed, if not for the stage, at least with the possibilities of the stage constantly in mind. Joyce goes to great pains to describe the local scene down to the smallest detail, perhaps his way of countering the extremely stylized, remote and flat scenery that Yeats had advocated – in 1904, once more, in an issue of *Samhain* – for the new Irish stage. By contrast, Joyce's houses, back yards, streets, pubs, churches and rooms are filled with all sorts of named objects: a rusty bicycle pump, an old election poster, dusty photographs, an iron bedstead, stacks of books and on and on: a conspicuous inventory of usable theatrical stock spurned by the revival. Mr Duffey's strictly furnished room in 'A Painful Case' seems to emerge directly from an actual list of stage properties; on the dining table in 'The Dead' every bit of available space is dramatically accounted for. 'Ivy Day in the Committee Room' is the story closest to a straightforward theatrical performance, a single stage with the actors appearing and disappearing through a single door, a shadow-play in which Yeats' recommendation for a 'shadowless light' in the same issue of *Samhain* just mentioned is scrupulously flouted.

But all these sometimes backward allusions are minor kidnappings into Joyce's prose of the Dublin theatre that ignored Joyce's Dublin. Far more important to Joyce was the theatrical spectacle Dublin itself presented. One of the ironies of bringing the stage to Dublin, Joyce must have thought, was that Dublin in many ways was already an immense stage. One of the most public-minded cities in the world, Dublin was filled – especially in the years at the beginning of the century when the questions of national identity were at their greatest intensity – with all sorts of off-stage actors, the professional Gael, the professional West Briton, the professional mystic, and the professional Dubliner who might be all or none of these depending on his mood, but who was always ready to put on a show, and speak out his public parts on the open streets.

It is not possible to reduce to a single cause the Dubliner's keenly developed sense of public drama. V. S. Pritchett, one of our wisest guides to the modern Dublin mind, would agree with Joyce in thinking it, to a degree at least, a form of evasion, a way of deflecting reality by turning it almost immediately into anecdote or legend. But Pritchett can see, too, that the Dubliner's dramatic impulse is also a means of enlivening reality's dull prospects, of making life more interesting than it actually is. There is a powerful undercurrent of play-making and playfulness on the Dublin streets, even behind the most malicious whispered insult. Outsiders who have probably heard too much about the endless harvest of creative spite and contention in the pubs are usually surprised to find that the victim, when seen, has never lost much stature or esteem by the attack. After all, he plays the same game too, and has now been given his turn to entertain the crowd. In fact, a large part of the mockery can be considered a popular form of very thinly disguised homage, raising a mere human being to the level of a Dublin topic. Surely there is something admiring in the exemplary double-edged Dublin comment on Oscar Wilde's father, a Dublin surgeon who had a reputation of never taking a bath: 'Why are Dr Wilde's nails always black? Because he scratches himself.'

For Joyce, though, evasion and the need to entertain at all costs could become pathological, and were symptoms of what he increasingly felt was the Dublin fear of confronting the private self without the benefit of the public mask. One of Joyce's major discoveries in *Dubliners* was the considerable power the public role has in determining the individual destiny. *Dubliners* is filled with Dubliners who enact the roles of church, politics, social convention, romantic fiction, but who have an enormous amount of trouble affirming or realizing an original impulse. Most of the stories show the individual always right on the far edge of becoming an extreme version of the predictable Dublin type. Though much has been made of Joyce's theory of 'epiphany', a term he never applied to *Dubliners*, there is very little revelation of the completely new. The stories invariably move toward an unmasking, but an unmasking that directs attention less to what the mask hides than to the nature of the mask itself.

Joyce was able to diagnose in *Dubliners* the unhealthy exaggeration of public roles partly because he had recognized it early on in his own character. He had become a celebrity, a Dublin 'artist', during his university days by playing the parts his student friends were only too ready to applaud. His favourite role of indifferent poet was appreciated as an elaborate act, though Joyce very likely invested more of himself in this 'character' than in any other. Gogarty liked to call him the wonderful mummer, and went out of his way to encourage Joyce as a public spectacle. But his very facility at acting out the expected roles made Joyce wary of becoming locked into a permanent part, of losing himself in his repeated impersonations.

For Joyce then, the various protests that greeted Yeats and the new Irish theatre could only add fuel to his self-perception that the Dubliner often had difficulty in separating the real from the theatrical. It was a theory repeatedly confirmed. The demonstrations he had witnessed at the performance of *The Countess Cathleen* were but the first of a series that were to hound the Abbey Theatre long after Joyce left Dublin. The reverse of the proposition makes an equal claim in Joyce's stories: the Dubliner is so used to public showmanship interrupting his daily rounds that there is the powerful temptation to take the eminently serious as mere theatre. Even the Easter Rising, according to Denis Johnston, was ridiculed as a poor show by a small crowd of hecklers he remembers standing by. They were very quickly disabused.

Closer to Joyce, and to *Dubliners*, Gogarty, especially during his student years, had a compulsive habit of metamorphosing ill fortune and human suffering out of the way by looking on all Dublin around him in terms of either good or bad entertainment. Everything, at one time even the burst aneurysm of a dying syphilitic sailor, could become the occasion of one of his spectacular witticisms. Gogarty was at least fair in making the same demands on himself, and he was nothing if not always extravagantly entertaining. For Joyce, however, no single public role, even that of the companionable comedian, should be allowed to speak for all human experience at all times.

One of Joyce's favourite literary devices consists in providing a catalogue of roles an individual has had to act out in his life. Most readers would remember Stephen's ironic description of his father in *A Portrait of the Artist as a Young Man* as 'a medical student, an oarsman, a tenor, an amateur actor, a shouting politician, a small landlord, a small investor, a drinker, a good fellow, a storyteller, somebody's secretary, something in a distillery, a taxgatherer, a bankrupt and at present a praiser of his own past'.

Not surprisingly, given Joyce's preoccupation with multiple Irish identities in 1904, he first uses the device in *Dubliners*. In 'Grace', he characterizes Mr M'Coy with the following list: 'He had been a clerk in the Midland Railway, a canvasser for advertisements for *The Irish Times* and for *The Freeman's Journal*, a town traveller for a coal firm on commission, a private inquiry agent, a clerk in the office of the Sub-Sheriff and he had recently become secretary to the City Coroner.'

Such a list might suggest a number of things about the person it describes, shiftiness of purpose, or perhaps even the curse of adaptability that Joyce mentions in his 'Day of the Rabblement' as one of the failures of the Irish theatre. But in *Dubliners* it suggests most of all that the individual has no character of his own outside the roles fortune and society have thrust him into. Certainly this is Joyce's vision of most of the characters in *Dubliners*. Even when they are shown actually choosing a part to play, such as the boy in 'Arab', or Little Chandler in 'A Little Cloud', they consistently blind themselves with the masks they willingly wear. All through the stories, Joyce's own fear of being trapped in the Dublin drama of public roles can be felt in every disappointed desire, every false position and every misdirection of the individual will.

Yet, despite all the private failure and public entrapment described in *Dubliners*, there are signs, especially in the later stories, that Joyce was capable of making claims for Dublin's special sense of public drama as a positive force, a gift rather than a disability. The distinction, as always in Joyce, resides in the degree of self-awareness the actor possesses when he takes on a part. Joyce had discovered his own individual purpose through a progressive dissatisfaction with single roles, a proof to him that perhaps not the roles themselves, but the attitudes of satisfaction, certitude or submission, were the veritable dangers.

He had discovered too, in the Dublin of 1904, that there is no such thing as a simple, absolute identity, Irish or otherwise, but a mysterious identity of many selves. All his major fictional characters, from Gabriel Conroy of 'The Dead' on through Stephen Dedalus and Leopold Bloom, must sift through a multitude of contradictory or false roles to discover themselves, but, paradoxically, can do so only by willingly acting out those same roles. Some roles are worth more than others, of course, but in any case no single role, to the exclusion of all others, can ever be absolutely adequate.

With this in mind, the early Joycean catalogue can be used to reveal a strength of will rather than the debilitating impulse of accommodation, lack of purpose and fatalism represented by the many roles of Simon Dedalus or Mr M'Coy. The year before he began *Dubliners*, in a book review of a biography of Giordano Bruno, Joyce uses the catalogue in just this approving sense: 'A Dominican monk, a gipsy professor, a commentator of old philosophies and a deviser of new ones, a playwright, a polemist, a counsel for his own defence, and, finally, a martyr burned at the stake. . . . Bruno, through all these modes and accidents (as he would have called them) of being, remains a consistent spiritual unity.' Joyce may have known, and at any rate would have certainly appreciated, Yeats' quite serious praise of William Morris as 'poet, socialist, romance-writer, artist, and upholsterer'.

Once the Dubliner realizes that he need not be bound to each and every role that fate and fortune present, the exaggerated public life of the city – its endless intriguing, its scandalizing, its love of contention, its keen nose for the pungent insult, even its sometimes cruel taste for derision and persecution – can be turned to advantage. What is important, as Stephen Dedalus reminds himself in *Ulysses*, on 16 June, 1904, less than two months before his autobiographer begins *Dubliners*, is to act, and to be acted on. By contending, the individual spirit is compelled to speak out, and the act of speaking out may very well reveal new and unknown powers of character. Here, in *Ulysses*, we have the Dublin theatre of restless self-discovery overcoming the Dublin theatre, in *Dubliners*, of the stationary masked rite.

Contention may liberate the spirit, and Joyce, in the middle of writing *Dubliners*, and looking back at Dublin from his turbulent life on the Continent, begins to admit that his own character owes much of its will and capacity for growth to having been forged in the greater turbulence of Dublin drama. If contention can liberate the spirit, it often liberates language at the same time. As Joyce well knew, the Dubliner who is adept at play-acting, at showing off, is often the first to detect the artificial and the pompous in others. Public speech in Dublin has a long history of being tested in this way, and Joyce, as he finished *Dubliners*, directs his attention more and more to the shamelessly exuberant, contentious, fiercely playful Dublin speech his later books openly celebrate.

'Ivy Day in the Committee Room' is a good example of a *Dubliners* story that looks forward to the big novels. Written almost entirely in dialogue, it illustrates the serious Joycean themes of loyal betrayal, inertia and misjudgement, but does so in a series of comic exchanges in which the Dublin love of spoken wit comes close to eclipsing all the familiar Dublin failings. It remains a typical *Dubliners* story in that each character stands hopelessly bound to a single role. But one of its major ironies is that they speak a language that has more life than they do; they spend much of their time repeating what they've heard all their lives – recitation is both the end and the key to the story – but they are as deaf to the full significance of what they hear as they are blind to the light of the day.

After 'The Dead', 'Ivy Day in the Committee Room' was Joyce's favourite story in *Dubliners*, and to my mind it marks an important turning point in his attitude towards the Dubliner he desired to present to the Irish revivalists, and to the world at large. He had read Yeats' complaint – in an issue of *Samhain* in, need it be said, 1904 – that Ibsen, one of Joyce's giants, lacked 'vivid language', and he would have heard most of the revivalists praise the superior Irish English of rural Ireland against what Synge three years later called the 'joyless and pallid' words of modern life. In the middle of writing his unsparing portraits of the unheroic, ineffectual, corrupted, clownish, but far from simple Dublin Irishman the newly elevated Irish stage refused to acknowledge, Joyce may have suddenly realized that the creative resources of Dublin English were, if, anything, closer to the 'fantastic, energetic, extravagant art' that Yeats had called for – *Samhain*, 1904 – than anything the Irish theatre had yet produced.

Joyce doesn't fully exploit those resources until the writing of *Ulysses*, but his 'contentious' stories, most of which were written after 'Ivy Day in the Committe Room', show him pitting Dublin voice against Dublin voice in a way that looks forward to the multiple voices and multiple styles of his later books. Together with 'Ivy Day in the Committee Room', 'Grace' and 'The Dead' must be among the loudest, most vocal stories in modern literature.

By writing *Dubliners* 'against' the exclusive Irish stage, Joyce revealed to himself that Dublin contained all the dramatic and verbal matter he would ever need. But more to the point, at least as far as this collection is concerned, he revealed to the Irish writers who followed him that Dublin was as rich a ground for their art as the untilled field of the Irish countryside. After *Dubliners* was finally published, in 1914, there was no need to make a case for the Dubliner as a legitimate Irishman. In fact, given his multiple identities, his duelling tongues, and his deeply divided loyalties, Joyce came to consider him the most faithful representative of all Irishmen. And from there it is perhaps but a short step to the condition of all men everywhere.

The impression Joyce stamped with his Dublin Irishman has been so strong that almost every major Irish writer of fiction has felt the need to come to terms with the Dublin variety of modern Irish life. They have done so in every literary form, the poem, the play, the novel, and especially in the brilliant, wholly revolutionary brand of writing that includes them all, the modern Dublin memoir.

But there has continued to be a special affinity between the Dublin writer and the short story. Joyce's achievement has for a long time overshadowed these later Dublin stories. *Dubliners*, by now, has reached far beyond Ireland, and is probably the single best-known collection of short stories written this century. Its influence on the development of the modern short story has been, and continues to be, enormous. But as this collection hopes to demonstrate, there are many other Dublin stories deserving of equal fame. Some of them, in fact, have already attained status as modern classics: Benedict Kiely's 'A Ball of Malt and Madame Butterfly', Samuel Beckett's 'Dante and the Lobster', Sean O'Faolain's 'Charlie's Greek', Mary Lavin's 'A Memory', James Plunkett's 'A Walk Through the Summer'. It wouldn't hurt to have at least two copies of each of these stories in the house.

A word needs to be said here about the actual choice of stories I include. Joyceans will surely notice that there are fifteen stories in all, exactly the number of stories in *Dubliners*. This was more haphazard than deliberate, and derives almost wholly from the amount of space I was allowed. I cannot pretend, however, that the coincidence makes me unhappy. I made no attempt to favour one type of Dublin story, nor one particular period of modern Dublin history. I did actively search out stories in which the special qualities of Dublin life enter into the narratives as an active force. For this reason, many stories, some of them quite good, that take place in Dublin, but that could, without any loss of interest, be placed in international surburbia, were eliminated. The main criterion of choice was simple: to include the best Dublin stories I could find, one story per author. And though I am fully satisfied with the collection as it stands, no amount of editorial pontificating should conceal a number of hard choices and painful omissions. In an ideal world, and with a hundred pages more, I would have gladly included stories by Val Mulkerns, William Trevor, Mervyn Wall, Julia O'Faolain and Ita Daly, to mention only a prized few.

In making my final choice, what continued to surprise me, in reading and rereading the stories, was the immense variety of style and subject they encompass. Oddly enough, there is very little sign of a direct influence of Joyce on the great majority of these writers. It's possible to recognize, for example, in O'Flaherty's 'The Tramp', the Joycean theme of Dublin paralysis preventing the two educated paupers from rousing themselves out of their hopeless lives of fear and habit. But O'Flaherty's vigorous natural man, with his very simple romantic vision of the open road, is a character that only O'Flaherty could make convincing.

It's possible too to recognize in George Moore's 'Sarah Gwynn' a Joycean insight into the crushing working world of the Dublin lower classes. Moore's collection of Irish rural stories, *The Untilled Field*, was published in 1903, and is thought by many to have influenced Joyce. It's an influence I find difficult to accept, even if we don't believe Joyce's statement to his brother that he first read the book several months after he began *Dubliners*, and that even then, he disliked it. There is only one story in *The Untilled Field* worthy of even the slightest story in *Dubliners*, and that is 'Home Sickness'. 'Sarah Moore', however, published twenty years after *The Untilled Field*, is an eccentric masterpiece, and Moore's treatment of the wealthy, solitary, furniture-demented doctor and the two deeply affectionate women, one a part-time prostitute and the other a future ex-nun, must rank among Moore's superior work. The final image of the swallow's nest – and of sacrificed family life – is a brilliant example of naturalistic symbolism.

Most of the writers in this collection, unlike Joyce, came to Dublin from other regions and other cities of Ireland. And most of them, again unlike Joyce, wrote their Dublin stories mid-way or late in their careers. By the time they began to deal with Dublin they had already developed powerful, mature voices of their own, and this may account for the great range of individual Dubliners they are able to depict.

What they do share with Joyce, and with each other, is an awareness of Dublin itself as a central element in each narrative, an intrusive presence that must be taken into account in any appreciation of the story's meaning.

If the Dubliners themselves in the stories differ widely, in class, social station, language, neighbourhood, religious and national creed, a few Dublin settings and situations are so common that they crop up again and again. The Dublin pub, for example, as Joyce well knew, is the authentic Dublin theatre, a stage that crowds out all competition, and that brings to life every block. It's quite capable of exerting an influence on a certain type of Dubliner far into the out-of-doors. All through James Stephens' sinister little Dublin parable, 'Schoolfellows', and Flann O'Brien's 'recorded' statement 'Drink and Time in Dublin' (in which shaky delirium, as usual, presses on with unshakable logic), there is the spectacle of the pub actively sending forth or hunting down its best actors. And when the characters of 'Ivy Day in the Committee Room' are not able to go to a pub, they transform the committee room into one with only a little help from outside. The stories of Kiely, Plunkett, Jordan and McGahern, all locate the pub at the driving heart of their narratives. After all, did not Yeats himself, late in his life, include the irreverent pub in a final injunction to future Irish poets in 'Under Ben Bulben': 'Sing the peasantry, and then/Hard-riding country gentlemen, /The holiness of monks, and after/Porter-drinkers' randy laughter.' This is one Yeatsian desire that has been grandly fulfilled by the modern Dublin story.

But as Joyce had anticipated all through *Dubliners*, Dublin is surpassingly prodigal of public theatre of all sorts, and there is far more than one type of stage in these stories. If there are any sceptics left, we need only consider the doctor's richly furnished room in 'Sarah Gwynn', the bare workhouse hospital ward in 'The Tramp', the very logical combination of pub and courtroom in Gogarty's 'Old Friery' – a complete short story hidden in an incomplete novel – or the otherwordly, neon-lit O'Connell Street in MacMahon's wonderfully lyrical 'Ballintierna in the Morning'.

Finally, however, whatever else binds these brilliantly varied stories together, they are bound most of all by the success with which they extend Joyce's achievement in *Dubliners* through almost a century of creative association between a single city and a single literary genre.

Much has been written lately about the many destructive changes that have plagued Dublin during the past several decades. But these are changes that can be found, sadly enough, in almost every city of the world. The restless, bulldozing architect, the illiterate town planner, the banner-intoxicated chamber of commerce, the manhandling automobile, all are part of an international climate of grievous urban tyrannies. My own beautiful town on the Maine, Angers, has recently cut down 200-year-old trees to build a parking lot for the local authorities, and, not satisfied, paid a Paris architect a great deal of money to throw together a commercial mall of concrete block and plexiglass billboards dead in the historical centre of the city. These are the common ills of the age. But what sets Dublin far, far apart, and it is good to remember this during the present year of Dublin celebration, has been a constant proof of an overbrimming creative spirit that has resisted all attempts to dry it up. The following stories, added to all the other novels, poems, plays and memoirs of modern Dublin, should strengthen an impression that has been impossible to contest for already many years, that Dublin, Ireland, against all the odds, has become the most astonishing literary city of modern times.

Ben Forkner
Angers, France
1988

Ivy Day in the Committee Room

JAMES JOYCE

Old Jack raked the cinders together with a piece of cardboard and spread them judiciously over the whitening dome of coals. When the dome was thinly covered his face lapsed into darkness but, as he set himself to fan the fire again, his crouching shadow ascended the opposite wall and his face slowly re-emerged into light. It was an old man's face, very bony and hairy. The moist blue eyes blinked at the fire and the moist mouth fell open at times, munching once or twice mechanically when it closed. When the cinders had caught he laid the piece of cardboard against the wall, sighed and said:

– That's better now, Mr O'Connor.

Mr O'Connor, a grey-haired young man, whose face was disfigured by many blotches and pimples, had just brought the tobacco for a cigarette into a shapely cylinder but when spoken to he undid his handiwork meditatively. Then he began to roll the tobacco again meditatively and after a moment's thought decided to lick the paper.

– Did Mr Tierney say when he'd be back? he asked in a husky falsetto.

– He didn't say.

Mr O'Connor put his cigarette into his mouth and began to search his pockets. He took out a pack of thin pasteboard cards.

– I'll get you a match, said the old man.

– Never mind, this'll do, said Mr O'Connor.

He selected one of the cards and read what was printed on it:

MUNICIPAL ELECTIONS
ROYAL EXCHANGE WARD

Mr Richard J. Tierney, P.L.G., respectfully solicits the favour of your vote and influence at the coming election in the Royal Exchange Ward

Mr O'Connor had been engaged by Mr Tierney's agent to canvass one part of the ward but, as the weather was inclement and his boots let in the wet, he spent a great part of the day sitting by the fire in the Committee Room in Wicklow Street with Jack, the old caretaker. They had been sitting thus since the short day had grown dark. It was the sixth of October, dismal and cold out of doors.

Mr O'Connor tore a strip off the card and, lighting it, lit his cigarette. As he did so the flame lit up a leaf of dark glossy ivy in the lapel of his coat. The old man watched him attentively and then, taking up the piece of cardboard again, began to fan the fire slowly while his companion smoked.

– Ah, yes, he said, continuing, it's hard to know what way to bring up children. Now who'd think he'd turn out like that! I sent him to the Christian Brothers and I done what I could for him, and there he goes boosing about. I tried to make him someway decent.

He replaced the cardboard wearily.

– Only I'm an old man now I'd change his tune for him. I'd take the stick to his back and beat him while I could stand over him – as I done many a time before. The mother, you know, she cocks him up with this and that. . . .

– That's what ruins children, said Mr O'Connor.

– To be sure it is, said the old man. And little thanks you get for it, only impudence. He takes th'upper hand of me whenever he sees I've a sup taken. What's the world coming to when sons speaks that way to their father?

– What age is he? said Mr O'Connor.

– Nineteen, said the old man.

– Why don't you put him to something?

– Sure, amn't I never done at the drunken bowsy ever since he left school? *I won't keep you*, I says. *You must get a job for yourself*. But, sure it's worse whenever he gets a job; he drinks it all.

Mr O'Connor shook his head in sympathy, and the old man fell silent, gazing into the fire. Someone opened the door of the room and called out:

– Hello! Is this a Freemasons' meeting?

– Who's that? said the old man.

– What are you doing in the dark? asked a voice.

– Is that you, Hynes? asked Mr O'Connor.

– Yes. What are you doing in the dark? said Mr Hynes, advancing into the light of the fire.

He was a tall slender young man with a light brown moustache. Imminent little drops of rain hung at the brim of his hat and the collar of his jacket-coat was turned up.

– Well, Mat, he said to Mr O'Connor, how goes it?

Mr O'Connor shook his head. The old man left the hearth and, after stumbling about the room, returned with two candlesticks which he thrust one after the other into the fire and carried to the table. A denuded room came into view and the fire lost all its cheerful colour. The walls of the room were bare except for a copy of an election address. In the middle of the room was a small table on which papers were heaped.

Mr Hynes leaned against the mantelpiece and asked:

– Has he paid you yet?

– Not yet, said Mr O'Connor. I hope to God he'll not leave us in the lurch to-night.

Mr Hynes laughed.

– O, he'll pay you. Never fear, he said.

– I hope he'll look smart about it if he means business, said Mr O'Connor.

– What do you think, Jack? said Mr Hynes satirically to the old man.

The old man returned to his seat by the fire, saying:

– It isn't but he has it, anyway. Not like the other tinker.

– What other tinker? said Mr Hynes.

– Colgan, said the old man scornfully.

– Is it because Colgan's a working-man you say that? What's the difference between a good honest bricklayer and a publican – eh? Hasn't the working-man as good a right to be in the Corporation as anyone else – ay, and a better right than those shoneens that are always hat in hand before any fellow with a handle to his name? Isn't that so, Mat? said Mr Hynes, addressing Mr O'Connor.

– I think you're right, said Mr O'Connor.

– One man is a plain honest man with no hunker-sliding about him. He goes in to represent the labour classes. This fellow you're working for only wants to get some job or other.

– Of course, the working-class should be represented, said the old man.

– The working-man, said Mr Hynes, gets all kicks and no halfpence. But it's labour produces everything. The working-man is not looking for fat jobs for his sons and nephews and cousins. The working-man is not going to drag the honour of Dublin in the mud to please a German monarch.

– How's that? said the old man.

– Don't you know they want to present an address of welcome to Edward Rex if he comes here next year? What do we want kowtowing to a foreign king?

– Our man won't vote for the address, said Mr O'Connor. He goes in on the Nationalist ticket.

– Won't he? said Mr Hynes. Wait till you see whether he will or not. I know him. Is it Tricky Dicky Tierney?

– By God! perhaps you're right, Joe, said Mr O'Connor. Anyway, I wish he'd turn up with the spondulics.

The three men fell silent. The old man began to rake more cinders together. Mr Hynes took off his hat, shook it and then turned down the collar of his coat, displaying, as he did so, an ivy leaf in the lapel.

– If this man was alive, he said, pointing to the leaf, we'd have no talk of an address of welcome.

– That's true, said Mr O'Connor.

– Musha, God be with them times! said the old man. There was some life in it then.

The room was silent again. Then a bustling little man with a snuffling nose and very cold ears pushed in the door. He walked over quickly to the fire, rubbing his hands as if he intended to produce a spark from them.

– No money, boys, he said.

– Sit down here, Mr Henchy, said the old man, offering him his chair.

– O, don't stir, Jack, don't stir, said Mr Henchy.

He nodded curtly to Mr Hynes and sat down on the chair which the old man vacated.

– Did you serve Aungier Street? he asked Mr O'Connor.

– Yes, said Mr O'Connor, beginning to search his pockets for memoranda.

– Did you call on Grimes?

– I did.

– Well? How does he stand?

– He wouldn't promise. He said: *I won't tell anyone what way I'm going to vote*. But I think he'll be all right.

– Why so?

– He asked me who the nominators were; and I told him. I mentioned Father Burke's name. I think it'll be all right.

Mr Henchy began to snuffle and to rub his hands over the fire at a terrific speed. Then he said:

– For the love of God, Jack, bring us a bit of coal. There must be some left.

The old man went out of the room.

– It's no go, said Mr Henchy, shaking his head. I asked the little shoeboy, but he said: *O, now, Mr Henchy, when I see the work going on properly I won't forget you, you may be sure*. Mean little tinker! 'Usha, how could he be anything else?

– What did I tell you, Mat? said Mr Hynes. Tricky Dicky Tierney.

– O, he's as tricky as they make 'em, said Mr Henchy. He hasn't got those little pigs' eyes for nothing. Blast his soul! Couldn't he pay up like a man instead of: *O, now, Mr Henchy, I must speak to Mr Fanning. . . . I've spent a lot of money?* Mean little shoeboy of hell! I suppose he forgets the time his little old father kept the hand-me-down shop in Mary's Lane.

– But is that a fact? asked Mr O'Connor.

– God, yes, said Mr Henchy. Did you never hear that? And the men used to go in on Sunday morning before the houses were open to buy a waistcoat or a trousers – moya! But Tricky Dicky's little old father always had a tricky little black bottle up in a corner. Do you mind now? That's that. That's where he first saw the light.

The old man returned with a few lumps of coal which he placed here and there on the fire.

– That's a nice how-do-you-do, said Mr O'Connor. How does he expect us to work for him if he won't stump up?

– I can't help it, said Mr Henchy. I expect to find the bailiffs in the hall when I go home.

Mr Hynes laughed and, shoving himself away from the mantelpiece with the aid of his shoulders, made ready to leave.

– It'll be all right when King Eddie comes, he said. Well, boys, I'm off for the present. See you later. 'Bye, 'bye.

He went out of the room slowly. Neither Mr Henchy nor the old man said anything but, just as the door was closing, Mr O'Connor, who had been staring moodily into the fire, called out suddenly:

– 'Bye, Joe.

Mr Henchy waited a few moments and then nodded in the direction of the door.

– Tell me, he said across the fire, what brings our friend in here? What does he want?

– 'Usha, poor Joe! said Mr O'Connor, throwing the end of his cigarette into the fire, he's hard up like the rest of us.

Mr Henchy snuffled vigorously and spat so copiously that he nearly put out the fire which uttered a hissing protest.

– To tell you my private and candid opinion, he said, I think he's a man from the other camp. He's a spy of Colgan's if you ask me. *Just go round and try and find out how they're getting on. They won't suspect you.* Do you twig?

– Ah, poor Joe is a decent skin, said Mr O'Connor.

– His father was a decent respectable man, Mr Henchy admitted: Poor old Larry Hynes! Many a good turn he did in his day! But I'm greatly afraid our friend is not nineteen carat. Damn it, I can understand a fellow being hard up but what I can't understand is a fellow sponging. Couldn't he have some spark of manhood about him?

– He doesn't get a warm welcome from me when he comes, said the old man. Let him work for his own side and not come spying around here.

– I don't know, said Mr O'Connor dubiously, as he took out cigarette-papers and tobacco. I think Joe Hynes is a straight man. He's a clever chap, too, with the pen. Do you remember that thing he wrote . . . ?

– Some of these hillsiders and fenians are a bit too clever if you

ask me, said Mr Henchy. Do you know what my private and candid
opinion is about some of those little jokers? I believe half of them
are in the pay of the Castle.

– There's no knowing, said the old man.

– O, but I know it for a fact, said Mr Henchy. They're Castle
hacks. . . . I don't say Hynes. . . . No, damn it, I think he's a
stroke above that. . . . But there's a certain little nobleman with a
cock-eye – you know the patriot I'm alluding to?

Mr O'Connor nodded.

– There's a lineal descendant of Major Sirr for you if you like! O,
the heart's blood of a patriot! That's a fellow now that'd sell his
country for fourpence – ay – and go down on his bended knees and
thank the Almighty Christ he had a country to sell.

There was a knock at the door.

– Come in! said Mr Henchy.

A person resembling a poor clergyman or a poor actor appeared
in the doorway. His black clothes were tightly buttoned on his
short body and it was impossible to say whether he wore a
clergyman's collar or a layman's because the collar of his shabby
frock-coat, the uncovered buttons of which reflected the candle-
light, was turned up about his neck. He wore a round hat of hard
black felt. His face, shining with raindrops, had the appearance of
damp yellow cheese save where two rosy spots indicated the
cheekbones. He opened his very long mouth suddenly to express
disappointment and at the same time opened wide his very bright
blue eyes to express pleasure and surprise.

– O, Father Keon! said Mr Henchy, jumping up from his chair.
Is that you? Come in!

– O, no, no, no! said Father Keon quickly, pursing his lips as if
he were addressing a child.

– Won't you come in and sit down?

– No, no, no! said Father Keon, speaking in a discreet indulgent
velvety voice. Don't let me disturb you now! I'm just looking for
Mr Fanning. . . .

– He's round at the *Black Eagle*, said Mr Henchy. But won't you
come in and sit down a minute?

– No, no, thank you. It was just a little business matter, said
Father Keon. Thank you, indeed.

He retreated from the doorway and Mr Henchy, seizing one of the candlesticks, went to the door to light him downstairs.

– O, don't trouble, I beg!

– No, but the stairs is so dark.

– No, no, I can see. . . . Thank you, indeed.

– Are you right now?

– All right, thanks. . . . Thanks.

Mr Henchy returned with the candlestick and put it on the table. He sat down again at the fire. There was silence for a few moments.

– Tell me, John, said Mr O'Connor, lighting his cigarette with another pasteboard card.

– Hm?

– What is he exactly?

– Ask me an easier one, said Mr Henchy.

– Fanning and himself seem to me very thick. They're often in Kavanagh's together. Is he a priest at all?

– 'Mmmyes, I believe so. . . . I think he's what you call a black sheep. We haven't many of them, thank God! but we have a few. . . . He's an unfortunate man of some kind. . . .

– And how does he knock it out? asked Mr O'Connor.

– That's another mystery.

– Is he attached to any chapel or church or institution or –

– No, said Mr Henchy. I think he's travelling on his own account. . . . God forgive me, he added, I thought he was the dozen of stout.

– Is there any chance of a drink itself? asked Mr O'Connor.'

– I'm dry too, said the old man.

– I asked that little shoeboy three times, said Mr Henchy, would he send up a dozen of stout. I asked him again now but he was leaning on the counter in his shirt-sleeves having a deep goster with Alderman Cowley.

– Why didn't you remind him? said Mr O'Connor.

– Well, I couldn't go over while he was talking to Alderman Cowley. I just waited till I caught his eye, and said: *About that little matter I was speaking to you about.* . . . *That'll be all right, Mr H.*, he said. Yerra, sure the little hop-o'-my-thumb has forgotten all about it.

– There's some deal on in that quarter, said Mr O'Connor

thoughtfully. I saw the three of them hard at it yesterday at Suffolk Street corner.

– I think I know the little game they're at, said Mr Henchy. You must owe the City Fathers money nowadays if you want to be made Lord Mayor. Then they'll make you Lord Mayor. By God! I'm thinking seriously of becoming a City Father myself. What do you think? Would I do for the job?

Mr O'Connor laughed.

– So far as owing money goes. . . .

– Driving out of the Mansion House, said Mr Henchy, in all my vermin, with Jack here standing up behind me in ¬ powdered wig – eh?

– And make me your private secretary, John.

– Yes. And I'll make Father Keon my private chaplain. We'll have a family party.

– Faith, Mr Henchy, said the old man, you'd keep up better style than some of them. I was talking one day to old Keegan, the porter. *And how do you like your new master, Pat?* says I to him. *You haven't much entertaining now*, says I. *Entertaining!* says he. *He'd live on the smell of an oil-rag.* And do you know what he told me? Now, I declare to God, I didn't believe him.

– What? said Mr Henchy and Mr O'Connor.

– He told me: *What do you think of a Lord Mayor of Dublin sending out for a pound of chops for his dinner? How's that for high living?* says he. *Wisha! wisha*, says I. *A pound of chops*, says he, *coming into the Mansion House. Wisha!* says I, *what kind of people is going at all now?*

At this point there was a knock at the door, and a boy put in his head.

– What is it? said the old man.

– From the *Black Eagle*, said the boy, walking in sideways and depositing a basket on the floor with a noise of shaken bottles.

The old man helped the boy to transfer the bottles from the basket to the table and counted the full tally. After the transfer the boy put his basket on his arm and asked:

– Any bottles?

– What bottles? said the old man.

– Won't you let us drink them first? said Mr Henchy.

– I was told to ask for bottles.

– Come back to-morrow, said the old man.

– Here, boy! said Mr Henchy, will you run over to O'Farrell's and ask him to lend us a corkscrew – for Mr Henchy, say. Tell him we won't keep it a minute. Leave the basket there.

The boy went out and Mr Henchy began to rub his hands cheerfully, saying:

– Ah, well, he's not so bad after all. He's as good as his word, anyhow.

– There's no tumblers, said the old man.

– O, don't let that trouble you, Jack, said Mr Henchy. Many's the good man before now drank out of the bottle.

– Anyway, it's better than nothing, said Mr O'Connor.

– He's not a bad sort, said Mr Henchy, only Fanning has such a loan of him. He means well, you know, in his own tinpot way.

The boy came back with the corkscrew. The old man opened three bottles and was handing back the corkscrew when Mr Henchy said to the boy:

– Would you like a drink, boy?

– If you please, sir, said the boy.

The old man opened another bottle grudgingly, and handed it to the boy.

– What age are you? he asked.

– Seventeen, said the boy.

As the old man said nothing further the boy took the bottle, said: *Here's my best respects, sir* to Mr Henchy, drank the contents, put the bottle back on the table and wiped his mouth with his sleeve. Then he took up the corkscrew and went out of the door sideways, muttering some form of salutation.

– That's the way it begins, said the old man.

– The thin end of the wedge, said Mr Henchy.

The old man distributed the three bottles which he had opened and the men drank from them simultaneously. After having drunk each placed his bottle on the mantelpiece within hand's reach and drew in a long breath of satisfaction.

– Well, I did a good day's work to-day, said Mr Henchy, after a pause.

– That so, John?

– Yes. I got him one or two sure things in Dawson Street,

Crofton and myself. Between ourselves, you know, Crofton (he's a decent chap, of course), but he's not worth a damn as a canvasser. He hasn't a word to throw to a dog. He stands and looks at the people while I do the talking.

Here two men entered the room. One of them was a very fat man, whose blue serge clothes seemed to be in danger of falling from his sloping figure. He had a big face which resembled a young ox's face in expression, staring blue eyes and a grizzled moustache. The other man, who was much younger and frailer, had a thin clean-shaven face. He wore a very high double collar and a wide-brimmed bowler hat.

– Hello, Crofton! said Mr Henchy to the fat man. Talk of the devil. . . .

– Where did the boose come from? asked the young man. Did the cow calve?

– O, of course, Lyons spots the drink first thing! said Mr O'Connor, laughing.

– Is that the way you chaps canvass, said Mr Lyons, and Crofton and I out in the cold and rain looking for votes?

– Why, blast your soul, said Mr Henchy, I'd get more votes in five minutes than you two'd get in a week.

– Open two bottles of stout, Jack, said Mr O'Connor.

– How can I? said the old man, when there's no corkscrew?

– Wait now, wait now! said Mr Henchy, getting up quickly. Did you ever see this little trick?

He took two bottles from the table and, carrying them to the fire, put them on the hob. Then he sat down again by the fire and took another drink from his bottle. Mr Lyons sat on the edge of the table, pushed his hat towards the nape of his neck and began to swing his legs.

– Which is my bottle? he asked.

– This lad, said Mr Henchy.

Mr Crofton sat down on a box and looked fixedly at the other bottle on the hob. He was silent for two reasons. The first reason, sufficient in itself, was that he had nothing to say; the second reason was that he considered his companions beneath him. He had been a canvasser for Wilkins, the Conservative, but when the Conservatives had withdrawn their man and, choosing the lesser of two evils, given their support to the Nationalist candidate, he had been engaged to work for Mr Tierney.

In a few minutes an apologetic *Pok!* was heard as the cork flew out of Mr Lyons' bottle. Mr Lyons jumped off the table, went to the fire, took his bottle and carried it back to the table.

– I was just telling them, Crofton, said Mr Henchy, that we got a good few votes to-day.

– Who did you get? asked Mr Lyons.

– Well, I got Parkes for one, and I got Atkinson for two, and I got Ward of Dawson Street. Fine old chap he is, too – regular old toff, old Conservative! *But isn't your candidate a Nationalist?* said he. *He's a respectable man*, said I. *He's in favour of whatever will benefit this country. He's a big rate-payer*, I said. *He has extensive house property in the city and three places of business and isn't it to his own advantage to keep down the rates? He's a prominent and respected citizen*, said I, *and a Poor Law Guardian, and he doesn't belong to any party, good, bad, or indifferent*. That's the way to talk to 'em.

– And what about the address to the King? said Mr Lyons, after drinking and smacking his lips.

– Listen to me, said Mr Henchy. What we want in this country, as I said to old Ward, is capital. The King's coming here will mean an influx of money into this country. The citizens of Dublin will benefit by it. Look at all the factories down by the quays there, idle! Look at all the money there is in the country if we only worked the old industries, the mills, the shipbuilding yards and factories. It's capital we want.

– But look here, John, said Mr O'Connor. Why should we welcome the King of England? Didn't Parnell himself . . .

– Parnell, said Mr Henchy, is dead. Now, here's the way I look at it. Here's this chap come to the throne after his old mother keeping him out of it till the man was grey. He's a man of the world, and he means well by us. He's a jolly fine decent fellow, if you ask me, and no damn nonsense about him. He just says to himself: *The old one never went to see these wild Irish. By Christ, I'll go myself and see what they're like*. And are we going to insult the man when he comes over here on a friendly visit? Eh? Isn't that right, Crofton?

Mr Crofton nodded his head.

– But after all now, said Mr Lyons argumentatively, King Edward's life, you know, is not the very . . .

– Let bygones be bygones, said Mr Henchy. I admire the man personally. He's just an ordinary knockabout like you and me. He's fond of his glass of grog and he's a bit of a rake, perhaps, and he's a good sportsman. Damn it, can't we Irish play fair?

– That's all very fine, said Mr Lyons. But look at the case of Parnell now.

– In the name of God, said Mr Henchy, where's the analogy between the two cases?

– What I mean, said Mr Lyons, is we have our ideals. Why, now, would we welcome a man like that? Do you think now after what he did Parnell was a fit man to lead us? And why, then, would we do it for Edward the Seventh?

– This is Parnell's anniversary, said Mr O'Connor, and don't let us stir up any bad blood. We all respect him now that he's dead and gone – even the Conservatives, he added, turning to Mr Crofton.

Pok! The tardy cork flew out of Mr Crofton's bottle. Mr Crofton got up from his box and went to the fire. As he returned with his capture he said in a deep voice:

– Our side of the house respects him because he was a gentle-man.

– Right you are, Crofton! said Mr Henchy fiercely. He was the only man that could keep that bag of cats in order. *Down, ye dogs! Lie down, ye curs!* That's the way he treated them. Come in, Joe! Come in! he called out, catching sight of Mr Hynes in the doorway.

Mr Hynes came in slowly.

– Open another bottle of stout, Jack, said Mr Henchy. O, I forgot there's no corkscrew! Here, show me one here and I'll put it at the fire.

The old man handed him another bottle and he placed it on the hob.

– Sit down, Joe, said Mr O'Connor, we're just talking about the Chief.

– Ay, ay! said Mr Henchy.

Mr Hynes sat on the side of the table near Mr Lyons but said nothing.

– There's one of them, anyhow, said Mr Henchy, that didn't renege him. By God, I'll say for you, Joe! No, by God, you stuck to him like a man!

– O, Joe, said Mr O'Connor suddenly. Give us that thing you wrote – do you remember? Have you got it on you?

– O, ay! said Mr Henchy. Give us that. Did you ever hear that, Crofton? Listen to this now: splendid thing.

– Go on, said Mr O'Connor. Fire away, Joe.

Mr Hynes did not seem to remember at once the piece to which they were alluding but, after reflecting a while, he said:

– O, that thing is it. . . . Sure, that's old now.

– Out with it, man! said Mr O'Connor.

– 'Sh, 'sh, said Mr Henchy. Now, Joe!

Mr Hynes hesitated a little longer. Then amid the silence he took off his hat, laid it on the table and stood up. He seemed to be rehearsing the piece in his mind. After a rather long pause he announced:

THE DEATH OF PARNELL

6th October 1891

He cleared his throat once or twice and then began to recite:

> *He is dead. Our Uncrowned King is dead.*
>   *O, Erin, mourn with grief and woe*
> *For he lies dead whom the fell gang*
>   *Of modern hypocrites laid low.*
>
> *He lies slain by the coward hounds*
>   *He raised to glory from the mire;*
> *And Erin's hopes and Erin's dreams*
>   *Perish upon her monarch's pyre.*
>
> *In palace, cabin or in cot*
>   *The Irish heart where'er it be*
> *Is bowed with woe – for he is gone*
> *Who would have wrought her destiny.*

He would have had his Erin famed,
The green flag gloriously unfurled,
Her statesmen, bards and warriors raised
Before the nations of the World.

He dreamed (alas, 'twas but a dream!)
Of Liberty: but as he strove
To clutch that idol, treachery
Sundered him from the thing he loved.

Shame on the coward caitiff hands
That smote their Lord or with a kiss
Betrayed him to the rabble-rout
Of fawning priests – no friends of his.

May everlasting shame consume
The memory of those who tried
To befoul and smear th' exalted name
Of one who spurned them in his pride.

He fell as fall the mighty ones,
Nobly undaunted to the last,
And death has now united him
With Erin's heroes of the past.

No sound of strife disturb his sleep!
Calmly he rests: no human pain
Or high ambition spurs him now
The peaks of glory to attain.

They had their way: they had him low.
But Erin, list, his spirit may
Rise, like the Phœnix from the flames,
When breaks the dawning of the day,

The day that brings us Freedom's reign.
And on that day may Erin well
Pledge in the cup she lifts to Joy
One grief – the memory of Parnell.

Mr Hynes sat down again on the table. When he had finished his recitation there was a silence and then a burst of clapping: even Mr

Lyons clapped. The applause continued for a little time. When it had ceased all the auditors drank from their bottles in silence.

Pok! The cork flew out of Mr Hynes' bottle, but Mr Hynes remained sitting, flushed and bareheaded on the table. He did not seem to have heard the invitation.

– Good man, Joe! said Mr O'Connor, taking out his cigarette papers and pouch the better to hide his emotion.

– What do you think of that, Crofton? cried Mr Henchy. Isn't that fine? What?

Mr Crofton said that it was a very fine piece of writing.

from *Dubliners*, 1914

Sarah Gwynn

GEORGE MOORE

On returning from the study door, whither he had accompanied the last patient, the doctor cast a glance of approbation at the two piles of gold and silver on his table, the gold slightly overtopping the silver; and considering them as a very adequate remuneration for his afternoon's work, Dr O'Reardon dropped into his great Chippendale armchair (the very one that Sir Stanley used to sit in – it had returned to Ely Place after a brief sojourn in Taylor's shop in Liffey Street), and ensconced amid its carvings, his thoughts ran on a tiresome woman for whose everlasting megrim he had written a prescription: five grains of carbonate of soda – a neighbour, an acquaintance, a garrulous woman, who never would take a hint but would go on talking, however many people were in the waiting-room; she paid her guinea, but rarely failed to waste two guineas' worth of his time, putting him past his complacency. He regretted these accesses of temper by the burnished brass of the fire-irons and the multi-coloured marble chimney-piece, and continued to recall his patients. Another woman engaged his thoughts; her rheumatoid arthritis perplexed him; she didn't seem to improve under his treatment and he was afraid he would have to try inoculations. These cases, he said, go commonly from bad to worse. A moment after he was thinking of a child he had examined that morning for heart, still uncertain whether the murmur that had come to his ear through the stethoscope meant specific disease or whether it might be attributed to poverty of blood. Another, a still more serious case, was remembered; and so that he might think better he closed his eyes, but began very soon to lose control over his thoughts, a veil seeming to rise and another to descend. He strove against sleep, but it was too late to rouse, and he must have slept for a long or a short time, which he could not say, but he must have slept deeply, for when the knocker of the front door awoke him he stared round the room, not recognizing it as his own, returning to consciousness of himself through recollections of the parlourmaid who had run out of the house that morning without saying a word to anybody (she had her wages yesterday). From the parlourmaid his thoughts turned to the cook, who must be upstairs, else she would have gone to the front door. Now who could the visitor be? A patient, most likely, though it was past four o'clock. For a doctor of his position to let a patient in was a breach of etiquette, but circumstances—— Another knock startled him from his meditation, and he returned from the front door followed by a sparely dressed woman, standing not much higher than his elbow.

All men and women resemble some animal, a friend had said one evening, and when he had pointed out many likenesses to cats and dogs, horses and hyenas, among his acquaintances, somebody said: And O'Reardon – what is he like? The answer came at once: a camel, and immediately everybody saw the resemblance: the small head, high nose, long lip, wide, drooping mouth. The story was an old one, almost out of currency, but the little starveling the doctor had just let into his house recalled it. If I am like a camel, he said to himself, what is this woman like? A squirrel? No; a squirrel is a gay boy. Before he could think again the little woman by his side began to tell that she had heard from Miss Lynch that he required a cook, and he listened, already won by a voice so pure and clear that his curiosity was stirred to see his visitor; and the little, blonde face, the upturned nose, and clear, eager eyes that appeared when the lamp was lighted seemed to be the girl he might have guessed if he had laid his mind to guessing – a tiny, thread-paper girl in a straw hat, an alpaca jacket, and a thin skirt that did not hide her broken boots, a starveling, and remembering what Miss Lynch had told him, he said: The cook must be in the house somewhere; she'll get you a cup of tea.

No, thank you, sir. I came here thinking you wanted a cook. The doctor answered that it was the parlourmaid who had left. Then you'll not be wanting a cook, sir? she broke in, without a trace of disappointment in her voice; she even seemed to the doctor relieved to hear that she was not required. I remember now, the doctor said. You were in a convent in Wales, weren't you?

Yes, sir.

Miss Lynch told me about you; but when you knocked I was

asleep and must have slept heavily, for I didn't know my own room when I awoke.

I am sorry I woke you, sir.

There's no need for you to be sorry. I'm glad you did, and that I went to the door. You were in a convent for nearly ten years, and because you answered the Sub-Prioress, or maybe the Prioress herself, sharply, they bundled you out, clapping a straw hat on your head and an alpaca jacket on your shoulders, giving you but your bare fare to Dublin, not caring——

Oh, but you mustn't talk like that, sir! It was all my fault. I spoke to our Sub-Prioress in a way that I shouldn't have. I lost my temper, and all the blame is with me. They did quite right to send me away, for they couldn't have kept me. You must believe what I say; indeed, I am speaking the truth, and no more than it. The doctor did not answer, and at the end of the pause the nun said: I doubt very much if I should suit you. I think I'll go.

You shall go, if you wish to go, in a minute or two, but I'd like to say a few words first. Miss Lynch mentioned that you would not hear a word said against the nuns, and advised me not to speak about the convent; but, as I have said, your knock awoke me, and I came to the door unable to collect my thoughts. That's how it happened, else I should not have spoken about the nuns. So, you see, there's no real reason for you to run away.

You want a cook, sir? The doctor answered that his cook had decided to stay, but the parlourmaid had left, and that if she would care to accept the situation he would be glad to engage her. I go out in the mornings, he continued, to my hospital or to visit my patients, and in the afternoons I receive patients from two till four. The wages are twenty-four pounds a year. I don't know your name.

My name is Sarah Gwynn, sir; and during the pause Dr O'Reardon was again attracted by the tiny face, lit by blue-grey nervous eyes. I hope you'll not refuse the situation, he said, for if you do Miss Lynch will be very angry with me for my indiscretion.

I should not like you to have it on your mind, sir, that the nuns behaved otherwise than rightly, and would sooner lose the situation than——

Miss Lynch, who is a Roman Catholic, doesn't take that view, but we need not trouble ourselves about the rights and wrongs.

You may have been overworked and tired; your nerves may have given way.

Yes, sir, that was it.

Sarah's vehement defence of her former friends and sisters in the Lord Jesus Christ had evoked the doctor's sympathy, and smitten by her originality, he determined not to lose her. You will require some clothes, he said, assuming that she had agreed to stay, and he went to his writing-table and took five pounds from the pile of gold. At the sight of so much money Sarah drew back, as if afraid. I should like you to buy the things you want before the shops close, he continued. Miss Lynch will advise you, perhaps accompany you, as you have only just arrived in Dublin.

I know Dublin, sir. I was here before.

Ah, so much the better. Well, I shall expect to see you when I return home for luncheon to-morrow.

You may be sure I'll come, sir, she answered from the door; and then remembering that the lock was a double one, he said: Allow me. The two handles must be turned at the same time.

Sarah passed out, and Dr O'Reardon had barely reseated himself in his chair before he began to regret the impulsive mood that had impelled him to take five pounds from the pile by his writing-pad and give them to a woman he might never see again. But she came recommended by Helena, a level-headed woman, and the doubt that had arisen was swept away, and its place was taken by a sudden and awful dread of breakages. For the woman who had left him had been ten years in a convent, where the concrete is nothing and the abstract everything, and to-morrow, if she returned (which she would, for Helena Lynch would not have sent her to him if she were not sure of her honesty), his cabinets filled with Bow and Chelsea would be in her charge; and the project of running after her with another five pounds, the price of a breach of agreement, started up in his mind. It was cowardice that kept him in his chair; and that night he slept but little, leaving the house for his hospital filled with misgivings of what would happen between ten and eleven, the time she would arrive. He felt that when he returned for luncheon at one o'clock he would be told that she had filled a cut-glass decanter with hot water, with the usual consequences, or that a Chelsea figure had been swept from the chimney-piece into the fender. And the oriental vases and the birds! He shuddered. The carved mirrors above the chimney-pieces she could not touch, but she might easily knock a carved garland from a sidetable with a sweeping brush.

His carriage continued to take him further and further from his cherished possessions, and if a capital operation had not been awaiting him, he would have turned back to leave a note saying that she was not to attempt any work, cleaning above all, before seeing him. As the carriage crossed Carlisle Bridge, he thought of his pictures, his collection and his own water-colours. A might-have-been lives on in the heart, almost a reproach, and the memories of the art that he had abandoned and that could never now be his, put the ex-nun out of the doctor's mind (it was thus that he now thought of her) till he arrived at the hospital.

II

At one o'clock O'Reardon returned along the quays, forgetful of the old shop in Liffey Street, deep in thoughts of an accident, one that every doctor dreads: death under an operation. The patient had not recovered consciousness, and Dr O'Reardon crossed Carlisle Bridge, passed Trinity College, reaching home without seeing or hearing, so absorbed that he did not recognize the smart young woman in cap and apron who met him in the passage. He asked her if luncheon was ready, and she answered that it would be in a few minutes; and it was not till she began to tell him that several had called to see him that morning that he roused a little and began to ask himself who the young woman was that remembered so clearly the messages given to her. On looking under the white cap he recognized the anxious face of the vagrant nun whom he had seen overnight, asking himself again what animal she resembled, if it was the white and red that had put a weasel into his head. But a weasel is white underneath and red above. Or was it her gait? She seemed to run forward and to stop suddenly, just like a weasel. Have you broken anything, Sarah?

Broken anything, sir? What makes you think that? Sarah resented the insinuation so sharply that the doctor had to plead that his thoughts were away, and he related the unfortunate operation, the failure of which he knew could not be laid to his charge, nor to that of the anaesthetist or the nurses. The man ought to have been operated upon earlier, he said.

And as with time his mind freed itself from qualms of conscience, he began to notice that life was passing pleasantly, a great deal of its smoothness seemingly owing to the diligence and care of his new parlourmaid. Since she came into his service plates ceased to be chipped; no Waterford glass had been broken, nor was his eye ever caught by a piece of ornamental carving knocked from a carven armchair. Nor did a cessation of breakages comprise all her qualities; she was now the parlourmaid that every doctor desires and never finds. Her service at table was excellent, though she had never attended at table before she came into his service. In six months she was more learned than the best of her predecessors. Everybody envied him. A dinner of twelve doctors could not be managed by two servants; another housemaid was called in, and Sarah's administration of the service was admirable. The plates were not put in the oven; they were heated by hot water; the entrées came out hot; the claret was neither hot nor cold but kept warm to just the right temperature. She reminded him that Mr——did not drink champagne; and when the doctor went into the country every Saturday to paint, and forgot to wash his brushes, when he remembered them they were washed. He had never had a parlourmaid to wash his brushes before. His palette was cleaned, too, and without disturbing the colours that he had set. Messages were delivered and appointments made that he could keep. Every month he discovered new qualities; economies were effected, and how she managed to supervise the household books without enraging the cook, he did not know, nor did he dare to enquire, but he noticed improvements everywhere, and also a change in Sarah herself.

She was a starveling when she came, shy and perplexed; now she had put on a little flesh and recovered her strength, and though her face could not be said to be as merry as a squirrel's, it was alive and pleasant. He noticed the neatness with which she wore her cap, her carefully brushed hair, and that when her attention wandered, which it did sometimes, a far-away look came into her pale grey eyes; and so he was moved to ask her if she was happy in her situation and had ceased to regret the convent, to think well of the nuns, but remembering the rebuff he had received on the first occasion, he refrained from putting any questions to her. From these absences she would return suddenly, and he often wondered if she was aware of her absent-mindedness; he thought she was not, and that she came and went unwittingly. Her face lighted up when he spoke to her; she would continue the dropped conversation and go out of the room, a little more abruptly, he thought, than at other times. Sarah is much improved in health, he said to himself, and fell to thinking what her secret might be, without doubting that all Sarah had told him of herself was true; but there was much in her life beyond the facts that she had been in a Welsh convent for ten years and had been turned out at a moment's notice for rudeness to her superiors. Her accent told him that she came from the County Down, and for a Down girl to find her way to a Welsh convent was queer enough to set the least curious wondering how she had wriggled out of her Protestantism to begin with, and subsequently into a convent in Wales.

It had come to his ears that Sarah missed Mass, which was strange, unless indeed she had changed in mind as much or more than she had physically, and he remembered her words in defence of the outrageous nuns, and her abrupt rising from her chair with the intention of refusing the situation he had offered her. That time may have revealed to her how cruelly she had been treated was quite possible. She had never spoken of it again. It was true that the opportunity had not occurred. But the other reports! His friends had seen Sarah late at night in Sackville Street and Grafton Street and round Trinity College; nor was she passing quickly through these streets on her way home, but loitering, peering into the faces of the passers-by like one in search of somebody. That his friends had met Sarah, or somebody they had mistaken for Sarah, was certain; but the thought that the reaction from the convent had driven her to lead a double life – his parlourmaid during the day, a whore on her evenings out – was a belief that none who knew her could entertain, for to know Sarah was to believe every word she said. Her exalted moods, her clear, pure voice—— No, it is not possible, he said; moreover, Helena would not have sent her here if she were not sure of her character, knowing how important it is to me. . . . His thoughts passed into a reverie of the days when

Helena had decided to work for her own living, and the excellent Health Inspector that had come out of his determination. But how had she come upon Sarah? All he knew was that they had met the day after Sarah arrived in Dublin in the straw hat and the alpaca jacket. It might be that Helena knew only Sarah's story; but it is not easy for one Catholic to deceive another with a tale of expulsion from a convent, and sharp-witted Helena, though a Catholic, was no fool, and he would learn Sarah's secret from Helena when she returned to Dublin.

The words came into his mind: she'll hardly recognize Sarah, so much improved is she, almost a good-looking girl; and hearing her laughing – her laughter came through the window with many sweet-scented airs from the garden – Sarah laughing with Michael! he said, and seeing her standing by the tall, lilac bushes, gathering purple bloom for his dinner-table, Michael, the gardener, drawing down the high branches with his rake, he began a letter to Helena, telling her of the coming of spring in his garden, the lilac in bloom, the buds swelling in the apple trees, waiting for the May-time. All the world, he said, yields to the gentle season, and it may be that it will find its way into Sarah's heart; her feet are certainly on the lilac path, and I should not be surprised overmuch (though I should be surprised), if you were to find her married to Michael when you return, a merry look in her eyes replacing the yearning look for something beyond the world, which you have not forgotten, so characteristic is it of her. . . . In the letter he was writing he would tell, too, of the secret which he was sure that Sarah was hiding from him – hiding, perhaps, from Helena. His thoughts were brought to an end by the arrival of a patient, and it was not till many days after that he discovered the half-written letter among some papers on his writing-table.

III

I cannot thank you enough, he wrote, for sending me Sarah, a most excellent, far-seeing servant, holding all the threads, managing everything, interested apparently in me and in me only; but behind this impersonal externality she lives her personal life, of which we know nothing. She has been with me now nearly a year, yet my knowledge of her is not greater to-day than it was before I saw her. I have learned, it is true, that she came originally from the north of Ireland; she didn't tell me, her accent told me, and I have been wondering if her bringing-up was Protestant and if she became a Catholic from caprice. Newman, I believe, went over for theological reasons, but theology cannot have been the motive that seduced Sarah, whose attendance at Mass is casual, uncertain, so I am told. Be this a lie or truth, she is no longer religious; indeed I doubt if she ever was religious. Then why did she, a Protestant presumably, become a Catholic and enter a convent? And why is she so silent about herself? The door opened behind him, and without turning round the doctor answered Sarah, who asked if he was busy: I am writing a letter to Miss Lynch; and he continued writing till his attention was attracted by the silence behind him. You heard me say that I was writing to Miss Lynch? Now, Sarah, if you have any message—— No, sir, I have no message, I have come to ask you for her address. You see, it was she who sent me to you, and may be able to get me another place, for I've come to tell you that I shall be leaving you at the end of the month. But if you would let me go sooner——

Leaving me, Sarah, at the end of the month! What do you mean? I understood that you were satisfied with your situation——

Yes, sir; the situation is all right and I am grateful, but it can't be helped.

Can't be helped! the doctor repeated. Everything can be helped. Tell me why you're leaving – why you're thinking of leaving. Is it wages? Tell me; there must a reason, and when I know the reason I shall be able to arrange.

There are things that cannot be arranged, sir, and this is one of them. As she spoke the words she moved towards the door, but the doctor rushed past her, saying: No, Sarah, no; you cannot leave the room until I hear why you want to leave me. It is not fair, nor is it right, for you to walk out of my house without giving a reason, like the parlourmaid you superseded. Are you going to be married, for if you are, that will be a sufficient reason?

No, sir; I am not going to get married.

He watched her face, and she returned to the writing-table with him. Now, sit down, Sarah, and tell me why you're leaving.

Well, sir, it is because the gardener wants to marry me.

But he hasn't interfered with you in any way?

No, sir; I've got no fault to find with him.

No fault to find except that he asked you to marry him?

But I can't marry him, sir. It would be better if you didn't ask me any more questions, indeed it would.

Am I to understand that you like the gardener?

He is all right, sir; I shouldn't mind if things were different.

Tell me, Sarah.

You wouldn't understand, sir; it would seem a lot of nonsense to you.

But everybody is nonsense to the next one. I would like to hear first of all why you left the north and why you became a Catholic.

I was always a Catholic, sir; my mother was a Catholic.

And your father?

Father was a Protestant, and mother went over when she married him. You see, in the County Down a Protestant can't marry a Catholic, for everybody would be against her. Mother wanted to bring me over with her, but I wouldn't go over, and that was the beginning of it.

Sarah stopped suddenly, and a little perplexed doctor and maid-servant stared at each other. I can't see, sir, how all this can interest you; but if you wish to hear it, I'll tell you the story, for I have been very happy here and am grateful to you, and, as you said, I can't leave without giving a reason. When mother went over I was twelve, and out in the fields at five o'clock in the morning pulling swedes and mangel-wurzels; the wurzels are the worst, for they have roots a foot long, and it was terribly hard work getting them up, for I wasn't as strong as the other girls. They all thought it hard work; our backs ached dreadfully when we went home to breakfast at eight o'clock.

And after breakfast?

After breakfast I had to go to school; and when school was over we began to feel the dread of next morning creeping over us, at least I did.

And to escape from the pulling of mangrel-wurzels you came to Dublin?

No, it wasn't that, sir. After a bit my stepfather was out of his luck; ten sheep died on him, the mare cast her foal; and we did not keep the bad luck to ourselves, for we shared it with the farmers round our way, and the talk began that somebody had put a curse on the County. If anything goes wrong in County Down it's the fault of the Catholics. I was the only Catholic there, and as I passed by some boys on a gate, one of them said: There goes the papish, and another picked it up and cried: To hell with the Pope and his witches. I took fright in case the story should get about and my feet be put in the fire till I confessed that I had sold my soul to the Devil. So I saved up a few pence every week till I had enough to bring me to Dublin, and one day after my morning's work on the farm, instead of coming in for dinner I walked into Belfast. It was a brave long walk, more than seven miles, so I had to buy some meat, and this left me with only a shilling above my railway fare. I was afraid to break into my shilling in Dublin, but by ten o'clock it was that cold I had to have a cup of tea. I hung round the coffee-stall, thinking I might hear where I could look for work in the morning, and then the stall-keeper closed for the night. A drizzle was coming on, and the policeman I spoke to told me I had better go to the workhouse. But I didn't know the road, and if they didn't take me in (and why should they? for I didn't belong to Dublin), I'd have to come all the way back again. Why back again? the doctor asked, and she said that she expected more luck about the parks. Then where? queried the doctor. Than in the streets round a workhouse, she answered. The late hour and the word luck put the thought of prostitution and begging into the doctor's mind, and it was with a sort of relief that he heard her say that on that night luck would have meant to her a bench where she could sit till daybreak. I was looking for one, she said, when a girl spoke to me. I think I heard you ask the policeman where you could get a lodging, said she; those were her very words; but I told her I had no money to pay for one, only a few pence. She asked me if I was from Dublin and I answered I was not, that I was from the County Down and had taken the train from Belfast that night. We walked on together. I said: You are out late, and she told me that she was out to meet somebody. But it's getting late, she said, and the rain is coming on again; if you stay out all night you'll be soaked. I told her I couldn't help that, for I had only a few pence and was afraid to go to a doss-house where the beds are threepence a night. She didn't answer me and I could see she was turning something over in her head. It was then that I began to take notice of her; I noticed her umbrella, for I had never had one myself, and wondered why she had spoken to me and let me walk by her side. She had a veil, too. Quite the lady, said I to myself, and no ill-looking girl either. She told me her name was Phyllis Hoey and that she worked in the daytime in a biscuit factory, and if I came with her in the morning I could get work there, not work that would be well paid for, but enough to pay for my lodging. As for food and clothes, well, that was another thing, she said. She told me to come in under her umbrella out of the rain, and I came up close, afraid at first to take her arm. We'll be fellow-workers in the morning, she said, and you can sleep with me to-night. I didn't know where she was taking me to. It was a long way, and it was all I could do to hold out till the end, and I can't tell you, sir, what a relief it was to get out of the darkness, to see her light a candle, and to catch sight of the bed. We slept soundly enough, and in the morning she took me to the factory. The manager wanted an extra girl, as it happened, and I would get eight shillings a week. As I only got three-and-six a week for pulling mangrel-wurzels, eight shillings seemed like a fortune. Why, said I to Phyllis as we went to the workroom, if you let me live with you we'll have sixteen shillings a week. We won't have all that, said Phyllis, for there are always fines; they generally manage to get a shilling a week out of us. Well, fifteen shillings, said I, and it was disheartening to hear her say that we'd have to pay more for the room now there were the two in it.

The day passed from eight o'clock in the morning until twelve, packing the biscuits in tin boxes, with every layer separated by paper, and they told me we mustn't let it get crumpled; if the Inspector found the least wrinkle in the paper, we had to unpack the box again, and as we were paid by piece-work I soon saw that like this we wouldn't get even six shillings a week maybe. At twelve there was an hour for dinner; as I'd had no breakfast I didn't know how I'd get through to the end of the day, and I wouldn't have if Phyllis hadn't taken me to a grub-shop, where she said most of the girls went for their food, the ones that wasn't living at home, and Phyllis paid for me, for I'd have no money till the end of the week.

But, said I, our dinners alone will cost us all we earn. Phyllis laughed and said that there were always extras; I thought she meant overtime, and we went back to the factory. It closed at seven. And on our way home I asked if we couldn't buy our food and cook it ourselves, and save half of what we spent in the grub-shop. But Phyllis was afraid that we'd not get back to the factory in time, and any saving we'd make would be lost in a fine. And so talking we got back to our room, where Phyllis began to dress herself out just as I'd seen her the night before, hat, umbrella and gloves, and as she didn't offer to take me with her, I stayed at home, waiting up till midnight. You mustn't wait up for me, she said, for if you do you'll be too tired to go to work. And what about you? said I, and waited for an answer, which I didn't get. She just went on undressing herself, taking out of her pocket more money than I knew she had gone out with.

It was that night as we lay down together that she said to me: Well, Sarah, you may just as well hear it now as later. A girl can't get a living out of the factory; it just keeps us employed in the daytime, and then the girls go out into Sackville Street, and there, or round about the Bank or in Grafton Street, the money's good – you can pick up half a sovereign or maybe a sovereign. But you don't find them along the pavement, said I. Our gentlemen friends give as much, ninny, she said, and I quickly understood that the factory girls, all the young ones at least, made their living, or the best part of it, on the streets, and that I'd have to do the same, for I couldn't thole going on sponging on Phyllis, who only fell away from the right course because there was no other way for a girl to get her living in Dublin, none that she knew of. I heard Phyllis fall asleep, but I couldn't sleep that night for thinking, it not seeming to me that I could go on the streets nor that I could stay at home while she did, for that would be like taunting her, living a lady's life at home and she walking out round and round, up one street and down another. That's how I saw her in my head all the night, afraid to come back without half a sovereign, and to take money earned her way seemed no better than earning it that way myself. Phyllis didn't try to persuade me; she said that every girl must do the best she can for herself. She had often heard of girls marrying in the end off the streets, but she didn't want to say a word that might lead me where I didn't want to go. She said she quite understood, but that there wouldn't be enough money for both of us if I didn't go, and in the end I might have been pushed into it, for I'm no better than Phyllis; and there never was a kinder soul, and maybe it's kindness that counts in the end.

And how was it that you escaped the street, Sarah?

No more than an accident, sir. We were at work all day in the factory, as I've told you, and while Phyllis was out from seven o'clock till half-past eleven or twelve, I used to sit sewing, trying to make a little money that way, and as it was summer time the nuns were out every evening in their garden. I forgot to tell you that our window overlooked a convent garden, a lovely garden, with big trees and green plots, and it was lovelier when the nuns came out and walked in twos and threes through the shadows. I had only known religion as a quarrelsome thing that set men throwing stones and beating each other with sticks, breaking windows and cursing each other, and I said: If I had time, I'd like to know more of the nuns, they seem so quiet and happy. But we were, as I've said, at work all day, and it wasn't till there was a strike in the factory that the days were our own, with no bell ringing and nobody to take our names as we went in. We could go and come as we liked, only there was the money; but as most of the girls got their living as I told you, sir, we could hold out. It was whilst the strike lasted that I went to the nuns' chapel to attend Mass, a thing we seldom had – on Sundays we had to sleep it out. The strike lasted a fortnight, and I heard a little more of the Catholic religion than was spoken about in the County Down. Phyllis said; If you have a feeling that way, tell the priest who hears your confession that you'd like instruction in the Catholic religion; he'll give it to you and jumping. So I did, and entered the Church just about when the strike was to end.

But, Sarah, I thought you were always a Catholic.

My mother was a Catholic and I was baptized one, as I've told you, but mother went over when I was a child; between twelve and thirteen I was at the time, so you see I had had no instruction, or very little, in my religion. I'd been a month in Dublin by this time and owed Phyllis more money than I would ever be able to pay her back, and I was thinking of going into service, which I ought to have done long before, but I knew nobody that would recommend me. Father Roland (that was the priest who instructed me) said he would recommend me, but he was a long time about it and things were going from bad to worse. It seemed that I would have to do in the end as Phyllis did, and it might have been like that if Father Roland hadn't said one day: Some nuns in Wales are looking out for lay sisters, but they are very poor and cannot afford to send you the price of your passage over; and you'll want money to buy the clothes you'll wear during your probationship. But where am I to get the money? I asked, and he spoke of putting by a little week by week; and I was going to tell him how I was living, but the story didn't seem one for a gentleman like him to hear. And it all seemed more hopeless than ever. Phyllis said nothing, but I knew she was thinking that I'd better come out with her of an evening. She was down on her luck; for nearly a week she had not met with any money, and we were as poor as we could be, but still I clung on to hope. I seemed very selfish to myself, but you see, I was only eighteen and knew nobody except Phyllis and the girls at the factory. If I had known then what I know now, I could have gone to an agent and got some charring, maybe a situation. But I'm making a long story out of it, and the telling of it will make no difference. I must leave you, sir.

I'll be able to tell you, Sarah, if you'll have to leave me when I have heard your story.

Well, sir, one night Phyllis came home in great spirits. She had met a gentleman who had been very kind to her and given her two pounds. We talked about him a long while, and Phyllis was to meet him next day. And when she came back about half-past eleven, that was her time, she said: I told him about you, and he says that he'll pay the money for the convent if you'll come to meet him. It wasn't for sin that he needed me; the man was really a very religious man and knew that he was doing wrong in lying with Phyllis, but he couldn't help himself; and that was why he told her he would give the money to get me into the convent. I was to pray for him in return.

And did you go to meet him, Sarah?

No, sir; for the next time Phyllis saw him he said that Phyllis's word was good enough for him, and that he'd give her the money, taking in return for it my promise to pray for him. Tell him, I said to Phyllis, that I will never cease to pray for him, and for you, too, dear Phyllis, though indeed it should be you to pray for me, so much does it seem that I'm the wicked one. And we spoke of the wages of sin. But Phyllis said: Dear, you wouldn't do it well; you're not suited to the life. It's well that you didn't.

She seems to be a very good girl, your Phyllis, the doctor said.

Yes, Phyllis is a good girl. There never was a better one, so good that it seemed to me, as I was saying, sir, that I was the wicked girl and Phyllis the good one. But that couldn't be, for the Church says different. Then I seemed to understand that every day I stayed in Dublin I was putting Phyllis into sins that she wouldn't commit if I wasn't with her. The night she went out to meet the gentleman again I prayed for them both all the time, and the money seemed hateful money she brought back. But there it was; it was earned, it was gotten, it would have to be spent, and it was better it should be spent on a good purpose than on a bad, so it seemed to me; and the next day we bought the clothes. Father Roland wrote to the nuns. A telegram came, and we went down to the boat together, crying all the way, for we were very sorry to part. Sir, I don't think I can go on telling you. It broke my heart to part with that girl; she'd been so good to me and we were such friends, and there was nothing for it now but we be to part for ever. I felt I was never going to see her again, and I think she felt the same about me.

Have you never tried to find her, Sarah?

Oh, sir, all my evenings out have been spent hunting for her round Merrion Square and round about College Green, up Sackville Street as far as the Rotunda, looking for her in the crowd. Now and again it seemed to me that I saw somebody like her, and I ran and looked into her face, but it was not Phyllis. I can't go on telling you the story, sir. I can't, indeed I can't. She laid her face in her hands and fell across the doctor's writing-table, her sobs alarming him, the big tears rolling from her eyelids down her swollen cheeks, even to her chin. If anybody were to call! The doctor waited, saying nothing, relying on silence to calm the girl's grief. At last he said: Let me hear the rest of the story. You went on board the boat and arrived at the convent – when?

In the late afternoon, sir, towards evening. I don't think I can tell you any more of it.

Yes, you can, Sarah. I cannot tell you whether you are to stay or go till I've heard the end.

Well, I don't know that there's much more to tell, sir. You can guess the rest, that I was very miserable at leaving Phyllis, and felt more and more as time went on that in God's sight there could not be much to choose between us, and at last I went with my story to the Mother Prioress.

To the Mother Prioress! the doctor repeated.

You see, I wanted to leave the convent and go back to Phyllis and tell her that I'd lead her life. In great grief one hasn't one's right thoughts. And when I came to the Prioress to tell her that I wasn't happy and what I had left behind, she said: My child, you can't go to a life of sin. Well, what can I do? I asked her, and she told me that there was one remedy for it all, and that was prayer. You see, she said, you are without money, without friends; you can't save Phyllis from the life she is leading, but you can pray for her. All things are in the hands of God; he alone can help. So I took the Prioress's advice and prayed. . . . After a time I was a postulant and then a novice, and when I had taken the final vows I seemed stronger. But there was always in my heart the pain that I had left Phyllis to a life of sin and gone away myself to a life of comfort and ease, with the hope of heaven at the end. I couldn't get it out of my head, and I wouldn't have been able to bear if it it hadn't been for the Mother Prioress, who was very good to me and understood that the lay sisters had as much right to hear Mass as the choir sisters. But her time came, as it will come to all of us, and the Prioress that came after her was quite different from the one that had gone.

It was she who turned you out of the convent, wasn't it? Sarah answered: Yes, sir, and continued her story drearily, telling that several lay sisters in the convent had died, and that many of those who remained were old women who had come to the end of their time, infirm, bed-ridden women: We had to attend on them in their cells and wheel them up and down the Broad Walk when there was a little sun. These old sisters were a great burden on the funds of the convent; I think the choir sisters felt it. And then two lay sisters died, young women who were not strong enough for the work. That was about three years ago, sir. So the convent was short of workers, and the choir sisters had to shift for themselves, and not being used to work they soon tired. So the Mother Prioress wrote to all the priests she knew for postulants, but the ones that answered her letters wanted to be choir sisters; none of them had fortunes, and the convent couldn't afford to take them without. So all the work fell upon us, and many days we didn't even get Mass. There was no time for private prayer; it was drudge, drudge all the day, and if half an hour or ten minutes did come, I was too tired to pray, and there seemed to be no hope for me to make up my arrears. My health, too, began to fail, and I was distracted by thoughts that I was failing in my duty towards Phyllis. The Prioress had told me I could only help Phyllis by my prayers, and in the last years there was no time. And what with bad health and thinking that I was remiss in my duty towards her and the man who had given me the money, one of the big dishes dropped out of my hand one day in the kitchen. The noise and the clatter of the pieces brought in the Sub-Prioress, who told me I wasn't worth my keep. I didn't answer her, but she brought the Prioress to see the kitchen, and everything was found fault with: it wasn't swept, and the crockery was chipped and broken – all through my carelessness. I don't know what they didn't find fault with that day, and they thrieped on me till at the last the blood went to my head and I spoke without knowing what I was saying, telling them that while they were walking idly in the garden we were working our lives away. Yes, I think I said that two nuns had died already of hard work and bad food, and that we had no time for prayer; that the nunnery was no house of prayer but just a sweaters' den, and that I'd sooner go back to a biscuit factory, where at all events I had the evenings to myself for prayer. I said many wrong things, but however wrong I was the Prioress shouldn't have turned me out of the convent after ten years of work. I stood up for her when I came here first, sir, when you spoke against her; but perhaps I am wrong now and was right then. And now you have had the whole story.

Not at all the story, Sarah.

Well, I know no more of it, sir.

You have not told me why you're leaving my service.

My duty is towards Phyllis, sir; I have promised her my prayers, and there's the man that paid for me, too, to be considered. If I married I would be having children and I'd have to look after them, and Phyllis would be forgotten; I couldn't be remembering her always except in a convent.

You've never told me, Sarah, how you met Miss Lynch. You must have met her the day you arrived in Dublin.

No, sir; it was the next day. I arrived in Dublin late in the evening, and after walking about Sackville Street, Bond Street, and round Trinity College, searching for Phyllis——

But you were ten years in the Welsh convent, and in ten years——

She may have married; she always looked to marry, I know that, but being in Dublin I had to look, for one never knows. I was just back where I was before, with this difference, that I had a sovereign. The nuns at the last moment said they'd let me have that much——

For ten years' work! chimed in Dr O'Reardon, but without noticing the interruption Sarah continued: It was all over again what it was before, myself asking the policeman to direct me, and when he heard I had money he said there was a woman in the street he lived in who would take me in. He directed me. There was in her house a child put out to nurse——

And Miss Lynch being a Health Inspector! said the doctor. I see it all!

But I wouldn't want you to think ill of the Welsh nuns, sir. You see, it was hard for them to keep me and I after saying to the Prioress that she was answerable for the lives of the lay sisters, and much of that sort. They couldn't have kept me, and I have reason to think they have suffered in their consciences ever since, for when I wrote to them to tell them where I was and that I'd like to enter another convent if they'd give me a brief, they wrote, leaving out many of the bad things I'd said, for they were in the wrong too themselves, and they felt it, I'm sure of it. I am leaving you, sir, with sorrow in my heart, for I cannot find Phyllis, though I have looked everywhere for her.

Phyllis may be dead.

Even so, sir, I must pray for her; we must pray for the dead. I know you Protestants don't, but we Catholics do. And I hope you'll forgive me, sir, if I've deceived you in anything, an' indeed I have that, for I only came into your service to earn enough money——

To go into another convent, the doctor interrupted.

Yes; that was at the back of my mind always.

Well, if that be your conviction, Sarah, you must go.

Now will it be putting you to an inconvenience if I don't stay my month?

It will, Sarah, but I haven't the heart to detain you. Peace of mind comes before everything else; and I dare say that I shall be able to get another parlourmaid within the next three days. And we part then, Sarah, for eternity.

Not for eternity, sir. We shall all meet in heaven, Catholics and Protestants alike.

And what about the broken-hearted man on the ladder clipping the ivy on the wall of my house?

Throwing out the sparrows' nests, sir. He said you told him to.

What is to be done, Sarah? Sweet-peas and sparrows are incompatible.

He's sorry to do it, sir. He showed me a nest with four little ones, and the moment I touched their beaks they opened them, thinking their father and mother were bringing them food.

You think more of the sparrows than of Michael, Sarah.

I'd think of him ready enough if it wasn't for my prayers.

The door closed. The doctor was alone again, and he continued his letter to Helena Lynch, hearing Michael's shears among the ivy.

from *In Single Strictness*, 1922

The Tramp

LIAM O'FLAHERTY

There were eight paupers in the convalescent yard of the work-house hospital. The yard was an oblong patch of cement with the dining room on one side and a high red-brick wall on the other. At one end was the urinal and at the other a little tarred wooden shed where there was a bathroom and a wash-house. It was very cold, for the sun had not yet risen over the buildings that crowded out the yard almost from the sky. It was a raw, bleak February morning, about eight o'clock.

The paupers had just come out from breakfast and stood about, uncertain what to do. What they had eaten only made them hungry and they stood shivering, making muffs of their coat sleeves, their little black woollen caps perched on their heads, some still chewing a last mouthful of bread, others scowling savagely at the ground as they conjured up memories of hearty meals eaten some time in the past.

As usual Michael Deignan and John Finnerty slouched off into the wash-house and leaned against the sink, while they banged their boots on the floor to keep warm. Deignan was very tall and lean. He had a pale melancholy face and there was something the matter with the iris of his right eye. It was not blue like the other eye, but of an uncertain yellowish colour that made one think, somehow, that he was a sly, cunning, deceitful fellow, a totally wrong impression. His hair was very grey around the temples and fair elsewhere. The fingers of his hands were ever so long and thin and he was always chewing at the nails and looking at the ground, wrapped in thought.

'It's very cold,' he said in a thin, weak, listless voice. It was almost inaudible.

'Yes,' replied Finnerty, gruffly, as he started up and heaved a loud sigh. 'Ah –' he began and then he stopped, snorted twice to clear his nose, and let his head fall on his chest. He was a middle-sized, thick-set fellow, still in good condition and fat in the face, which was round and rosy, with grey eyes and very white teeth. His black hair was grown long and curled about his ears. His hands were round, soft and white, like a schoolmaster's.

The two of them stood leaning their backs against the washstand and stamped their feet in a moody silence for several minutes and then the tramp who had been admitted to the hospital the previous night wandered into the wash-house. He appeared silently at the entrance of the shed and paused there for a moment while his tiny blue eyes darted around piercingly yet softly, just as a graceful wild animal might look through a clump of trees in a forest. His squat low body, standing between the tarred doorposts of the shed with the concrete wall behind and the grey sky overhead, was after a fashion menacing with the power and vitality it seemed to exude. So it seemed at least to the two dejected, listless paupers within the shed. They looked at the tramp with a mournful vexed expression and an envious gleam in their eyes and a furrowing of their foreheads and a shrinking of their flesh from this fresh dominant coarse lump of aggressive wandering life, so different to their own jaded, terror-stricken lives. Each thought, 'Look at the red fat face of that vile tramp. Look at his fierce insulting eyes, that stare you in the face as boldly as a lion, or a child, and are impudent enough to have a gentle expression at the back of them, unconscious of malice. Look at that huge black beard that covers all his face and neck except the eyes and the nose and a narrow red slit for the mouth. My God, what throat muscles and what hair on his chest, on a day like this too, when I would die of cold to expose my chest that way!'

So each thought and neither spoke. As the tramp grinned foolishly – he just opened his beard, exposed red lips and red gums with stray blackened teeth scattered about them and then closed the beard again – the two paupers made no response. The two of them were educated men, and without meaning it they shrank from associating with the unseemly dirty tramp on terms of equality, just as they spent the day in the wash-house in the cold, so as to keep away from the other paupers.

The tramp took no further notice of them. He went to the back of the shed and stood there looking out of the door and chewing tobacco. The other two men, conscious of his presence and irritated by it, fidgeted about and scowled. At last the tramp looked at Deignan, grinned, fumbled in his coat pocket, took out a crumpled cigarette and handed it to Deignan with another grin and a nodding of his head. But he did not speak.

Deignan had not smoked a cigarette for a week. As he looked at it for a moment in wonder, his bowels ached with desire for the little thin, crumpled, dirt-stained roll of tobacco held between the thumb and forefinger of the tramp's gnarled and mud-caked hand. Then with a contortion of his face as he tried to swallow his breath he muttered, 'You're a brick,' and stretched out a trembling hand. In three seconds the cigarette was lit and he was inhaling the first delicious puff of drug-laden smoke. His face lit up with a kind of delicious happiness. His eyes sparkled. He took three puffs and was handing the cigarette to his friend when the tramp spoke.

'No, keep it yerself, towny,' he said in his even, effortless, soft voice. 'I've got another for him.'

And then when the two paupers were smoking, their listlessness vanished and they became cheerful and talkative. The two cigarettes broke down the barriers of distrust and contempt between themselves and the tramp. His unexpected act of generosity had counteracted his beard and the degraded condition of his clothes. He was not wearing a pauper's uniform, but patched corduroy trousers and numbers of waistcoats and tattered coats of all colours, piled indiscriminately on his body and held together not by buttons but by a cord tied around his waist. They accepted him as a friend. They began to talk to him.

'You just came in for the night?' asked Deignan. There was still a condescending tone in the cultured accents.

The tramp nodded. Then after several seconds he rolled his tobacco to the other cheek, spat on the floor and hitched up his trousers.

'Yes,' he said, 'I walked from Drogheda yesterday and I landed in Dublin as tired as a dog. I said to myself that the only place to go was in here. I needed a wash, a good bed and a rest, and I had only ninepence, a piece of steak, a few spuds and an onion. If I bought a bed they'd be all gone and now I've had a good sleep, a warm bath, and I still have my ninepence and my grub. I'll start off soon as I get out at eleven o'clock and maybe walk fifteen miles before I put up for the night somewhere.'

'But how did you get into the hospital ward?' asked Finnerty, eyeing the tramp with a jealous look. The cigarette had accentuated Finnerty's feeling of hunger, and he was irritated at the confident way the tramp talked of walking fifteen miles that day and putting up somewhere afterwards.

'How did I get in?' said the tramp. 'That's easy. I got a rash on my right leg this three years. It always gets me into the hospital when I strike a workhouse. It's easy.'

Again there was a silence. The tramp shuffled to the door and looked out into the yard. The sky overhead was still grey and bleak. The water that had been poured over the concrete yard to wash it two hours before still glistened in drops and lay in little pools here and there. There was no heat in the air to dry it.

The other six paupers, three old men with sticks, two young men and a youth whose pale face was covered with pimples, were all going about uncertainly, talking in a tired way and peering greedily in through the windows of the dining room, where old Neddy, the pauper in charge of the dining room, was preparing the bread and milk for the dinner ration. The tramp glanced around at all this and then shrugged his shoulders and shuffled back to the end of the wash-house.

'How long have you been in here?' he asked Deignan.

Deignan stubbed the remainder of his cigarette against his boot, put the quenched piece in the lining of his cap and then said, 'I've been here six months.'

'Educated man?' said the tramp. Deignan nodded. The tramp looked at him, went to the door and spat and then came back to his former position:

'I'll say you're a fool,' he said quite coolly. 'There doesn't look to be anything the matter with you. In spite of your hair, I bet you're no more than thirty-five. Eh?'

'That's just right about my age, but –'

'Hold on,' said the tramp. 'You are as fit as a fiddle, this is a spring morning, and yer loafing in here and eating yer heart out with hunger and misery instead of taking to the roads. What, man! You're mad. That's all there's to it.' He made a noise with his tongue as if driving a horse and began to clap his hands on his bare chest. Every time he hit his chest there was a dull heavy sound like distant thunder. The noise was so loud that Deignan could not speak until the tramp stopped beating his chest. He stood wriggling his lips and winking his right eye in irritation against what the tramp had said and jealousy of the man's strength and endurance, beating his bare hairy chest that way on such a perishing day. The blows would crush Deignan's ribs and the exposure would give him pneumonia.

'It's all very well for you to talk,' he began querulously. Then he stopped and looked at the tramp. It occurred to him that it would be ridiculous to talk to a tramp about personal matters. But there was something aggressive and dominant and yet absolutely unemotional in the tramp's fierce stare that drove out that feeling of contempt. Instead Deignan felt spurred to defend himself. 'How could you understand me?' he continued. 'As far as you can see I am all right. I have no disease but a slight rash on my back and that comes from underfeeding, from hunger and . . . and depression. My mind is sick. But of course you don't understand that.'

'Quite right,' said Finnerty, blowing cigarette smoke through his nostrils moodily. 'I often envy those who don't think. I wish I were a farm labourer.'

'Huh.' The tramp uttered the exclamation in a heavy roar. Then he laughed loudly and deeply, stamped his feet and banged his chest. His black beard shook with laughter. 'Mother of Mercy,' he cried, 'I'll be damned but you make me laugh, the two of you.'

The two shuffled with their feet and coughed and said nothing. They became instantly ashamed of their contemptuous thoughts for the tramp, he who a few minutes before had given them cigarettes. They suddenly realized that they were paupers, degraded people, and contemptible people for feeling superior to a fellow man because he was a tramp. They said nothing. The tramp stopped laughing and became serious.

'Now look here,' he said to Deignan, 'what were you in civilian life, as they say to soldiers, what did you do before you came in here?'

'Oh, the last job I had was a solicitor's clerk,' murmured Deignan, biting his nails. 'But that was only a stop-gap, I can't say that I ever had anything permanent. Somehow I always seemed to drift. When I left college I tried for the Consular Service and failed. Then I stayed at home for a year at my mother's place in Tyrone. She has a little estate there. Then I came to Dublin here. I got disgusted hanging around at home. I fancied everybody was pitying me. I saw everybody getting married or doing something while I only loafed about, living on my mother. So I left. Landed here with two portmanteaux and eighty-one pounds. It's six years ago next fifteenth of May. A beautiful sunny day it was too.'

Deignan's plaintive voice drifted away into silence and he gnawed his nails and stared at the ground. Finnerty was trying to get a last puff from the end of his cigarette. He was trying to hold the end between his thumbs and puckered up his lips as if he were trying to drink boiling milk. The tramp silently handed him another cigarette and then he turned to Deignan.

'What did ye do with the eighty-one quid?' he said. 'Did ye drink it or give it to the women?'

Finnerty, cheered by the second cigarette which he had just lit, uttered a deep guffaw and said, 'Ha, the women, blast them, they're the curse of many a man's life,' but Deignan started up and his face paled and his lips twitched.

'I can assure you,' he said, 'that I never touched a woman in my life.' He paused as if to clear his mind of the horror that the tramp's suggestion had aroused in him. 'No, I can't say I drank it. I can't say I did anything at all. I just drifted from one job to another. Somehow, it seemed to me that nothing big could come my way and that it didn't matter very much how I spent my life, because I would be a failure anyway. Maybe I did drink too much once in a while, or dropped a few pounds at a race meeting, but nothing of any account. No, I came down just because I seemed naturally to drift downwards and I couldn't muster up courage to stop myself. I . . . I've been here six months. . . . I suppose I'll die here.'

'Well I'll be damned,' said the tramp. He folded his arms on his chest, and his chest heaved in and out with his excited breathing. He kept looking at Deignan and nodding his head. Finnerty, who had heard Deignan's story hundreds of times with numberless details, shrugged his shoulders, sniffed and said: 'Begob, it's a funny world. Though I'm damn sure that I wouldn't be here only for women and drink.'

'No?' said the tramp. 'How do you make that out?'

'No, by Jiminy,' said Finnerty, blowing out a cloud of blue smoke through his mouth as he talked. 'I'd be a rich man to-day only for drink and women.' He crossed his feet and leaned jauntily back against the washstand, with his hands held in front of him, the fingers of the right hand tapping the back of the left. His fat round face, with the heavy jaw, turned sideways towards the doorway, looked selfish, stupid and cruel. He laughed and said in an undertone, 'Oh boys, oh boys, when I come to think of it.' Then he coughed and shrugged his shoulders. 'Would you believe it,' he said turning to the tramp, 'I've spent five thousand pounds within the last twelve months? It's a fact. Upon my soul I have. I curse the day I got hold of that money. Until two years ago I was a happy man, I had one of the best schools in the south of Ireland. Then an aunt of mine came home from America and stayed in the house with my mother and myself. She died within six months and left mother five thousand pounds. I got it out of the old woman's hands, God forgive me, and then . . . Oh well.' Finnerty shook his head solemnly, raised his eyebrows and sighed. 'I'm not sorry,' he continued, leering at a black spot on the concrete floor of the wash-house. 'I could count the number of days I was sober on my fingers and thumbs. And now I'd give a month of my life for a cup of tea and a hunk of bread.' He stamped about clapping his hands and laughing raucously. His bull neck shook when he laughed. Then he scowled again and said, 'Wish I had a penny. That's nine o'clock striking. I'm starving with the hunger.'

'Eh? Hungry?' The tramp had fallen into a kind of doze while Finnerty had been talking. He started up, scratched his bare neck and then rummaged within his upper garments mumbling to himself. At last he drew forth a little bag from which he took three pennies. He handed the pennies to Finnerty. 'Get chuck for the three of us,' he said.

Finnerty's eyes gleamed, he licked his lower lip with his tongue and then he darted out without saying a word.

In the workhouse hospital a custom had grown up, since goodness knows when, that the pauper in charge of the dining room was allowed to filch a little from the hospital rations, of tea, bread and soup, and then sell them to the paupers again as extras at nine o'clock in the morning for a penny a portion. This fraudulent practice was overlooked by the ward master; for he himself filched all his rations from the paupers' hospital supply and he did it with the connivance of the workhouse master, who was himself culpable in other ways and was therefore prevented by fear from checking his subordinates. But Finnerty did not concern himself with these things. He dived into the dining room, held up the three pennies before old Neddy's face and whispered 'Three'. Neddy, a lean wrinkled old pauper with a very thick red under-lip like a Negro, was standing in front of the fire with his hands folded under his dirty check apron. He counted the three pennies, mumbling, and then put them in his pocket. During twenty years he had collected ninety-three pounds in that manner. He had no relatives to whom he could bequeath the money, he never spent any and he never would leave the workhouse until his death, but he kept on collecting the money. It was his only pleasure in life. When he had collected a shilling in pennies he changed it into silver and the silver in due course into banknotes.

'They say he has a hundred pounds,' thought Finnerty, his mouth dry with greed, as he watched Neddy put away the pennies. 'Wish I knew where it was. I'd strangle him here and now and make a run for it. A hundred pounds. I'd eat and eat and eat and then I'd drink and drink.'

The tramp and Deignan never spoke a word until Finnerty came back, carrying three bowls of tea and three hunks of bread on a white deal board. Deignan and Finnerty immediately began to gulp their tea and tear at the bread, but the tramp merely took a little sip at the tea and then took up his piece of bread, broke it in two, and gave a piece to each of the paupers.

'I'm not hungry,' he said. 'I've got my dinner with me, and as soon as I get out along the road in the open country I'm going to sit down and cook it. And it's going to be a real spring day, too. Look at that sun.'

The sun had at last mounted the wall. It was streaming into the yard lighting up everything. It was not yet warm, but it was cheering and invigorating. And the sky had become a clear pure blue colour.

'Doesn't it make ye want to jump and shout,' cried the tramp, joyously stamping about. He had become very excited, seeing the sun.

'I'm afraid I'd rather see a good dinner in front of me,' muttered Finnerty with his mouth full of bread.

'What about you, towny?' said the tramp, standing in front of Deignan. 'Wouldn't ye like to be walking along a mountain road now with a river flowing under yer feet in a valley and the sun tearing at yer spine?'

Deignan looked out wistfully, smiled for a moment dreamily and then sighed and shook his head. He sipped his tea and said nothing. The tramp went to the back of the shed. Nobody spoke until they had finished the bread and tea. Finnerty collected the bowls.

'I'll take these back,' he said, 'and maybe I might get sent over to the cookhouse for something.'

He went away and didn't come back. The tramp and Deignan fell into a contemplative doze. Neither spoke until the clock struck ten. The tramp shrugged himself and, coming over to Deignan, tapped him on the arm.

'I was thinking of what you said about . . . about how you spent your life, and I thought to myself, "Well that poor man is telling the truth and he's a decent fellow, and it's a pity to see him wasting his life in here." That's just what I said to myself. As for that other fellow. He's no good. He's a liar. He'll go back again to his school or maybe somewhere else. But neither you nor I are fit to be respectable citizens. The two of us were born for the road, towny. Only you never had the courage of your convictions.'

The tramp went to the door and spat. Deignan had been looking at him in wonder while he was talking and now he shifted his position restlessly and furrowed his forehead.

'I can't follow you,' he said nervously and he opened his mouth to continue, when again he suddenly remembered that the man was a tramp and that it would not be good form to argue with him on matters of moral conduct.

'Of course ye can't,' said the tramp, shuffling back to his

position. Then he stuck his hands within his sleeves and shifted his tobacco to his other cheek. 'I know why you can't follow me. You're a Catholic, you believe in Jesus Christ and the Blessed Virgin and the priests and a heaven hereafter. You like to be called respectable, and to pay your debts. You were born a free man like myself, but you didn't have the courage . . .'

'Look here, man,' cried Deignan in a shocked and angry voice, 'stop talking that rubbish. You have been very kind about – er – cigarettes and food, but I can't allow you to blaspheme our holy religion in my presence.'

The tramp laughed noiselessly. There was silence for several moments. Then the tramp went up to Deignan, shook him fiercely by the right arm and shouted in his ear. 'You're the biggest fool I ever met.' Then he laughed aloud and went back to his place. Deignan began to think that the tramp was mad and he grew calm and said nothing.

'Listen here,' said the tramp. 'I was born disreputable. My mother was a fisherman's daughter and my lawful father was a farm labourer, but my real father was a nobleman and I knew it when I was ten years old. That's what gave me a disreputable outlook on life. My father gave mother money to educate me, and of course she wanted to make me a priest. I said to myself, I might as well be one thing as another. But at the age of twenty-three when I was within two years of ordination a servant girl had a child and I got expelled. She followed me, but I deserted her after six months. She lost her looks after the birth of the child. I never clapped eyes on her or the child since.' He paused and giggled. Deignan bit his lip and his face contorted with disgust.

'I took to the road then,' said the tramp. 'I said to myself that it was a foolish game trying to do anything in this world but sleep and eat and enjoy the sun and the earth and the sea and the rain. That was twenty-two years ago. And I'm proud to say that I never did a day's work since and never did a fellowman an injury. That's my religion and it's a good one. Live like the birds, free. That's the only way for a free man to live. Look at yourself in a looking-glass. I'm ten years older than you and yet you look old enough to be my father. Come, man, take to the road with me to-day. I know you're a decent fellow, so I'll show you the ropes. In six months from now you'll forget you were ever a pauper or a clerk. What d'ye say?'

Deignan mused, looking at the ground.

'Anything would be better than this,' he muttered. 'But . . . Good Lord, becoming a tramp! I may have some chance of getting back to respectable life from here, but once I became a tramp I should be lost.'

'Lost? What would you lose?'

Deignan shrugged his shoulders.

'I might get a job. Somebody might discover me here. Somebody might die. Anything might happen. But if I went on the road . . .' He shrugged his shoulders again.

'So you prefer to remain a pauper?' said the tramp with an impudent, half-contemptuous grin. Deignan winced and he felt a sudden mad longing grow within his head to do something mad and reckless.

'You're a fine fellow,' continued the tramp; 'you prefer to rot in idleness here with old men and useless wrecks to coming out into the free air. What, man! Pull yerself together and come over now with me and apply for yer discharge. We'll foot it out together down south. What d'ye say?'

'By Jove, I think I will!' Deignan with a gleam in his eyes. He began to trot excitedly around the shed, going to the door and looking up at the sky, and coming back again and looking at the ground, fidgeting with his hands and feet. 'D'ye think, would it be all right?' he kept saying to the tramp.

'Sure it will be all right,' the tramp kept answering. 'Come on with me to the ward master and ask for your discharge.'

But Deignan would not leave the shed. He had never in all his life been able to come to a decision on an important matter.

'Do you think, would it be all right?' he kept saying.

'Oh damn it and curse it for a story,' said the tramp at last, 'stay where you are and good day to you. I'm off.'

He shuffled out of the shed and across the yard. Deignan put out his hand and took a few steps forward.

'I say –' he began and then stopped again. His brain was in a whirl thinking of green fields, mountain rivers, hills clad in blue mists, larks singing over clover fields, but something made him unable to loosen his legs, so that they could run after the tramp.

'I say –' he began again, and then he stopped and his face shivered and beads of sweat came out on his forehead.

He could not make up his mind.

from *Spring Sowing*, 1924

Schoolfellows

JAMES STEPHENS

I

We had been at school together and I remembered him perfectly
well, for he had been a clever and prominent boy. He won prizes for
being at the top of his class; and prizes for good behaviour; and
prizes for games. Whatever prizes were going we knew that he
should get them; and, although he was pleasant about it, he knew it
himself.

He saw me first, and he shouted and waved his hat, but I had
jumped on a tram already in motion. He ran after me for quite a
distance; but the trams only stop at regular places, and he could not
keep up: he fell behind, and was soon left far behind.

I had intended jumping off to shake his hand; but I thought, so
fast did he run, that he would catch up; and then the tram went
quicker and quicker; and quite a stream of cars and taxis were in
the way; so that when the tram did stop he was out of sight. Also I
was in a hurry to get home.

Going home I marvelled for a few moments that he should have
run so hard after me. He ran almost – desperately.

'It would strain every ounce of a man's strength to run like that!'
I said.

And his eyes had glared as he ran!

'Poor old chap!' I thought. 'He must have wanted to speak to me
very badly.'

Three or four days afterwards I met him again; and we talked
together for a while on the footpath. Then, at whose suggestion I do
not remember, we moved into the bar of an hotel near by.

We drank several glasses of something; for which, noticing that
his hat was crumpled and his coat sleeves shiny, I paid. We spoke of
the old days at school and he told me of men whom he had met, but
whom I had not heard of for a long time. Such old schoolfellows as I

did know of I mentioned, and in every instance he took their addresses down on a piece of paper.

He asked what I was doing and how I was succeeding and where I lived; and this latter information he pencilled also on his piece of paper.

'My memory is getting bad,' he said with a smile.

Every few minutes he murmured into our schoolday conversation –

'Whew! Isn't it hot!'

And at other times, laughing a little, apologizing a little, he said:

'I am terribly thirsty to-day; it's the heat I suppose.'

I had not noticed that it was particularly hot; but we are as different in our skins as we are in our souls, and one man's heat may be tepid enough to his neighbour.

II

Then I met him frequently. One goes home usually at the same hour and by the same road; and it was on these home-goings and on this beaten track that we met.

Somehow, but by what subtle machinery I cannot recall, we always elbowed one another into a bar; and, as his hat was not getting less crumpled nor his coat less shiny, I paid for whatever liquor was consumed.

One can do anything for a long time without noticing it, and the paying for a few drinks is not likely to weigh on the memory. Still, we end by noticing everything; and perhaps I noticed it the earlier because liquor does not agree with me. I never mentioned that fact to anyone, being slightly ashamed of it, but I knew it very woefully myself by the indigestion which for two or three days followed on even a modest consumption of alcohol.

So it was that setting homeward one evening on the habitual track I turned very deliberately from it; and, with the slightest feeling of irritation, I went homewards by another route: and each night that followed I took this new path.

I did not see him for some weeks, and then one evening he hailed me on the new road. When I turned at the call and saw him running – he was running – I was annoyed, and, as we shook hands, I became aware that it was not so much the liquor I was trying to side-track as my old schoolfellow.

He walked with me for quite a distance; and he talked more volubly than was his wont. He talked excitedly; and his eyes searched the streets ahead as they widened out before our steps, or as they were instantly and largely visible when we turned a corner. A certain malicious feeling was in my mind as we paced together; I thought:

'There is no public-house on this road.'

Before we parted he borrowed a half-sovereign from me saying that he would pay it back in a day or two, but I cheerfully bade adieu to the coin as I handed it over, and thought also that I was bidding a lengthy adieu to him.

'I won't meet him for quite a while,' I said to myself; and that proved to be true.

III

Nevertheless when a fair month had elapsed I did meet him again, and we marched together in a silence which was but sparsely interrupted by speech.

He had apparently prospected my new route, for he informed me that a certain midway side-street was a short cut; and midway in this side-street we found a public-house.

I went into this public-house with the equable pulse of a man who has no true grievance; for, I should have been able to provide against a contingency which even the worst-equipped prophet might have predicted.

As often as his glass was emptied I saw that it was refilled; but, and perhaps with a certain ostentation, I refrained myself from the cup.

Of course, one drink leads to another, and the path between each is conversational. My duty it appeared was to supply the drinks, but I thought it just that he should supply the conversation.

I had myself a fund of silence which might have been uncomfortable to a different companion, and against which he was forced to deploy many verbal battalions.

We had now met quite a number of times. He had exhausted our schooldays as a topic; he knew nothing about politics or literature or city scandal, and talk about weather dies of inanition in less than a minute; and yet – he may have groaned at the necessity – there had to be fashioned a conversational bridge which should unite drink to drink, or drinks must cease.

In such a case a man will talk about himself. It is one's last subject; but it is a subject upon which, given the preliminary push, one may wax eternally eloquent.

He rehearsed to me a serial tale of unmerited calamity, and of hardship by field and flood; of woes against which he had been unable to provide, and against which no man could battle; and of accidents so attuned to the chords of fiction that one knew they had to be true. He had been to rustic-sounding places in England and to Spanish-sounding places in America; and from each of these places an undefined but complete misfortune had uprooted him and chased him as with a stick. So by devious, circuitous, unbelievable routes he had come home again.

One cannot be utterly silent unless one is dead, and then possibly one makes a crackle with one's bones; so I spoke:

'You are glad to be home again,' I queried.

He was glad; but he was glad dubiously and with reservations. Misfortune had his address, and here or elsewhere could thump a hand upon his shoulder.

His people were not treating him decently, it appeared. They had been content to see him return from outlandish latitudes, but since then they had not given him a fair show.

Domestic goblins hinted at, not spoken, but which one sensed to be grisly, half detached themselves from between the drinks. He was not staying with his people. They made him an allowance. You could not call it an allowance either: they paid him a weekly sum. Weekly sum was a large way of putting it, for you cannot do much on fifteen shillings a week: that sum per week would hardly pay for, for –

'The drinks,' I put in brightly; for one cannot be persistently morose in jovial company.

'I must be off,' I said, and I filled the chink of silence which followed on my remark with a waving hand and the bustle of my hasty departure.

IV

Two evenings afterwards he met me again.

We did not shake hands; and my salutation was so brief as not really to merit that name.

He fell in beside me and made a number of remarks about the weather; which, if they were as difficult to make as they were to listen to, must have been exceedingly troublesome to him. One saw him searching as in bottomless pits for something to say; and he hauled a verbal wisp from these profundities with the labour of one who drags miseries up a mountain.

The man was pitiable, and I pitied him. I went alternately hot and cold. I blushed for him and for myself; for the stones under our feet and for the light clouds that went scudding above our heads; and in another instant I was pale with rage at his shameful, shameless persistence. I thrust my hands into my pockets, because they were no longer hands but fists; and because they tingled and were inclined to jerk without authority from me.

We came to the midway, cross-street which as well as being a short cut was the avenue to a public-house; and he dragged slightly at the crossing as I held to my course.

'This is the longest way,' he murmured.

'I prefer it,' I replied.

After a moment he said:

'You always go home this way.'

'I shall go a different way to-morrow,' I replied.

'What way?' he enquired timidly.

'I must think that out,' said I.

With that I stood and resolutely bade him goodbye. We both moved a pace from each other, and then he turned again, flurriedly, and asked me for the loan of a half a crown.

He wanted it to get a – a – a –

I gave it to him hurriedly and walked away, prickling with a sensation of weariness and excitement as of one who has been worried by a dog but has managed to get away from it.

Then I did not see him for two days, but of course I knew that I should meet him, and the knowledge was as exasperating as any kind of knowledge could be.

V

It was quite early in the morning; and he was waiting outside my house. He accompanied me to the tram, and on the way asked me for a half a crown. I did not give it, and I did not reply to him.

As I was getting on the tram he lowered his demand and asked me urgently for sixpence. I did not answer nor look at him, but got on my tram and rode away in such a condition of nervous fury that I could have assaulted the conductor who asked me to pay my fare.

When I reached home that evening he was still waiting for me; at least, he was there, and he may have hung about all day; or he may have arrived just in time to catch me.

At the sight of him all the irritation which had almost insensibly been adding to and multiplying and storing itself in my mind, fused together into one sole consciousness of rage which not even a language of curses could make explicit enough to suit my need of expression. I swore when I saw him; and I cursed him openly when he came to me with the sly, timid, outfacing bearing, which had become for me his bearing.

He began at once; for all pretence was gone, and all the barriers of reserve and decency were down. He did not care what I thought of him: nor did he heed in the least what I said to him. He did not care about anything except only by a means; by every means; by cajolery, or savagery, or sentimentality, to get or screw or torment some money out of me.

I knew as we stood glaring and panting that to get the few pence he wanted he would have killed me with as little compunction as one would kill a moth which had fluttered into the room; and I knew that with as little pity I could have slaughtered him as he stood there.

He wanted sixpence, and I swore that I would see him dead before I gave it to him. He wanted twopence and I swore I would see him damned before I gave him a penny.

I moved away, but he followed me clawing my sleeve and whining:

'Twopence; you can spare twopence: what is twopence to you? If I had twopence and a fellow asked me for it I'd give it to him: twopence. . . .'

I turned and smashed my fist into his face. His head jerked upwards, and he went staggering backwards and fell backwards into the road; as he staggered the blood jetted out of his nose.

He picked himself up and came over to me bloody, and dusty, and cautious, and deprecating with a smile that was a leer. . . .

'Now will you give me twopence?' he said.

I turned then and I ran from him as if I were running for my life. As I went I could hear him padding behind me, but he was in no condition, and I left him easily behind. And every time I saw him after that I ran.

from *Etched in Moonlight*, 1928

Dante and the Lobster

SAMUEL BECKETT

It was morning and Belacqua was stuck in the first of the canti in
the moon. He was so bogged that he could move neither backward
nor forward. Blissful Beatrice was there, Dante also, and she
explained the spots on the moon to him. She showed him in the first
place where he was at fault, then she put up her own explanation.
She had it from God, therefore he could rely on its being accurate in
every particular. All he had to do was to follow her step by step.
Part one, the refutation, was plain sailing. She made her point
clearly, she said what she had to say without fuss or loss of time.
But part two, the demonstration, was so dense that Belacqua could
not make head or tail of it. The disproof, the reproof, that was
patent. But then came the proof, a rapid shorthand of the real facts,
and Belacqua was bogged indeed. Bored also, impatient to get on to
Piccarda. Still he pored over the enigma, he would not concede
himself conquered, he would understand at least the meanings of
the words, the order in which they were spoken and the nature of
the satisfaction that they conferred on the misinformed poet, so
that when they were ended he was refreshed and could raise his
heavy head, intending to return thanks and make formal retraction
of his old opinion.

He was still running his brain against this impenetrable passage
when he heard midday strike. At once he switched his mind off its
task. He scooped his fingers under the book and shovelled it back
till it lay wholly on his palms. The Divine Comedy face upward on
the lectern of his palms. Thus disposed he raised it under his nose
and there he slammed it shut. He held it aloft for a time, squinting
at it angrily, pressing the boards inwards with the heels of his
hands. Then he laid it aside.

He leaned back in his chair to feel his mind subside and the itch
of this mean quodlibet die down. Nothing could be done until his
mind got better and was still, which gradually it did. Then he

ventured to consider what he had to do next. There was always something that one had to do next. Three large obligations presented themselves. First lunch, then the lobster, then the Italian lesson. That would do to be going on with. After the Italian lesson he had no very clear idea. No doubt some niggling curriculum had been drawn up by someone for the late afternoon and evening, but he did not know what. In any case it did not matter. What did matter was: one, lunch; two, the lobster; three, the Italian lesson. That was more than enough to be going on with.

Lunch, to come off at all, was a very nice affair. If his lunch was to be enjoyable, and it could be very enjoyable indeed, he must be left in absolute tranquillity to prepare it. But if he were disturbed now, if some brisk tattler were to come bouncing in now with a big idea or a petition, he might just as well not eat at all, for the food would turn to bitterness on his palate or, worse again, taste of nothing. He must be left strictly alone, he must have complete quiet and privacy, to prepare the food for his lunch.

The first thing to do was to lock the door. Now nobody could come at him. He deployed an old *Herald* and smoothed i. out on the table. The rather handsome face of McCabe the assassin stared up at him. Then he lit the gasring and unhooked the square flat toaster, asbestos grill, from its nail and set it precisely on the flame. He found he had to lower the flame. Toast must not on any account be done too rapidly. For bread to be toasted as it ought, through and through, it must be done on a mild steady flame. Otherwise you only charred the outsides and left the pith as sodden as before. If there was one thing he abominated more than another it was to feel his teeth meet in a bathos of pith and dough. And it was so easy to do the thing properly. So, he thought, having regulated the flow and adjusted the grill, by the time I have the bread cut that will be just right. Now the long barrel-loaf came out of its biscuit-tin and had its end evened off on the face of McCabe. Two inexorable drives with the bread-saw and a pair of neat rounds of raw bread, the main elements of his meal, lay before him, awaiting his pleasure. The stump of the loaf went back into prison, the crumbs, as though there were no such thing as a sparrow in the wide world, were swept in a fever away, and the slices snatched up and carried to the grill. All these preliminaries were very hasty and impersonal.

It was now that real skill began to be required, it was at this point that the average person began to make a hash of the entire proceedings. He laid his cheek against the soft of the bread, it was spongy and warm, alive. But he would very soon take that plush feel off it, by God but he would very quickly take that fat white look off its face. He lowered the gas a suspicion and plaqued one flabby slab plump down on the glowing fabric, but very pat and precise, so that the whole resembled the Japanese flag. Then on top, there not being room for the two to do evenly side by side, and if you did not do them evenly you might just as well save yourself the trouble of doing them at all, the other round was set to warm. When the first candidate was done, which was only when it was black through and through, it changed places with its comrade, so that now it in its turn lay on top, done to a dead end, black and smoking, waiting till as much could be said of the other.

For the tiller of the field the thing was simple, he had it from his mother. The spots were Cain with his truss of thorns, dispossessed, cursed from the earth, fugitive and vagabond. The moon was that countenance fallen and branded, seared with the first stigma of God's pity, that an outcast might not die quickly. It was a mix-up in the mind of the tiller, but that did not matter. It had been good enough for his mother, it was good enough for him.

Belacqua on his knees before the flame, poring over the grill, controlled every phase of the broiling. It took time, but if a thing was worth doing at all it was worth doing well, that was a true saying. Long before the end the room was full of smoke and the reek of burning. He switched off the gas, when all that human care and skill could do had been done, and restored the toaster to its nail. This was an act of dilapidation, for it seared a great weal in the paper. This was hooliganism pure and simple. What the hell did he care? Was it his wall? The same hopeless paper had been there fifty years. It was livid with age. It could not be disimproved.

Next a thick paste of Savora, salt and Cayenne on each round, well worked in while the pores were still open with the heat. No butter, God forbid, just a good forment of mustard and salt and pepper on each round. Butter was a blunder, it made the toast soggy. Buttered toast was all right for Senior Fellows and Salvationists, for such as had nothing but false teeth in their heads.

It was no good at all to a fairly strong young rose like Belacqua. This meal that he was at such pains to make ready, he would devour it with a sense of rapture and victory, it would be like smiting the sledded Polacks on the ice. He would snap at it with closed eyes, he would gnash it into a pulp, he would vanquish it utterly with his fangs. Then the anguish of pungency, the pang of the spices, as each mouthful died, scorching his palate, bringing tears.

But he was not yet all set, there was yet much to be done. He had burnt his offering, he had not fully dressed it. Yes, he had put the horse behind the tumbrel.

He clapped the toasted rounds together, he brought them smartly together like cymbals, they clave the one to the other on the viscid salve of Savora. Then he wrapped them up for the time being in any old sheet of paper. Then he made himself ready for the road.

Now the great thing was to avoid being accosted. To be stopped at this stage and have conversational nuisance committed all over him would be a disaster. His whole being was straining forward towards the joy in store. If he were accosted now he might just as well fling his lunch into the gutter and walk straight back home. Sometimes his hunger, more of mind, I need scarcely say, than of body, for this meal amounted to such a frenzy that he would not have hesitated to strike any man rash enough to buttonhole and baulk him, he would have shouldered him out of his path without ceremony. Woe betide the meddler who crossed him when his mind was really set on this meal.

He threaded his way rapidly, his head bowed, through a familiar labyrinth of lanes and suddenly dived into a little family grocery. In the shop they were not surprised. Most days, about this hour, he shot in off the street in this way.

The slab of cheese was prepared. Separated since morning from the piece, it was only waiting for Belacqua to call and take it. Gorgonzola cheese. He knew a man who came from Gorgonzola, his name was Angelo. He had been born in Nice but all his youth had been spent in Gorgonzola. He knew where to look for it. Every day it was there, in the same corner, waiting to be called for. They were very decent obliging people.

He looked sceptically at the cut of cheese. He turned it over on its back to see was the other side any better. The other side was worse.

They had laid it better side up, they had practised that little deception. Who shall blame them? He rubbed it. It was sweating. That was something. He stooped and smelt it. A faint fragrance of corruption. What good was that? He didn't want fragrance, he wasn't a bloody gourmet, he wanted a good stench. What he wanted was a good green stenching rotten lump of Gorgonzola cheese, alive, and by God he would have it.

He looked fiercely at the grocer.

'What's that?' he demanded.

The grocer writhed.

'Well?' demanded Belacqua, he was without fear when roused, 'is that the best you can do?'

'In the length and breadth of Dublin' said the grocer 'you won't find a rottener bit this minute.'

Belacqua was furious. The impudent dogsbody, for two pins he would assault him.

'It won't do' he cried, 'do you hear me, it won't do at all. I won't have it.' He ground his teeth.

The grocer, instead of simply washing his hands like Pilate, flung out his arms in a wild crucified gesture of supplication. Sullenly Belacqua undid his packet and slipped the cadaverous tablet of cheese between the hard cold black boards of the toast. He stumped to the door where he whirled round however.

'You heard me?' he cried.

'Sir' said the grocer. This was not a question, nor yet an expression of acquiescence. The tone in which it was let fall made it quite impossible to know what was in the man's mind. It was a most ingenious riposte.

'I tell you' said Belacqua with great heat 'this won't do at all. If you can't do better than this' he raised the hand that held the packet 'I shall be obliged to go for my cheese elsewhere. Do you mark me?'

'Sir' said the grocer.

He came to the threshold of his store and watched the indignant customer hobble away. Belacqua had a spavined gait, his feet were in ruins, he suffered with them almost continuously. Even in the night they took over from the corns and hammer-toes, and carried on. So that he would press the fringes of his feet desperately against the endrail of the bed or better again, reach down with his hand and drag them up and back towards the instep. Skill and patience could disperse the pain, but there it was, complicating his night's rest.

The grocer, without closing his eyes or taking them off the receding figure, blew his nose in the skirt of his apron. Being a warm-hearted human man he felt sympathy and pity for this queer customer who always looked ill and dejected. But at the same time he was a small tradesman, don't forget that, with a small trades-man's sense of personal dignity and what was what. Thruppence, he cast it up, thruppence worth of cheese per day, one and a tanner per week. No, he would fawn on no man for that, no, not on the best in the land. He had his pride.

Stumbling along by devious ways towards the lowly public where he was expected, in the sense that the entry of his grotesque person would provoke no comment or laughter, Belacqua gradual-ly got the upper hand of his choler. Now that lunch was as good as a fait accompli, because the incontinent bosthoons of his own class, itching to pass on a big idea or inflict an appointment, were seldom at large in this shabby quarter of the city, he was free to consider items two and three, the lobster and the lesson, in closer detail.

At a quarter to three he was due at the school. Say five to three. The public closed, the fishmonger reopened, at half-past two. Assuming then that his lousy old bitch of an aunt had given her order in good time that morning, with strict injunctions that it should be ready and waiting so that her blackguard boy should on no account be delayed when he called for it first thing in the afternoon, it would be time enough if he left the public as it closed, he could remain on till the last moment. Benissimo. He had half-a-crown. That was two pints of draught anyway and perhaps a bottle to wind up with. Their bottled stout was particularly excellent and well up. And he would still be left with enough coppers to buy a *Herald* and take a tram if he felt tired or was pinched for time. Always assuming, of course, that the lobster was all ready to be handed over. God damn these tradesmen, he thought, you can never rely on them. He had not done an exercise but that did not matter. His Professoressa was so charming and remarkable. Signorina Adriana Ottolenghi! He did not believe it possible for a woman to be more intelligent or better informed than the little Ottolenghi. So he had set her on a pedestal in his mind,

apart from other women. She had said last day that they would read
Il Cinque Maggio together. But she would not mind if he told her,
as he proposed to, in Italian, he would frame a shining phrase on his
way from the public, that he would prefer to postpone the Cinque
Maggio to another occasion. Manzoni was an old woman,
Napoleon was another. Napoleone di mezza calzetta, fa l'amore a
Giacominetta. Why did he think of Manzoni as an old woman?
Why did he do him that injustice? Pellico was another. They were
all old maids, suffragettes. He must ask his Signorina where he
could have received that impression, that the nineteenth century in
Italy was full of old hens trying to cluck like Pindar. Carducci was
another. Also about the spots on the moon. If she could not tell him
there and then she would make it up, only too gladly, against the
next time. Everything was all set now and in order. Bating, of
course, the lobster, which had to remain an incalculable factor. He
must just hope for the best. And expect the worst, he thought gaily,
diving into the public, as usual.

Belacqua drew near to the school, quite happy, for all had gone
swimmingly. The lunch had been a notable success, it would abide
as a standard in his mind. Indeed he could not imagine its ever
being superseded. And such a pale soapy piece of cheese to prove so
strong! He must only conclude that he had been abusing himself all
these years in relating the strength of cheese directly to its green-
ness. We live and learn, that was a true saying. Also his teeth and
jaws had been in heaven, splinters of vanquished toast spraying
forth at each gnash. It was like eating glass. His mouth burned and
ached with the exploit. Then the food had been further spiced by
the intelligence, transmitted in a low tragic voice across the counter
by Oliver the improver, that the Malahide murderer's petition for
mercy, signed by half the land, having been rejected, the man must
swing at dawn in Mountjoy and nothing could save him. Ellis the
hangman was even now on his way. Belacqua, tearing at the
sandwich and swilling the precious stout, pondered on McCabe in
his cell.

  The lobster was ready after all, the man handed it over instanter,
and with such a pleasant smile. Really a little bit of courtesy and
goodwill went a long way in this world. A smile and a cheerful word

from a common working-man and the face of the world was brightened. And it was so easy, a mere question of muscular control.

'Lepping' he said cheerfully, handing it over.

'Lepping?' said Belacqua. What on earth was that?

'Lepping fresh, sir' said the man, 'fresh in this morning.'

Now Belacqua, on the analogy of mackerel and other fish that he had heard described as lepping fresh when they had been taken but an hour or two previously, supposed the man to mean that the lobster had very recently been killed.

Signorina Adriana Ottolenghi was waiting in the little front room off the hall, which Belacqua was naturally inclined to think of rather as the vestibule. That was her room, the Italian room. On the same side, but at the back, was the French room. God knows where the German room was. Who cared about the German room anyway?

He hung up his coat and hat, laid the long knobby brown-paper parcel on the hall-table, and went prestly in to the Ottolenghi.

After about half-an-hour of this and that obiter, she complimented him on his grasp of the language.

'You make rapid progress' she said in her ruined voice.

There subsisted as much of the Ottolenghi as might be expected to of the person of a lady of a certain age who had found being young and beautiful and pure more of a bore than anything else.

Belacqua, dissembling his great pleasure, laid open the moon enigma.

'Yes' she said 'I know the passage. It is a famous teaser. Off-hand I cannot tell you, but I will look it up when I get home.'

The sweet creature! She would look it up in her big Dante when she got home. What a woman!

'It occurred to me' she said 'apropos of I don't know what, that you might do worse than make up Dante's rare movements of compassion in Hell. That used to be' her past tenses were always sorrowful 'a favourite question.'

He assumed an expression of profundity.

'In that connexion' he said 'I recall one superb pun anyway: "qui vive la pietà quando è ben morta . . ."'

She said nothing.

'Is it not a great phrase?' he gushed.

She said nothing.

'Now' he said like a fool 'I wonder how you could translate that?'

Still she said nothing. Then:

'Do you think' she murmured 'it is absolutely necessary to translate it?'

Sounds as of conflict were borne in from the hall. Then silence. A knuckle tambourined on the door, it flew open and lo it was Mlle Glain, the French instructress, clutching her cat, her eyes out on stalks, in a state of the greatest agitation.

'Oh' she gasped 'forgive me. I intrude, but what was in the bag?'

'The bag?' said the Ottolenghi.

Mlle Glain took a French step forward.

'The parcel' she buried her face in the cat 'the parcel in the hall.'

Belacqua spoke up composedly.

'Mine' he said, 'a fish.'

He did not know the French for lobster. Fish would do very well. Fish had been good enough for Jesus Christ, Son of God, Saviour. It was good enough for Mlle Glain.

'Oh' said Mlle Glain, inexpressibly relieved, 'I caught him in the nick of time.' She administered a tap to the cat. 'He would have tore it to flitters.'

Belacqua began to feel a little anxious.

'Did he actually get at it?' he said.

'No no' said Mlle Glain 'I caught him just in time. But I did not know' with a bluestocking snigger 'what it might be, so I thought I had better come and ask.'

Base prying bitch.

The Ottolenghi was faintly amused.

'Puisqu'il n'y a pas de mal . . .' she said with great fatigue and elegance.

'Heureusement' it was clear at once that Mlle Glain was devout 'heureusement'.

Chastening the cat with little skelps she took herself off. The grey hairs of her maidenhead screamed at Belacqua. A devout, virginal bluestocking, honing after a penny's worth of scandal.

'Where were we?' said Belacqua.

But Neapolitan patience has its limits.

'Where are we ever?' cried the Ottolenghi, 'where we were, as we were.'

Belacqua drew near to the house of his aunt. Let us call it Winter, that dusk may fall now and a moon rise. At the corner of the street a horse was down and a man sat on its head. I know, thought Belacqua, that that is considered the right thing to do. But why? A lamplighter flew by on his bike, tilting with his pole at the standards, jousting a little yellow light into the evening. A poorly dressed couple stood in the bay of a pretentious gateway, she sagging against the railings, her head lowered, he standing facing her. He stood up close to her, his hands dangled by his sides. Where we were, thought Belacqua, as we were. He walked on, gripping his parcel. Why not piety and pity both, even down below? Why not mercy and Godliness together? A little mercy in the stress of sacrifice, a little mercy to rejoice against judgment. He thought of Jonah and the gourd and the pity of a jealous God on Nineveh. And poor McCabe, he would get it in the neck at dawn. What was he doing now, how was he feeling? He would relish one more meal, one more night.

His aunt was in the garden, tending whatever flowers die at that time of year. She embraced him and together they went down into the bowels of the earth, into the kitchen in the basement. She took the parcel and undid it and abruptly the lobster was on the table, on the oilcloth, discovered.

'They assured me it was fresh' said Belacqua.

Suddenly he saw the creature move, this neuter creature. Definitely it changed its position. His hand flew to his mouth.

'Christ!' he said 'it's alive.'

His aunt looked at the lobster. It moved again. It made a faint nervous act of life on the oilcloth. They stood above it, looking down on it, exposed cruciform on the oilcloth. It shuddered again. Belacqua felt he would be sick.

'My God' he whined 'it's alive, what'll we do?'

The aunt simply had to laugh. She bustled off to the pantry to fetch her smart apron, leaving him goggling down at the lobster, and came back with it on and her sleeves rolled up, all business.

'Well' she said 'it is to be hoped so, indeed.'

'All this time' muttered Belacqua. Then, suddenly aware of her hideous equipment: 'What are you going to do?' he cried.

'Boil the beast' she said, 'what else?'

'But it's not dead' protested Belacqua 'you can't boil it like that.'

She looked at him in astonishment. Had he taken leave of his senses.

'Have sense' she said sharply, 'lobsters are always boiled alive. They must be.' She caught up the lobster and laid it on its back. It trembled. 'They feel nothing' she said.

In the depths of the sea it had crept into the cruel pot. For hours, in the midst of its enemies, it had breathed secretly. It had survived the Frenchwoman's cat and his witless clutch. Now it was going alive into scalding water. It had to. Take into the air my quiet breath.

Belacqua looked at the old parchment of her face, grey in the dim kitchen.

'You make a fuss' she said angrily 'and upset me and then lash into it for your dinner.'

She lifted the lobster clear of the table. It had about thirty seconds to live.

Well, thought Belacqua, it's a quick death, God help us all.

It is not.

from *More Pricks than Kicks*, 1934

Old Friery

OLIVER ST JOHN GOGARTY

I

Hosanna the Barrister was to meet Old Friery the Coroner in Golly's back at ten. It was getting on for eleven now. Christy Friery was called 'old', not exactly for his age, but for the length of time he had been before the public as City Coroner. He was just as often called Red Friery, on account of the red beard from under which his belly began, and into which his two long cheeks flowed like pink blubber from a pair of foxy eyes with yellow-white lashes, some of which were stubbed at the ends like the legs of a fly, as a result of his attempts to light a cigarette in a breeze. He always wore a black silk hat and a black frock-coat, with a black alpaca waistcoat to keep him cool and yet professional. It was said that the tailor who had taken his measure was out of pocket because he had not taken it as quickly as the bookmakers.

Hosanna the Barrister was different. He was a tall, thin, low-shouldered man with a sudden stomach like the protuberance of a sea-horse, and a mangy moustache and eyebrows, which he used for concentrating or brow-beating, and full florid lips, purple and exuberant, suggesting a Moor or a pair of earthworms on their honeymoon. An unblinking glass eye gave his countenance a fixed regard which suggested unwavering loyalty and steadfastness. He was a ready barrister, with a voice which could rant like a street preacher or whisper as insinuatingly as a charwoman ordering a glass of plain. When shouting he was at his best – *in excelsis*, in fact; that is why he was called Hosanna, though his family name was Bumleigh. Juniors called him when in full blast the Fog Horn, but it was a bad nickname, for a fog horn does not make a fog but is used in time of fog, whereas his roars and vapourings produced each other, and the result was confounded confusion. He was too easily seen through to be a hypocrite; but he was useful as a second-rate work of art is useful: it exemplifies the obstacles to perfection. 'Nobody can be superior to nothing,' as Barney says; but if the half failures were not there, it would be hard to know who were the better advocates.

For all the humbug which was inseparable from his profession, he was a man of upright life so far as conduct went, thanks to his having read on the barrows more second-hand smutty books than anyone in Dublin. Others held – but what did they know? – that his virtue was due to accompanying the four honest solicitors who were addicted to Art on their triennial trips to Paris. They may have come to this conclusion from a 'show me your company and I'll tell you what you are'. But this could not be right either, because he owed a considerable amount of his practice to his association with Lad Lane and other 'whereases'.

Now, instead of being supported by shady solicitors, he was supporting one, for Old Friery as a solicitor was about the shadiest in Dublin – a qualification which would have been more becoming to the rôle of Coroner among the unhouselled shades of the morgue than to the rôle of attorney.

Old Friery the Coroner came into Golly's snug and took his breakfast, which consisted of an aspirin and a naggin of malt.

'Go easy with the water,' he said, as Golly emptied the naggin into a half-pint tumbler. 'I wouldn't have to take this at all if it wasn't for the wind that gets congealed round me heart.'

Mr Golly stood back, halted, and surveyed him. He went back another little bit, to gather way as it were, and then came forward bravely like an engine preparing to shunt.

'Isn't it you that's in luck?' And he stared hard at Friery.

Friery, whose nerves were on edge, didn't relish the stare.

'I wouldn't have noticed it if you hadn't told me,' said the Coroner dryly. 'I'm up to-day in the Recorder's Court. Where is the luck?'

'It's here in me waistcoat pocket,' Golly replied. 'You spoke of the wind getting congealed round your heart?'

'If it wasn't round me heart it might be round worse. I'm moidered from this blasted flatulence. It takes a naggin to break it every morning.'

'I suffered something shocking from it myself until I got this. I

haven't tried them yet. But they'll cure anything from lumbago to a
smoking chimney. I have it from the horse's mouth, first shot.' He
tapped a box of pills.

'The horse's mouth' was an unhappy metaphor. It jarred on
Friery, who lost a race which he would have won (talking of horses'
mouths) 'if the bastard had only put out his tongue'. Horse's
mouth!

'I'll just stop two and give you four,' said the generous Mr Golly.

The Coroner took one and put the rest of the pills in an empty
matchbox, which with difficulty he returned to his waistcoat
pocket.

'Do you expect me to swallow this without a drink?' he asked.

Mr Golly, who was not prepared for the complication, slowly
obliged.

'Why can't that bloody fellow Bumleigh keep his appointment?
He should have been here hours ago. I'll have to be getting off.' As
he displayed no haste, and as it was the third time in an hour that
the Coroner 'had to be getting off', he had evidently used words
which were not 'operative'.

'What do you take to open your stomach in the morning?' he
asked to humour Golly, who had stood the drink.

'Anything at all,' said Golly, 'that will break the wind and let the
food in. There was a chemist fellow called Hoey in here one day and
he explained the whole thing to me. Of course I disagree with him –
that is, I'd be sorry to go the whole way with him. He's only a
chemist, not a doctor. He said it wasn't wind.'

'Then what did he explain?' asked the Coroner hopelessly.

'He explained why your heart goes rolling round in the morning
and your stomach fills with air.'

'I wish to God he had my heart,' said the Coroner.

'"It's not wind at all," sez Hoey, "but it's your stomach that
swells up like a pig's bladder. The minute it bulges up to hit the
heart there's hell to pay," sez he.'

'He's not far wrong,' said Friery the Coroner.

'"Yer heart is like a bull-frog leppin' on a bladder. No wonder
yer agitated in the mornings." Them's the very words he used.'

'Who's this fellow Hoey?' the Coroner asked, interested.

'He's a kind of chemist's assistant. Of course he's not a doctor.

But I've two prime boys here now and they're coming on nicely in the curriculum and that sort of thing,' Mr Golly explained.

A tapping on the glass panel of the door announced Bumleigh.

To a question, he replied: 'A dry ginger ale.'

When Mr Golly reappeared Bumleigh spoke so confidentially to Friery that Golly, recognizing 'legal stuff and all that kind of thing', felt himself constrained to withdraw.

'The ould huer comes along,' Friery explained. '"I have just this lump sum that himself left me, and I'd like you to invest it for me, sir," sez she.'

'And the lady was?' Hosanna asked.

'The Toucher's relict, of course. I thought I told you.'

Bumleigh nodded sententiously and hummed. 'Invest?' he whispered equivocally.

'She might have meant me to put it into a brewery, but I would do no such thing. Not I. Why should I? Invest a poor woman's legacy in drink, is it?'

'To spend money on drink would have been highly reprehensible. What will you have?' asked Bumleigh the Barrister.

The Coroner indicated his tumbler as if he resented the superfluous question. Everyone knew that he had to take whiskey because beer or porter made him fat.

Bumleigh threw back his Cantrell and Cochrane with a relish and reluctantly ordered a large Jameson for his companion.

'"I've something gilt-edged," sez I, "something that can't go wrong, something that will give you an interest as well as multiply your capital if we don't spoil the market,"' Friery continued. '"Something that will leave you comfortable for your old age. Leave it to me," sez I. With that, she left the monkey and went out.'

'An organ-grinder's widow?'

Contemptuously Friery went on: 'I rang up a few of the boys to get it on in dribs and drabs on the course for the four-thirty at Baldoyle. None of these huers of bookmakers will take a bet from me lately, not even in honest cash. Well, after a hard morning's work on the telephone I got four ponies on.'

'On four ponies,' Bumleigh suggested. He was answered by a glance of contempt.

'Well, you know what happened? Jayshus, if the bastard had only put out his tongue!'

'And she is now taking proceedings?'

'Proceedings, is it? I'm proceeding to Green Street this morning, and I want you to defend me before that old goat, Falconer the Recorder.'

Hosanna nodded sententiously, and said 'Hum.'

'Stop that bumming or you'll drive me mad. Christ! To look at you one would think that I was for the Jug. You might think that I hadn't obeyed instructions or that I did something dishonest. Instead of helping me out, you are Job's comforter. Can't you work yourself into one of your righteous wraths and bloody well roar like Hell's blazes? Tell them where they get off; and the criminal scandal of suspecting the City Coroner. And then give them a squirt of tears, and say that never in your life did you hear of a more blackmailing attempt to get blood out of a most respected sportsman. Didn't I breed the Artful Dodger? Holy God, do you know who I am at all?'

'Is all the money gone?' asked Bumleigh the Barrister noncommittally.

The Coroner raised his hands as if he were rising from the sea. He did not see why there should be fees between colleagues.

Hosanna whistled softly, pointed his eyebrows at the ceiling, and coming down to earth, gulped his mineral.

'Suppose we make a clean breast of it?'

'Clean breast me neck! Wasn't the horse pulled? How could anything be clean from that stable? I tell ye we're up against a gang of twisters and copers. There was trickery in it from the word "Go"!'

Bumleigh nodded sententiously.

'Honest to God, Bumleigh, you'd think I had done something dishonest. And I up against a gang of rogues! Who the hell is briefing you, anyway?'

'Tell me nothing, tell me nothing!' Bumleigh implored. 'The less I know, the better I am. But calm yourself, my friend. I was only wishing that your case was, shall we say, more difficult to defend. Had it been a straightforward case – that is' – he checked himself to choose a word that would be nearer, all things considered, to *le mot juste* than 'straightforward' – 'what I mean is, you know in Law, that the worse the case the better. I'm not sure that I have the forensic skill to deal with a simple and uncomplicated action; yet yours is not very far from one. But tell me no more, 'twould only complicate the brief. It is well that you happen to be a solicitor or I couldn't take instructions at all.' He sighed and placed his hand over his diaphragm. He groaned inaudibly and then raised his hand genteely to his mouth.

'Those gaseous waters!'

'Coddin' apart, try one of these; they cured me. I know what's wrong with you.' The Coroner took the matchbox, after a struggle, from his waistcoat-pocket, which the protuberance of his belly kept closed. 'Try one of these.'

'What are they?'

'They are for the wind. I got them from Golly before you came in. He suffers from flatulence himself.'

'May I keep it until we are in Court?'

Friery nodded, using his belly for an ash-tray when his cigarette-ash fell.

'Have you got an empty matchbox?'

Bumleigh fumbled, for he did not smoke and a matchbox was not among his possessions.

'You can put it in your spectacle case.'

II

The Recorder, a white old man, was in his restless dotage. You never knew what side he'd be on. If he favoured you at the beginning of a case you might be in gaol at the end.

'And who is this widow?' he asked.

'She isn't a widow, your Lordship,' Lad Lane, the counsel for the plaintiff, said.

'Nonsense! I am distinctly under the impression that she is the widow of Toucher Duff. You said so yourself.'

'I said "relict", your Lordship. She is a lady who lived as his housekeeper with the lately departed sportsman.'

The Recorder sat up and glared over his spectacles at the woman who, acting on instructions, was sobbing quietly, for she had been told that when Counsel produced his handkerchief she was to break down. On a second and emergency production she was to collapse. This was round one.

'You mean that she was living with him?' the Recorder demanded.

Bumleigh groaned, disedified. His foot touched Friery's under the table. Apparently all so far was going well. A prostitute against a man of repute.

'Speak up, my good woman, and stop that sniffling. Tell the court, were you living with this – this – what's his name? – this Toucher person?'

'I was living with him, me Lord.'

Bumleigh saw victory in the offing.

'And now you are unprotected. It's a serious offence to rob the defenceless.' The Recorder was unaccountable!

'Your Lordship!'

'Sit down, Mr Bumleigh!'

Bumleigh groaned and rumbled internally. Friery tapped him over his spectacle case. Bumleigh took the hint.

'How came you to meet the defendant?'

'When he was holding an inquest on the Toucher.'

'Your – your paramour?'

Having not the faintest notion what 'paramour' meant, she answered: 'He always treated me well.'

'Continue.'

'The Toucher sez Old Friery was one of those –'

'Mr Friery!' the Recorder corrected.

The result of this was to confuse the plaintiff. She looked in vain for the handkerchief. The Recorder came to her aid.

'You have just told us that the Coroner here held an inquest on – on – Go on – and that you were favourably impressed.'

'Well, he let him be removed before the things got stale for the wake.'

'And that was enough to make you entrust him with all you possessed?'

'He often defended the Toucher when he got himself mixed up with the polis. And he defended me for the Margarine.'

The Recorder held up the court. 'Margurine,' he corrected, hardening the g.

'Margurine' brought back to mind one of Friery's forensic triumphs in the very court where now he found himself arraigned. The Recorder, who was given to endless irrelevant soliloquies, was trying the present plaintiff, who, months before, was accused of selling margarine as butter. She was defended by Friery.

'The pronunciation of this word must be settled before I can permit the hearing of this case to continue. After all, it is necessary to know what we are talking about –' 'Hear, hear!' said a solitary voice in the gallery, but it was unsupported. 'It is a matter of first principles – pronunciation. There seems to be a difference of opinion about the value of the g. Is it soft as in "marjarine" or hard? – I confess that I myself incline to a hard g as in "margurine".'

Friery, who knew that this could go on for an hour, was growing impatient. He interrupted: 'My client has settled that question to her own satisfaction. She called it "butter". That's why she's here.'

But it was Christy Friery himself was here now.

'It is obvious that you trusted him,' the Recorder remarked.

'The defendant does not deny receiving this money and dissipating it – Mr Bumleigh?'

Bumleigh rose to address the court. He began on a low key. He used a well-known gambit.

'Never has it been my experience to defend so important a civic official from a more trivial charge, or one coming from a more unsavoury source. What have we here? We have a woman, a self-confessed prostitute, arraigning a most respectable solicitor. She charges him with having misappropriated monies – for that is what it amounts to. No, no, Mr Lane me Lad.'

'Your Worship?' Mr Lad Lane was motioned down. That raised the voice of Bumleigh to stentorian pitch. He roared: 'A goat-toothed woman against the City Coroner!' He flung his gown off his arm as he pointed dramatically to Friery, whom he nearly hit upon the head. 'And how, and from what, and from whom did she receive the money?'

'From the Toucher who once caused a scene at Baldoyle with the Coroner, while he had occasion to conduct some members of the Vice-regal Party over the course.'

'It was only Lord Dudley's jockey, me Lord.'

'Silence!' roared Bumleigh in a voice that murdered silence.

'When he found himself accosted by the late Toucher, who seized him by the arms and whispered dramatically, "Don't let them see me."'

'Who were the people by whom he did not wish to be seen?' The Recorder inquired.

'The bookmakers, your Worship.'

'So this woman's paramour was not *persona grata* with bookmakers?'

'He was, your Worship. He was only pretending. He was attempting a confidence trick.'

'It is all very confusing. Proceed, Mr Bumleigh.'

'"Don't let them see me talking to you. Your bet would not be worth placing if they knew it was me gave you the tip. And they'd blame me for robbing them. Oh, don't let them see me!" While this confidence trick was being played –'

'Confidence trick!' Lad Lane echoed disconcertingly.

'I said confidence trick, for there is no other name for the means whereby this bookies' tout obtained the money which has now gone rightly back to those from whom it came. Every racegoer, every sportsman knows' – his voice fell to its insinuating semitone – 'in which category I have reason to include your Worship.'

'But not as a betting man, Mr Bumleigh. Not as a gambler!'

Bumleigh bowed, corrected. A bad break.

'We have here money from a contaminated source. I have a story of "instructions" to this conscientious solicitor. And what were those instructions? What were they. I ask Heaven.'

'You'll be on surer ground if you confine yourself to where you're known,' Lad Lane remarked. 'They were – and let this not be highly passed over – we have the plaintiff's own admission. What did she tell the Coroner? What were her instruction? "Invest it for me."' He looked round the court and glared horribly at the door, through which a large policeman, who had slipped out for 'a small one', was just then returning. That worthy fell back concussed by the voice of conscience.

'She told him to invest.'

'That is admitted, Mr Bumleigh.'

This caused the air to lose some vibrations and, unstimulated by the echoes of his own production, The orator had to begin again.

'"Invest," I said. Now what does "invest" mean? What does it connote to bookmakers, touts of whom this unfortunate female's partner in sin was one! What does it mean but to put the money on a horse? I submit – I submit that this woman, impressed by the integrity of the Coroner exercising his solemn function and investigating the awful problem of death, tried to take advantage of his fair credit with those who accept bets (a sad practice, I regret to say; almost a reprehensible practice) and to get him to put her money on in his own name. What else does "invest" mean to the sporting fraternity? What did this lecherous leman mean?' He swung round with the centrifugal force of his own question and pointed his eyebrows like the ears of an alert horse at two maiden sisters whom Friery had done out of five hundred pounds at the beginning of the flat-racing season.

'I said lecherous leman, and I mean it. Who is this leman?' He roared, and wriggled his wrists high in the air. 'Who is this leman?'

At this moment a spare old man with a wizened face – dead but for its intelligent bright eyes – and a broken nose that appeared to have been tattooed on the bridge or stricken by a cinder clinker, stood up at the back of the court. It was Tommy Monks, the Brummagem Bantam, hero of a hundred fights, one time champion of the Midlands. He was half deaf from the impact of a thousand punches. He had never heard so clearly since he was a young man. He thought that Hosanna was asking him about his one-time manager, so he stood up to him and answered:

'He was a wrong 'un all right.'

Having spoken, he subsided with his head lowered to keep the shouting off his point. The fetid court-house retched and re-echoed. The Impeachment of Warren Hastings was as nothing compared with the invective of Bumleigh bombinating at his best. 'Who is this lech –'

Lad Lane threw in his handkerchief; his client took the count.

'I perceive that the lady has fainted. Revive her, constable.' The Recorder extended his water carafe and tumbler.

The plaintiff had the good fortune to awake just in time.

'It's a heart attack!' she whispered. 'Dr Nedley says, "When she gets them, bring her into Hedigan's and make her take a large brandy or a few balls of malt."' She swooned again. She was half restored by a 'Baby Power'.

The Recorder appeared to be relieved.

'Could you modulate your voice, Mr Bumleigh?' he said, and then, in tones of kindness, asked the convalescent – 'Tell me, how came you to be associated with Mr Duff, and how long did this – this liason last?'

'His Worship is addressing you,' the police constable whispered.

'After me other sister died, your Worship.'

'Had he two – had you two – had you a sister?'

'I had. And when she died I was the only one he had left.'

The Recorder jerked his head swiftly from side to side like a goalkeeper expecting a shot from dribbling forwards. Then he shouted reproachfully, 'She was his sister, Mr Bumleigh! Is not that so, my good woman?'

'But I never said I wasn't. I never told a lie.'

Now it was Bumleigh who was in distress; he appeared to have some of the symptoms of acute colic. He looked reproachfully at Friery. That worthy surreptitiously suggested that it was time for tears. Forget the flatulence.

'We have here,' continued Bumleigh in a voice that contained the immemorial woe of the world since Time began its human story, 'we have on the one side a woman associated with those racegoing gangs that infest the racecourses of England, and are about to begin their nefarious operations in our hitherto crimeless country. And on the other side, at my hand here, is one of the most respected and beloved citizens who ever held public offfice in any country. A friend of the poor, a general comforter of the distressed. When a body has been taken from the Liffey after long immersion, and the wife of the unfortunate human being who was "Found Drowned" approaches the Morgue to try to identify in death what had been in life her bread-winner, is she confronted with red tape or the corpse? No; but with the Coroner. This kindly man makes it his business – nay, his duty – to attend what has become the last home of the unfortunate or the suicide, and to meet there the distressed relatives of whosoever – pardon me – of whomsoever has been laid out on the Morgue's melancholy slate. Does he persecute the bereaved with questions? No. What does he do? He does all that a man may do, and let us hope it is not always in vain – he comforts the afflicted and releases the corpse in time for the wake and the sad, insolvent obsequies of the poor. That, your Lordship, is our City Coroner. What city on the broad surface of the earth has a coroner to compare to him? When I think of all the affliction with which it is his lot to be confronted, when I see in my mind's eye the windows in shawls dragging along their fatherless children, I think of Friery the Coroner, the Comforter. I see his kindly pat on the head for the bereaved and bereft' (still speaking, he leant sideways to indicate with flattened hand the height of the toddler's head), 'and I can hardly withhold a manly tear. I –' He sobbed, griped with emotion and the pill that had as it appears been thoughtfully and propitously administered, and a large tear was the result. It rolled down his gown. The Coroner bowed his head, overwhelmed by his own benevolence. A tear struck the back of his client's chubby hand. 'I am not ashamed of my feelings, your Lordship. You too have had experience in this court of much of the misery that exists among the poor. You have protected them by long sentences from the rascal and the rogue. Now I ask you to protect this benevolent citizen from the machinations of the racegangs and the footpads and other ruffians who are at the back of this conspiracy of blackmail. I have done.' He sat down, snorting with emotion.

'Really, it seems to me that this is not a simple matter at all. It must be inquired into. I will remand the defendant for a week in protective custody. Of course, now that you have reminded me, you will understand that no stigma accrues to it. It is merely a measure for his own safety.'

Friery shook the tear from the back of his hand in disgust and scowled at Bumleigh. 'You overdid it,' he whispered. 'You hypocritical old hulk! Why the hell didn't you cut out that protection blather? Now you have me in Mountjoy, and there's not the least use in appealing to that old goat.'

Bumleigh, who was always dignified, forbore to reply rudely. 'You nearly poisoned me with your pill. It went the wrong way,' was all he said. He left the court with hastening steps. He was resigned to the ingratitude which marks the daily round. This time he was 'on the run' and no mistake!

Friery called after him, 'You must have taken the pill upside down,' which only made it worse because it showed a lack of sympathy; for who can tell when a pill is upside down? It was to the direction of its action he probably referred.

III

Lad Lane and Bumleigh were drawn together by a great bond of sympathy: they were married to sisters. They were left without illusions about each other; and their regard for each was more equable than high. It is not surprising, therefore, to find them changing sides, exchanging briefs, and slanging each other with all the gusto that advocates can assume when they are paid for being sincere. When the bond is remembered we can forget what might need explanation, the reversal of their rôles. When Friery emerges from the cynically named Mountjoy he finds that he is being prosecuted by his former Counsel and defended by his former prosecutor, Lad Lane. I was on the point of being surprised myself until I realized that it would reveal an ignorance of forensic procedure. Who or what is a prisoner, to set a bound to the march of a great advocate? Friery was not surprised.

Bumleigh rose to his full height. He looked pale and dishevelled, like a vulture moulting. His solemn agony had not yet faded from him. He remembered the pill. He opened for the plaintiff in the tones of one weighed down by a sense of injustice done. He suggested by his appearance that all the world's injustice had afflicted himself.

'We have here a poor woman who is the sister of the dead Duff. She went to live with him on the death of her older sister. Your Worship has before you the spectacle of Miss Duff, a woman twice bereaved.'

'Mrs Aggie Durkin, saving yer presence, a decent married woman, even though I am a widow and all that.'

'Aggie Durkin?'

'Short for Antoinette, mc Lordship.'

'A woman thrice bereaved,' Bumleigh continued. When he had

recovered from the shock of the plaintiff's recognizing Counsel without the mediation of a solicitor, he accepted it was a breach of etiquette, instructions from the plaintiff on the field, as it were. 'She entrusts her little legacy to the City Coroner, who, taking advantage of his high office and of the confidence implied by it, squanders on the fortuitous fields of Baldoyle the hard-earned money of this widow and thrice-bereaved worker. I do not know, nay, I would not care to know that infamy could go deeper. I would not care to know,' he repeated, wagging his head, 'lest my faith in the truth and goodness of human nature be destroyed. There is at root true worth in all men, even in some criminals. That worth is hard to find and is, if present at all, at a low level in the Coroner.'

Lad Lane interrupted with, 'My dear brethren, –'

'This was the manner of the distribution of the lady's savings. It was – you have heard the word "invested" in four ponies – that is, to use racing parlance, until the monkey was exhausted by other pony transactions.'

'There is a society – I believe there is a society in this town, Mr Bumleigh,' said the Recorder, 'known as the Society for the Prevention of Cruelty to Animals. I fail to see why it should permit such an exhibition in such a public place. I hope the monkey has recovered.'

'If the monkey could be recovered, your Worship, we wouldn't be here at all,' Lad Lane informed the Recorder.

Bumleigh in affected despair sat down.

'Get up,' said Lad Lane, 'and go on with your menagger-ey.'

'The g is soft in "menagerie", Mr Lane, soft,' said the Recorder. 'Was it at a circus, was it at a circus that the money was lost?'

'No, at Baldoyle races. He put the monkey on in a series of ponies. No bookmaker would deal directly with the Coroner. He had difficulty in investing it.'

'It is very all confusing. Where is the money now?'

'Lost,' moaned Bumleigh, 'through a betrayal of trust.'

'How much is lost?'

'The whole monkey.'

'But a monkey is not money?' the Recorder roared.

'I said I thought that I had made it clear,' said Bumleigh

penitentially, 'that I spoke in racing parlance: a monkey is five hundred pounds.'

The Recorder jerked himself high on his seat. 'And have I been kept for two days listening to a case over which I have no jurisdiction? You know well, or you ought to know well, that I cannot – this court cannot deal with sums in excess of fifty pounds. The case should never have been brought before me at all. Take it where you like, Mr Bumleigh. But take it out of my court. And when you appear before me again I will request you not to use horse copers' slang. Dismissed!'

That is how Counsel saved Friery the Coroner. And Friery was grateful to him, for, as he explained afterwards to his friends who were congratulating him, 'It's better not to have Bumleigh with you, but against you, if he is to do you any good.'

An attack of virtuous indignation afflicted Friery:

'I'd rather be a whore any day of the week than one of those barristers. A whore sells her body; but a barrister sells his bloody mind to the highest bidder. A whore can call her soul her own.' The idea of Friery as a whore was overwhelming. Falstaff as the Witch of Brentford! But Old Friery! Why, he couldn't get a fidelity guarantee to set up even as the Whores' Bank.

from *Tumbling in the Hay*, 1939

Drink and Time in Dublin

FLANN O'BRIEN

A RECORDED STATEMENT

– Did you go to that picture *The Lost Weekend*?

– *I did.*

– I never seen such tripe.

– *What was wrong with it?*

– O it was all right, of course – bits of it was good. Your man in the jigs inside in the bed and the bat flying in to kill the mouse, that was *damn* good. I'll tell you another good bit. Hiding the bottles in the jax. And there was no monkey business about that because I tried it since meself. It works but you have to use the half pint bottles. Up the chimbley is another place I thought of and do you know the ledge affair above windows?

– *I do.*

– That's another place but you could get a hell of a fall reaching up there on a ladder or standing on chairs with big books on them. And of course you can always tie the small bottles to the underneath of your mattress.

– *I suppose you can.*

– But what are you to do with the empties if you stop in bed drinking? There's a snag there. I often thought they should have malt in lemonade syphons.

– *Why didn't you like the rest of* The Lost Weekend?

– Sure haven't I been through far worse weekends meself – you know that as well as I do. Sure Lord save us I could tell you yarns. I'd be a rich man if I had a shilling for every morning I was down in the markets at seven o'clock in the slippers with the trousers pulled on over the pyjamas and the overcoat buttoned up to the neck in the middle of the summer. Sure don't be talking man.

– *I suppose the markets are very congested in the mornings?*

– With drunks? I don't know. I never looked round any time I was there.

– *When were you last there?*

– The time the wife went down to Cork last November. I won't forget that business in a hurry. That was a scatter and a half. Did I never tell you about that? O be God, don't get me on to *that* affair.

– *Was it the worst ever?*

– It was and it wasn't but I got the fright of me life. I'll tell you a damn good one. You won't believe this but it's a true bill. This is one of the best you ever heard.

– *I'll believe anything you say.*

– In the morning I brought the wife down to Kingsbridge in a taxi. I wasn't thinking of drink at all, hadn't touched it for four months, but when I paid the taxi off at the station instead of going back in it, the wife gave me a look. Said nothing, of course – after the last row I was for keeping off the beer for a year. But somehow she put the thing into me head. This was about nine o'clock, I suppose. I'll give you three guesses where I found meself at ten past nine in *another taxi?*

– *Where?*

– Above in the markets. And there wasn't a more surprised man than meself. Of course in a way it's a good thing to start at it early in the morning because with no food and all the rest of it you're finished at four o'clock and you're home again and stuffed in bed. It's the late nights that's the killer, two and three in the morning, getting poisoned in shebeens and all classes of hooky stuff, wrong change, and a taxi man on the touch. After nights like that it's a strong man that'll be up at the markets in time next morning.

– *What happened after the day you got back at four?*

– Up at the markets next morning *before* they were open. There was another chap there but I didn't look at him. I couldn't tell you what age he was or how bad he was. There was no four o'clock stuff that day. I was around the markets till twelve or so. Then off up town and I have meself shaved be a barber. Then up to a certain hotel and straight into the bar. There's a whole crowd there that I know. What are you going to have and so on. No no, have a large one. So-and-so's getting married on Tuesday. Me other man's wife has had a baby. You know the stuff? Well Lord save us I had a terrible tank of malt in me that day! I had a feed in the middle of it because I remember scalding myself with hot coffee and I never touch the coffee at all only after a feed. Of course I don't remember what happened me but I was in the flat the next morning with the clothes half off. I was supposed to be staying with the brother-in-law, of course, when the wife was away. But sure it's the old dog for the hard road. Drunk or sober I went back to me own place. As a matter of fact I never went near the brother-in-law at all. Be this time I was well into the malt. Out with me again feeling like death on wires and I'm inside in the local curing meself for hours, spilling stuff all over the place with the shake in the hand. Then into the barber's and after that off up again to the hotel for more malt. I'll give you a tip. Always drink in hotels. If you're in there you're in for a feed, or you've just had a feed, or you've an appointment there to see a fellow, and you're having a small one to pass the time. It looks very bad being in bars during the daytime. It's a thing to watch, that.

– *What happened then?*

– What do you think happened? What could happen? I get meself into a quiet corner and I start lowering them good-o. I don't know what happened me, of course. I met a few pals and there is some business about a greyhound out in Cloghran. It was either being bought or being sold and I go along in the taxi and where we were and where we weren't I couldn't tell you. I fall asleep on a chair in some house in town and next thing I wake up perished with the cold and as sick as I ever was in me life. Next thing I know I'm above in the markets. Taxis everywhere of course, no food only the plate of soup in the hotel, and be this time the cheque-book is in and out of the pocket *three or four times a day*, standing drinks all round, kicking up a barney in the lavatory with other drunks, looking for me 'rights' when I was refused drink – O, blotto, there's no other word for it. I seen some of the cheques since. *The writing!* A pal carts me home in a taxi. How long this goes on I don't know. I'm all right in the middle of the day but in the mornings I'm nearly too weak to walk and the shakes getting worse every day. Be this time I'm getting frightened of meself. Lookat here, mister-me-man, I say to meself, this'll have to stop. I was afraid the heart might give out, that was the only thing I was afraid of. Then I meet a pal of mine that's a doctor. This is inside in the hotel. There's only one man for you, he says, and that's sleep. Will you go home and go to bed if I get you something that'll make you sleep? Certainly, I said. I suppose this was about four or half four. Very well, says he, I'll write you out a prescription. He writes one out on hotel notepaper. I send for a porter. Go across with this, says I, to the nearest chemist shop and get this stuff for me and here's two bob for yourself. Of course I'm at the whiskey all the time. Your man comes back with a box of long-shaped green pills. You'll want to be careful with that stuff, the doctor says, that stuff's very dangerous. If you take one now and take another when you get home, you'll get a very good sleep but don't take any more till to-morrow night because that stuff's very dangerous. So I take one. But I know the doctor doesn't know how bad I am. I didn't tell him the whole story, no damn fear. So out with me to the jax where I take another one. Then back for a drink, still as wide-awake as a lark. You'll have to go home now, the doctor says, we can't have you passing out here, that stuff acts very quickly. Well, I have one more drink and off with me, *in a bus*, mind you, to the flat. I'm very surprised on the bus to find meself so wide-awake, looking out at people and reading the signs on shops. Then I begin to get afraid that the stuff is too weak and that I'll be lying awake for the rest of the evening and all night. To hell with it, I say to meself, we'll chance two more and let that be the end of it. Down went two more in the bus. I get there and into the flat. I'm still wide-awake and nothing will do me only one more pill for luck. I get into bed. I don't remember putting the head on the pillow, I wouldn't go out quicker if you hit me over the head with a crow-bar.

– *You probably took a dangerous over-dose.*

– Next thing I know I'm awake. It's dark. I sit up. There's matches there and I strike one. I look at the watch. The watch is stopped. I get up and look at the clock. Of course the clock is stopped, hasn't been wound for days. I don't know what time it is. I'm a bit upset about this. I turn on the wireless. It takes about a year to heat up and would you believe me I try a dozen stations all over the place and not one of them is telling what the time is. Of course I knew there was no point in trying American stations. I'm very disappointed because I sort of expected a voice to say 'It is now

seven thirty p.m.' or whatever the time was. I turn off the wireless
and begin to wonder. I don't know what time it is. *Then*, bedamnit,
another thing strikes me. *What day is it?* How long have I been
asleep with that dose? Well lookat, I got a hell of a fright when I
found I didn't know what day it was. I got one hell of a fright.

   – *Was there not an accumulation of milk-bottles or newspapers?*

   – There wasn't – all that was stopped because I was supposed to
be staying with the brother-in-law. What do I do? On with all the
clothes and out to find what time it is and what day it is. The funny
thing is that I'm not feeling too bad. Off with me down the street.
There's lights showing in the houses. That means it's night-time
and not early in the morning. Then I see a bus. That means it's not
yet half-nine, because they stopped at half-nine that time. Then I
see a clock. It's twenty past nine! But I still don't know what day it
is and it's too late to buy an evening paper. There's only one thing –
into a pub and get a look at one. So I march into the nearest, very
quiet and correct and say a bottle of stout please. All the other
customers look very sober and I think they are all talking very low.
When the man brings me the bottle I say to him I beg your pardon
but I had a few bob on a horse today, could you give me a look at an
evening paper? The man looks at me and says what horse was it? It
was like a blow in the face to me, that question! I can't answer at all
at first and then I stutter something about Hartigan's horses. None
of them horses won a race today, the man says, and there was a
paper here but it's gone. So I drink up the bottle and march out. It's
funny, finding out about the day. You can't stop a man in the street
and say have you got the right day please? God knows what would
happen if you done that. I know be now that it's no use telling lies
about horses, so in with me to another pub, order a bottle and ask
the man has he got an evening paper. The missus has it upstairs, he
says, there's nothing on it anyway. I now begin to think the best
thing is to dial O on the phone, ask for Inquiries and find out that
way. I'm on me way to a call-box when I begin to think that's a very
bad idea. The girl might say hold on and I'll find out, I hang on
there like a mug and next thing the box is surrounded by Guards
and ambulances and attendants with ropes. No fear, says I to
meself, there's going to be no work on the phone for me! Into
another pub. I have the wind up now and no mistake. How long

was I knocked out be the drugs? A day? Two days? Was I in the bed *for a week*? Suddenly I see a sight that gladdens me heart. Away down at the end of the pub there's an oul' fellow reading an evening paper with a magnifying glass. I take a mouthful of stout, steady meself, and march down to him. Me mind is made up: if he doesn't hand over the paper, I'll kill him. Down I go. Excuse me, says I, snatching the paper away from him and he still keeps looking through the glass with no paper there, I think he was deaf as well as half blind. Then I read the date – I suppose it was the first time the date was the big news on a paper. It says 'Thursday, 22nd November, 1945.' I never enjoyed a bit of news so much. I hand back the paper and says thanks very much, sir, for the loan of your paper. Then I go back to finish me stout, very happy and pleased with me own cuteness. Another man, I say to meself, would ask people, make a show of himself and maybe get locked up. But not me. I'm smart. Then begob I nearly choked.

– *What was the cause of that?*

– To-day is Thursday, I say to meself. Fair enough. But *what . . . day did I go to bed?* What's the use of knowing to-day's Thursday if I don't know when I went to bed? I still don't know whether I've been asleep for a day or a week! I nearly fell down on the floor. I am back where I started. Only I am feeling weaker and be now I have the wind up in gales. The heart begins to knock so loud that I'm afraid the man behind the counter will hear it and order me out.

– *What did you do?*

– Lookat here, me friend, I say to meself, take it easy. Go back now to the flat and take it easy for a while. This'll all end up all right, everything comes right in the latter end. Worse than this happened many's a man. And back to the flat I go. I collapse down into a chair with the hat still on me head, I sink the face down in me hands, and try to think. I'm like that for maybe five minutes. Then, *suddenly*, I know the answer! Without help from papers or clocks or people, I know how long I am there sleeping under the green pills! How did I know? Think that one out! How would *you* know if you were in the same boat?

(Before continuing, readers may wish to accept the sufferer's challenge.)

– *I am thinking.*

– Don't talk to me about calendars or hunger or anything like that. It's no use – you won't guess. You wouldn't think of it in a million years. Look. My face is in my hands – like this. Suddenly I notice the face is smooth. I'm not badly in need of a shave. That means it *must* be the same day I went to bed on! Maybe the stomach or something woke me up for a second or so. If I'd stopped in bed, I was off asleep again in a minute. But I got up to find the time and that's what ruined me! Now do you get it? Because when I went back to bed that night, I didn't waken till the middle of the next day.

– *You asked me how I would have found out how long I had been there after finding that the day was Thursday. I have no guarantee that a person in your condition would not get up and shave in his sleep. There was a better way.*

– There was no other way.

– *There was. If I were in your place I would have looked at the date on the prescription!*

from *Irish Writing*, No. 1, 1946

Ballintierna in the Morning

BRYAN MACMAHON

One clear cold morning in November two young men boarded a south-bound train in Kingsbridge Station, Dublin. Both were bareheaded and wore shabby tweed overcoats. That they were fitters was a fact indicated by a black timber attaché case which one of the men was carrying; there were also tell-tale smudges of grease on their cuffs and on the edges of their overcoat pockets. Their names were Bernie Byrne and Arthur Lowe: they were being sent by their firm to repair the boiler of a country Creamery in County Kildare.

Byrne was an albino; his complexion was over-fresh and his eyes were the eyes of a tamed white rodent. His hair was cut short to avoid attracting undue attention, but the irrepressible pink of his body had bubbled up through his scalp. His expression had a disconcerting trick of trading idiocy for sagacity at the most unexpected moments. Arthur Lowe's face gave promise of being cadaverous before he was twenty-five. He had a facial tic. He was so sallow that one could not imagine his intestines to be other than grey rubber tubes. His humour, of which he was extremely niggardly, was slow, droll and deliberate. His dyspepsia, already chronic, had made him a person subject to sudden bouts of unreasoning irritation.

During the journey down – a bare hour's run – they remained standing in the corridor with their elbows resting on the horizontal guard-bar of a window. Since they were young, they resented the fact that they were wearing their working clothes while travelling – this was the reason that they did not enter a compartment. The corridor was ammoniac and stale and had little to offer them except the beginnings of train-queasiness. Despite this they found the ride slightly exhilarating, and it was with an unmistakable, if indeed somewhat subdued, sense of adventure that they looked out into the widening day. People passing to the lavatory crushed by them with barely articulated apologies. The young men gave room with excessive readiness as if to compensate with manners what they lacked in clothes. Looking downwards at an angle of forty-five degrees Byrne saw in the compartment behind him a sickish girl of four or five who was mouthing biscuits. The compartment was crowded; at a station he heard a stout woman praise the virtues of Aylesbury ducks. Some time afterwards he heard a voice from the other side of the compartment begin: 'There's nothing on earth the matter with my husband, but. . . .'

The men alighted at a small station in County Kildare. An impish boy of twelve with a red head and a freckled face met them. That he was a playboy was instantly obvious. His face cracked up with contagious glee as he asked:

'Are ye the men to mend the Creamery?'

'We are!'

The albino was laughing. The boy's face set for a moment as he examined Byrne's face and eyes. The albino resented the examination.

'The manager says I'm to show ye the way. If ye like, I'll get the case sent up in a Creamery car and ye can take the short-cut across the bog?'

'Across the bog?'

'Aye!'

'That'll suit me fine,' said Byrne.

The boy roared at the porter who, on closer inspection, proved also to have a red head and was obviously a brother of the guide: 'Hey, Mick, send that up in the next car!'

When they came out of the station they saw the trees. From an old oak depended the tattered remnants of summer finery now eked out in ragged brown bunting; a mendicant beech held out in emaciated hands the last of its unspent coppers; the furze was flecked with in-between-season gold. Beneath the trees they saw the bogland. As they approached it they lost interest in the trees and were taken with the as yet finite landscape. Following the boy they crossed the fence between the trees and were then on the floor of the bog.

Before them a turf bank reared itself in a great black rectangular box with planed-away corners. Drawing near they saw that, close

to the surface, this rampart had crazied into fissures that had oozed
irregularly shaped knobs of semi-dried peat. Clean rushes in tight
clumps sprang from the chocolate-coloured ground. Bogholes were
filled with ink or quicksilver according to the light's quirk. A not
repulsive odour of old sulphur came up out of the mould underfoot.

Their guide was agility itself. He sprang to a step in the black
bog-wall, gained purchase and leaped up. The two young men
followed. Then they saw the countryside in its entirety. It had all
the variety of a display of tweeds in a shop window. Under their feet
it was prune and orange and vermilion, with sometimes a lichen
blazing up in a brilliant green. The leathery heather swished
hungrily around their boots. The large white bones of fallen and
stripped trees were flung here and there in the canyons of the
cutaway. The sun had bleached them and the wind had antlered
them. Two or three newly erected labourers' cottages were placed
around the periphery of the bog: what with their red roofs, green
doors, white walls and tarred plinths they had a wholly fictitious
prettiness. A disconsolate black cow moved dully beside each of
these dwellings. The sky was a wash of grey clouds. On the near
horizon they saw the scarlet and white hulk of the Creamery.
Beyond it were the crisp orthodox hills of the Irish skyline.

The men strode along, singularly braced by the morning air. To
breathe it was in itself an adventure. Since the ground underfoot
was reasonably dry they had the sensation of walking on eider-
downs. On their left they saw a hollow square carpeted with *fionnán*
as white as wood fibre. It was growing in great tufts which were
heavily matted in one another. The hollow seemed as snug as the
bottom of a delf-crate. Their guide dropped into this hollow, at the
same time signalling to the men not to make unnecessary noise.
Byrne and Lowe followed warily. The youngster had his hands
extended with the palms turned backwards. He was tiptoeing
forward, his pert head turning this way and that. Suddenly he
stood stockstill and the wings of his nostrils widened. His eyes were
fixed on a tuft of grass before him. Seeing him standing thus the
two men halted. Then the boy threw himself forward on the
ground. Lying prone he scrambled into a ball, bringing his knees
up to him and clawing at his belly. The men heard a squeal coming

from beneath the boy. For all the world it sounded like the complaint of an injured infant.

'I have him! I have him! I so-hoed the hare!' The youngster's voice was blotched with an excitement which immediately communicated itself to the men who began to laugh and query eagerly. Lowe's tic began to beat furiously. Meanwhile the little actor was making the most of his moment on the stage. He rolled over to his knees, thence to his feet, all the while clutching something in the pit of his stomach. Then the men saw the elongated whitish body trimmed with red-brown fur. They saw the cut and carve of the great hind legs, the squashed ears and the huge protuberant eyes. Carefully the boy gathered the animal together, all the while keeping the hind legs under firm control.

All three grew strangely intimate after sharing this experience together. With a nod of his head the boy indicated the hare's form in the grass. The albino immediately crouched and bared the snug little arch. They all saw where the bones of the hare's buttocks had bared the dark clay. Byrne and Lowe in turn placed the backs of their hands on the floor of the form and remarked that it was still warm. As they stood up, each man shrank and shrank in imagination until he was a hare in the form peering out at the world through the tangled stems of the grasses.

Then Bernie Byrne asked: 'Hey! what are you going to do with him?'

This was a question the boy had not asked himself previously. He took refuge in a laughing vagueness. But the act in him suddenly provided the answer.

'I don't know . . . unless I kill him!'

'Will you give him to me?' asked the albino.

'Alive?'

'Yes, alive!'

'Sure I'll give him to you. I'll put him in a bag above at the Creamery and you can take him with you.'

Arthur Lowe had recovered his moroseness. 'What do you want him for?'

'I don't know. . . . I'll do something with him.' Byrne smiled and grew remote. This withdrawal irked Lowe who said, 'Come on or we'll never get this job done.'

It was night when they returned to the city. A frosty river-wind caused them to shudder as they emerged from the station. Arthur Lowe was carrying the timber case: Byrne had the hare in a bag. They took a bus to O'Connell Bridge.

Looking up the great thoroughfare, Byrne suddenly discovered that he had been granted the power to view his city with novel eyes. For one thing the balusters of the bridge were now wondrously white. The diffused light in the street was almost as impalpable as floating powder: it hung in a layer perhaps twenty feet in height and then it fined upwards into the windless city rigging. Over this was the unremembered night sky. Dan O'Connell himself and his satellites in bronze had all fused to form a drowsy octopus; Nelson was a cold hero on an eminence waiting to be quickened by a brilliant anecdote. The trams were lively enough, but they had gone to great pains to conceal their pattering feet. To the left and right Neon displayed its inability to form a right angle. Now and again a ragamuffin wind, shot with gaseous green slime, clambered up the ladders in the river walls and shrugged its facile way in and out of the arcades and the ice-cream parlours. The curves of the lamp-standards interpreted benevolence in terms of cement.

The people, too, had altered. In a remote nook in the street cerulean lanterns were busy transforming the passers-by into death's heads. The theatre queues were composed of sexless, friendless, kinless persons who had voluntarily assembled thus in batches to make it easy for them to be gathered to God. The managements of the eating-houses had scraped circles or triangles or squares or lunes in the frosted rear glass of their windows through which the prudent could observe the imprudent eating lime-green hens. Objects in breeches and skirts trod on the grey-green cellar lights and applauded themselves for their intrepidity. A girl with her partner passed by hurriedly; a shell-pink dance frock was showing below her dark coat. Suddenly she leaned forward and, egging her face onwards to a gambler's vivacity, said sweetly, 'But Joseph . . .' Two workmen passed by; one of them was saying vehemently and gutturally, 'Play yer cards, I said, play yer cards.'

The albino had halted by the O'Connell Monument. His eyes were luminous in the dark.

'Hey!' called Lowe. 'Whatta yeh doin'?'

Byrne did not answer. He stepped softly in under the statue where it was semi-dark. He ripped the slip-knot on the sack's mouth, caught the sack by the bottom, and spilled the hare out on the ground. The animal was cramped: he gave three sorry hops, then crouched against the base of the statue. Above him Octopus O'Connell gave no indication of ambling.

(A hare is composed of three delightful ovals with swivels at the neck and loins. First there is the great oval of the body, balanced above and below by the smaller ovals of the head and hind quarters. The oval of the hind quarters is fragmentary but may be indicated satisfactorily enough by a simple illustration. The flexible ears are propellers, the tail a rudder. After that it is a question of power propelling a mechanism that is in perfect equipoise.

But wherever the power of the animal is generated, it finds expression in the spatulate hind legs which have the gift of spurning the world. Spurning the world – that's the secret out! That is what makes the hare so surpassingly gallant and his beholders so chagrined and superstitious.)

Sallowface was very quiet as he watched the albino. The tic flicked in his morose features. His face cleared as he gradually acquitted his companion of black-guardism. Byrne had begun to smile curiously; he crouched with legs set well apart. His two palms began to aim the hare towards the lighted street. The animal moved in the desired direction but, as yet, his gait consisted of despicable lopes. There was no indication that he could be so transcendently swift. Suddenly he stopped and began to cosy himself on a tram-track. Then he looked like an illustration of a hare in a child's picture-book. A breath of river-wind came upon him and eddied his fur; this wind also edged the albino's anger. He stripped his teeth and shouted, 'Yeh-Yeh-Yeh!' He raced his heavy boots and cried 'Hulla-hulla-hulla!' as he slipped his imaginary hounds. The somnolent hare became suddenly charged with action. First he sprang erect until he was a vibrant red loop laced with white shadow. His ears were tubed to the street. Then he began to pelt up mid-road. All the while the maniacal teeth of the albino were volleying 'Yeh-Yeh-Yeh!' behind him.

At first the hare's passing occasioned little comment. The people continued to stilt along or stand in lack-lustre lumps. Then someone began to cry out 'The Hare! The Hare!'

(You have seen the breeze impishly test the flexibility of a barley field; you have seen a child's hand ruffle the tassels of a country-woman's shawl; you have seen a window-wind bring to life the dead hair of a deskful of schoolgirls.)

'The Hare! The Hare!'

Passion sprang up in the people as if it were a Jack-in-the-Box. The alert among the six thousand persons began to gesticulate and run. 'The Hare! The Hare!' they shouted. The street rocked in its own uproar. The rushing, roaring people miraculously had sons and sisters and friends.

'The Hare! The Hare!'

Meanwhile the animate talisman darted here and there, setting his red torch to the golden thatch of the street. Now and again he stopped abruptly. When he did so, no part of the street was hidden from his exophthalmic-goitrous eyes. His ability to stop was amazing. There was no doubt whatsoever that he was terrified, yet his body was incapable of demonstrating dread and thus his terror masqueraded as alertness. He seemed to be aware that the milling people were roaring for his blood. And the people? They continued to demonstrate that mankind is a huge wind-rocked stone balanced on a cliff-face. Either that or (absurdity of absurdities) the greyhound is present in everyone, together with the bittern, the plaice and the elephant.

Then the blazing galleon of a tram bore down upon the animal. He lost the sense of his exits. He raced towards the lighted street wall which miraculously opened before him in the form of an entrance to a subterranean barber's shop. He sped downwards, breaking the many parallel gleams of the metal stair-treads.

The barbers stood in reverent ranks attending to the customers. With long cool hops the hare passed through and went in the half-open doorway of an inner storeroom which was roofed at its farthest end by opaque cellar-lights. The room had a repulsive smell compounded of superannuated combs and hair-oil in semi-rusty tins. Along one wall was a long bench. The hare lay down beneath it.

The crowd from the street surged down the stairway. They were

a shade intimidated when they saw the hieratic gestures of the
barbers. The head barber came forward – he also owned the
premises – and began to shepherd the intruders with his scissors
and comb. His name was Richard Collis and he had the urbanity
that has come to be associated with commercial competence. The
man had a skull the shape of an inflated pig-bladder; his complexion, though a trifle over-scarlet, was undoubtedly first class.
The points of his moustache were his twin-treasures and compen-
sated in some measure for a childless marriage. His thinning hair
was as a large cross placed on his bare shoulders. With every step he
took towards the intruders he filched the significance from their
entrance and made it appear a vulgar brawl.

'It's a hare, mister.'

'A hare's after coming into your shop.'

They took refuge in defeated laughter and the inevitable puns.

Richard Collis brought the full searchlight of his suavity to bear
on the crowd on the stairway. Those nearest him were light-
blinded by its rays. But his rear was unguarded: he felt the
nick-snip of the many scissors die down behind him and whenever
a snip did come it seemed as if one of the younger barbers were
cocking a snook at his poll. He turned to his staff and rebuked them
with a glance. The music of scissors and razor began again, but at a
much slower tempo. Turning once more, he found the people at
the head of the stairway quite merry and mutinous. It took all his
charm and tact to expel them without appearing undignified.

Then a young barber pointed and said: 'He's gone into the room,
sir.'

Richard Collis asked his customer to hold him excused. He
entered the store-room, switched on the light and closed the door
softly behind him. He saw the hare beneath the bench – a brown
huddle which had achieved an unmistakable domesticity. The
animal's panting was difficult to apprehend. Step by step the
barber stole nearer. The hare swivelled his head but did not move
away. Richard Collis got down on his knees. The hare watched
him, first with friendliness, then with apathy. There came a sudden
lull in the minor thunder of boots on the cellar lights. The barber
stayed thus watching the hare for an appreciable while.

Then Richard Collis's countenance sagged, spruced, then sagged irretrievably. The skin of his face, as yet under some small control, proved to be covering a volatile squirming flesh. Unsuspected nerves jerked in patches like wind-flaws on still water. His tongue had ballooned and was filling his mouth. His lower lip essayed speech a few times before it succeeded.

'Wisha, God be with you, Ballintierna in the morning!'

He continued to kneel thus in trance while high in his mind the years clinked by like silver beads. Gradually his face grew less ruined. At last the renewed thunder of the boots on the cellar-glass aroused him. Then he arose and returned to his shop, closing the door reverently behind him.

from *The Lion Tamer & Other Stories*, 1948

A Walk Through the Summer

JAMES PLUNKETT

I

At intervals while he walked, the man, who was old, allowed his stick to touch the railings which bounded the plot about the ivy-covered church. It was not a very well-cared plot. The grasses had grown high with summer and there were tall dandelions about the notice board. The notice itself had loosened with heat. Already one corner folded limply away from the wood. The loose end made no stir, the grasses stood perfectly still under the glowing sky. The notice read, 'I Am The Way The Truth And The Life.' It was the end of a summer evening.

Almost opposite the board, the print on which was large and aggressive, the old man stood still and listened. He was blind. He was also lost. He stood at the edge of the path and would have crossed if he had known for certain that some light still remained. But the silence, the heavy feel of the air about his face, the motionlessness and warmth suggested summer darkness. He allowed his stick to rest against the path's edge until a distant door dragged on its weatherboard. Then the blind man began to make tapping noises without moving from his position.

Casey stepped out into the summer evening. The quietness made him hesitate before descending the steps. He acknowledged the sky with its remote streaks of colour behind long rolling furrows of black cloud. For Casey it was a pregnant evening, an hour of decision. He thought uneasily of Barbara, who had probably spent the day at the sea with John and the children. His own evening had gone on some exercises in counterpoint, several dreary and unrewarding hours spent in the overfurnished room which Mrs O'Keeffe provided in addition to his meals for the all-in sum of three pounds per week. It was reasonable, Casey knew. Yet he found it expensive. The weekend trip to Galway was likely to prove expensive too. After a moment he dropped his cigarette over the railings, dug one hand deep into his pocket and took the steps slowly.

In a house some miles away Barbara shook sand from a towel and heard John leaving the bathroom upstairs. He always bathed immediately on their return from the sea. She shouted up to him:

'Who's coming tonight? Will there be a crowd?'

'Only the Manpowers. He wants to discuss the Cork trip. I put all the rest off as best I could.'

'My God – why didn't you say. Did you ask them for dinner?'

'No. I can take the Manpowers in small doses only.'

'Did you put Tom off?'

'Who?'

'Tom Casey.'

'Why?'

'Because I think I asked him. It could be embarrassing. I didn't know about the ghastly Manpowers.'

She listened carefully for his answer.

'Don't worry. We'll have some music anyway.' She folded the brightly coloured towel before resuming.

'What shall we play?'

'Darling, let's not gossip. I'm mother naked.'

'Sorry.'

'We'll put on the new issues from the Haydn Society. Do you think?'

'Chamber music. The Manpowers will be furious.'

'Damn the Manpowers,' John shouted back. 'Just give them plenty to drink.'

She heard him scampering towards the bedroom.

They met at the notice board. The aggressive letters were familiar to Casey.

'Can I help you?'

'I was looking for Ravensdale Avenue.'

'It's certainly not around here.'

'A road with houses only just built.'

'There are no new houses around here. A little further on there's the river. Then Ballsbridge.'

'Them railings behind me?'

'They surround the church.'

The blind man misunderstood and crossed himself. Casey smiled. 'It's not that kind of church,' he said gently.

The blind man cursed at his mistake.

'I've a little time to spare. I'll help you to try some of the back roads.'

The blind man allowed him to take his arm and shuffled along beside him, muttering angrily to himself. Casey, without minding very much, noticed he had not been thanked.

The girl who looked after the children for Barbara got them to bed. They were overtired and cross. They emptied little mounds of fine sand from their sandals and quarrelled with each other. There were three of them, two boys and a girl. Then she made tea in Russian fashion for Barbara who liked it that way after a day on the sands. She would sit for an hour perhaps, being lazy, hardly talking, until it seemed time to ask John to pour a drink while she changed and prepared for her guests.

The girl sat down dutifully opposite to her. She was a Pole, a refugee Barbara had offered to take care of. A couple of years before she had come from a world of devastated homes, a chaos of maimed people and orphaned children, so remote from the untouched safety of Dublin that few who met her realized that it had had any real existence. But they treated her with kindness. She was almost, but not quite, one of the family. Barbara sipped the tea and studied the young, grave face which seemed absorbed in the piece of knitting she had automatically picked up. It was not a pretty face, but foreign and strange and therefore different enough, Barbara knew, to prove attractive. Barbara herself was very pretty, in a well-groomed very feminine way. Her hands were particularly beautiful and delicate; her face, at thirty-four, quite unlined and untouched, perhaps because whatever she thought or felt never seemed quite to reach it. Nature had shaped her to go with the rich, warm room, the novels, the records, the Russian tea. And Barbara, for her part, encouraged nature.

'You had a dreadfully boring afternoon, I'm sure.' Her voice, too, was very beautiful.

The head above the knitting shook emphatically.

'Oh, no.'

'It's such a nuisance not having room. John and I were wishing you were with us.'

'That was kind.'

'If I'd known John was going to Cork tomorrow I could have got out of weekending with the Burkes. But he never tells me these things. You'll have the children to manage all on your own.'

'I do not mind.'

'It's only for the weekend of course. I'll get back on Monday afternoon.'

'I hope you have a lovely time.'

'Not in Galway, dear. Lough Corrib is such a bore. Festooned with fishermen.'

The brows puckered for a moment at the unfamiliar phrase, the eyes lifted enquiringly, then returned to the knitting. Barbara sipped her tea. Everything was working out nicely.

II

'If I could only get the feel of the streets,' the blind man complained. He hurried his step. There was no purpose in doing so, Casey knew, but he quickened also. It was quite a hopeless quest. Two or three times, when asked what road they were on, Casey was unable to say.

'Can't you ask someone?'

'There's no one about.'

'You live near at hand. It seems queer you don't know.'

'There are no nameplates,' Casey patiently explained.

'You can't read nameplates in the dark, anyway.'

'It's not altogether dark.'

'The dark leaves you just as helpless as I am. You don't have to make excuses. I'm not a fool.'

Casey, his arm linked in that of the blind man, grew tired and noticed that his companion smelled. It was a faint smell, a pitiable smell really because it sprang, in all probability, from helplessness and infirmity. It was also, of course, the result of poverty. Poverty nearly always smelled. Casey, for all he himself knew, might possess his own peculiar odour. It would be fainter though, because he was a little more capable and a little less poor. It was all very natural. Clothes worn for too long often caused it. Also a condition of the health. Casey was aware always of living on the fringe of such a world, saved only from its indignity by youth and a touch of fastidiousness.

They emerged from the leafy quietude of an elegant backwater onto the main road. Traffic passed on its way down the coast. Neon signs flashed in various colours, though not brilliantly, for the sky was not as yet dark. The clock of the Royal Dublin Society chimed.

'Where are we now?' the old man enquired.

'Ballsbridge,' Casey told him. He found himself saying it with a touch of triumph, as though it had been necessary to prove it by demonstration. That brought both of them to a standstill.

'Look,' Casey said, 'it's ten o'clock.'

The blind man screwed up his face unpleasantly.

'I mightn't be able to see,' he said, 'but I can hear a clock as well as the next.'

'You might let me finish,' Casey objected. 'It's ten o'clock and I want a drink before they close at half past. Would you like one?'

'Is it far?'

'Across the road.'

'I've no money.'

'I'll stand you one.'

'All right so,' the blind man said, 'but watch the traffic.'

'I think you can trust me.'

'Damn the thing I'll trust for many a long day after this.' As they crossed the road the blind man explained himself.

'I'll have nothing but the height of bad luck this night,' he predicted, 'and me after saluting a bloody Protestant church.'

The bar was pretty crowded. They moved down towards the end. As people were clearing a passage for the blind man a familiar voice rang out. It was Ellis.

Ellis, like Casey, knew the loneliness of furnished rooms and moved in a world of small salaries. In return for such respect-abilities as a post office savings account and the renunciation of alcohol and tobacco it offered a tenuous measure of security – even the possibility, ultimately, of marriage to a respectable girl. These were ideals which Ellis had deliberately pondered and then contemptuously rejected.

As they came over he lowered his paper and there was a pint of stout on the counter in front of him.

'What'll you have?'

'A pint,' Casey said.

'And your friend?'

'I'll leave it to yourself,' the blind man answered.

'That's what the jarvey said. I suppose it means whiskey.'

He called for a pint and a small Jameson.

'Not Jameson,' the blind man said. 'Jameson's is a Protestant crowd. Get me Powers.'

Ellis raised his eyebrows at Casey. Casey smiled tolerantly. Ellis shrugged and amended the order. Then he tapped the racing page with the back of his hand and said:

'There's where I should have gone today. The Curragh. I'd have had the first two favourites. Then I'd have backed Canty's mount – I'd reliable information and it came in at tens.'

Casey, his mind on Barbara and the fact that he was on the eve of arranging an adulterous weekend, found it hard to concentrate. But he managed to say:

'What put you off?'

'Oul Pringle had a liver on in the office and I didn't want to ask for the time off. So instead I went to the dogs after tea and lost a bloody stack. Here's health.'

The drinks had arrived. Ellis put the whiskey glass in the blind man's hand and poured some water into it.

'There's a drop of holy water to go with it,' he said. The blind man's hand shook with anger.

'Don't mock at God, young man,' he said, 'don't try to be smart about God.' He raised the glass unexpectedly and emptied it at a swallow. Then he put it down with a bang which very nearly shattered it. Ellis waited for some time for the customary salutation. None came.

Motioning him not to mind, Casey said, 'Good luck.'

Ellis acknowledged and said, 'I suppose you spent the day in virtuous pursuits.'

'At harmony and counterpoint exercises.'

'Ah. Messrs Bach and Beethoven. How are they keeping?'

Casey smiled and said, 'Deceased – I fear.'

'For God's sake,' Ellis exclaimed, as though the news was unexpected. 'That was very sudden.'

'It's the way of us all,' Casey said, falling in with his mood. 'Here today and gone tomorrow.'

'It's Mrs Bach I pity most. All them children. Twenty – isn't it?'

'Twenty-seven,' Casey corrected.

Ellis made a slow, clicking noise with his tongue.

'Have you two gentlemen lost someone,' the blind man asked. He had gathered little of the conversation.

'Bach and Beethoven,' Ellis explained. 'It's a great shock.'

The blind man's face grimaced unpleasantly once again. He said, 'Death comes for all.' There was a belligerent note in his voice. The thought seemed to satisfy some need in him. Perhaps it was the fact that all infirmity fell away in that one universal infirmity. Ultimately all men would be equal.

'You're right,' Casey agreed. 'That's a day we'll all see.'

'If God spares us,' Ellis added without a smile.

It was Ellis who posed the question at closing time. They had drunk rather fast, partly because the blind man kept emptying everything immediately it was placed in front of him. He knocked each drink back and then stared ahead of him, his jaws champing most of the time and his lips dribbling now and then from one side. At times some inner anger showed in his face, at other times greed. Near closing time Ellis asked:

'Are you going out to John's?'

'What put that into your head?'

'It's Friday. Don't you want to hear some music?'

'I've had my bellyful of music today,' Casey evaded. He had hoped Ellis would not be going.

'Then – the divine Barbara . . . ?' Ellis had said similar things in the past. Casey found it hard to assess just how much he guessed. He decided not to comment.

'What about our friend?'

'Shunt him off.'

'We can't do that. He's still lost.'

'We'd better bring him with us so. We haven't time to go messing round.'

'What about John?'

'John is a philanthropist.'

Casey doubtfully supposed it would be all right. It was an unexpected complication.

'You'll get a meal,' Ellis said to the blind man. 'And we'll get you home.'

The blind man hesitantly accepted. He appeared to be suspicious.

They took a bus. Ellis deliberately deposited the blind man in a seat apart and led Casey to the back.

'That's not a very appealing specimen of afflicted humanity,' he explained.

'What can we do. If we left him home we'd miss our last bus.'

Ellis said: 'I know. Duty before everything. I hope you have the fare.'

'Barely.'

'That's why I'm going to John's, if you want to know. I'm going to knock him for a tenner.'

'Everybody knocks John for money. It's a bit thick, in a way.'

'Better than knocking him for his wife.'

Casey stiffened. Ellis only meant it as a joke.

'I don't think that's funny.'

'Don't mind me,' Ellis said, 'I like saying things like that. As a matter of fact, she has an eye for you. You could nearly have a go there.'

'I don't want to discuss it.'

But Ellis kept on. He pushed his hat back and produced two packets of potato crisps from his pocket.

'Have a chew,' he offered.

Casey refused. Ellis put back the second packet and tore his own open. He stuffed a wad of crisps into his mouth.

'I'm not offering jembo over there any. He drank enough free whiskey to satisfy a bishop. That's another good reason for going to John's. We'll get something to eat. I'd nothing for tea except a sandwich I managed to lift in the canteen today. It fell off one of the trays onto the floor.'

'What did you do – put your foot on it?'

'Dropped my napkin over it. A bloody lovely sandwich. You should have seen your woman when she came back to pick it up and throw it out. She didn't know Ellis had it safe in his arse pocket.'

Casey smiled again and looked out the window. The bus had swung onto a looping road which skirted the bay. Tall streetlamps spread long orange streaks on the full waters and the stream of air which raked through the open glass panel smelled of the sea. Ellis crumpled the empty crisp bag with a sigh and flung it on the floor.

'That'd be a pleasurable night's work,' he observed.

'What?'

'The fair Barbara.'

Casey once again controlled the anger which in the eyes of Ellis would betray him, if he allowed it to show. Ellis, he felt, was pumping for information.

'I want happiness – not pleasure.'

'Happiness is not without pleasure.'

'But pleasure can be without happiness.'

Ellis looked astounded. He opened the second packet of crisps.

'I'll need a bit of nourishment to sort that one out,' he said.

'Happiness is the object – pleasure merely the accident. The object is legitimate, but the accident may operate in conflict with the object.'

'Illustration required,' Ellis invited, his mouth full of crisps.

'All right. Drink too much and you get a head. Result – unhappiness. Eat too much and you get sick. Result – ditto.'

'Mysterioso Profoundo.'

'You should read Aquinas.'

'Ah. Aquinas. How's he keeping?'

'Deceased also,' Casey said, to draw the subject further away from its beginnings.

'It's terrible,' Ellis said, 'all the old crowd dropping off one by one.' He shook out the bag and three small crisps fell into his hand. He gazed at them sadly, then showed them to Casey.

'There you are,' he said, 'there's only a few of us left.'

III

'I think that's about all,' Mr Manpower said. 'The main thing is to keep the American end interested.'

When he spoke of business he spoke with authority.

'Bloody dreary,' John said, and Mrs Manpower, a refined, spinsterish woman, looked startled. Mr Manpower used such expressions frequently. But a well-bred person, who had been to university. And before the ladies.

'Why can't Wallace come to Dublin?' John complained.

'He never does. He never flies from New York. Always comes by boat. And he won't trust any form of Irish transport.' Mr Manpower paused. 'You keep a good drop, John,' he added, eyeing his glass with great friendliness.

'Have some more,' John invited.

'Henry,' Mrs Manpower warned.

'Do me good,' Mr Manpower said easily.

A gentle snore drew their attention to a presence they had almost forgotten. A long, thin, aristocratic form lay sleeping in an easy chair.

'Poor Haddington,' Barbara apologized. She gently relieved the long fingers of a glass which dangled perilously from them and placed it on a shelf.

'How did he get here. He couldn't have driven out.'

'The bus,' John explained. 'He comes now and then. He was a dear friend of my father's.'

'One doesn't expect it really,' Mrs Manpower suggested carefully, 'certainly not from a professor.'

'That's what you call scholarly drinking,' Mr Manpower enthused.

'I think it most unbecoming,' Mrs Manpower reproved, making it clear that she was going to stick to her guns.

Mr Manpower winked vulgarly at John. 'Good thing for her,' he said jovially, indicating his infuriated spouse, 'that I'm only half educated.'

John pretended to be amused, and Barbara, because Mr Manpower was of considerable financial importance, managed a thin smile. Then she said sweetly:

'Don't you think, darling, a little music would be amusing.'

IV

The bus left them at its lonely terminus, a point of the bay marked by a few shops and a road which ran steeply uphill between tall hedges. As they climbed, the blind man linked between them, they saw it reverse and make its way back along the road below, a small smear of light pursued at water level by its own reflection. The blind man, who was puffing with exertion, stopped and suddenly lost his temper.

'What sort of a fool am I to be led on a wild goose chase like this?' he demanded. 'What class of a heathen hideout are youse heading for at this unholy hour of the night?'

'We're heading for records and novelties,' Ellis assured him, 'long hair and sturdy bank balances. You'll find it eminently respectable.'

After a while they turned into the tree-lined avenue. At the end stood the house, well-lit, self-assured, master of its own well-kept grounds.

'How do you think they'll take it,' Ellis asked, meaning the blind man.

'You're the one who said it was going to be all right.'

'That was approximately an hour ago.'

'So you've changed your mind?'

'That is what distinguishes man from the brute. The cow chews the cud. But does it get any nearer inventing the milking machine? When man ruminates he moves from idea to idea. I have been ruminating.'

'I'll say this for your frined,' the blind man confessed to Casey, 'he's an eloquent young blade.'

'You mean you've developed cold feet,' Casey grumbled. 'You'd better go to the front door with our friend. I'll slip round the back and explain matters.'

The French windows at the back stood open to the night. A piano trio of Haydn grew louder as Casey approached, his feet crunching on the gravel. The occupants of the room sat around in various attitudes of attention. Each had a drink. Though he had sat in it so many times the soft lighting and the warm luxury of the room affected Casey pleasantly. Money and graciousness did not always go together as they did so flawlessly here. Barbara, who was facing the windows sat up and said:

'Tom.'

'My dear Tom,' John greeted, rising.

'I'm interrupting,' Casey apologized. Then he explained quickly about the blind man.

'Delighted,' John said. 'Is he a musician?'

'No. An ignorant and rather aggressive old man who smells.'

'Oh, no,' Barbara said.

The Manpowers detached themselves from contemplation of the music in order to look surprised.

'This is delightful,' John said. 'Bring him in.'

'Good evening, everybody,' Casey said generally. The Manpowers switched on automatic smiles and went back with alacrity to the music. Casey went through to the hall door where Ellis was waiting with the blind man. Between them they brought him into the room and seated him down. John asked him if he would have a drink but Barbara said, 'Please, John.' John smiled at everybody and said sorry. When the music had finished the guests expressed their opinions.

'Damn good,' Mr Manpower applauded. 'You're a powerful man for the music.' His wife made a great show of pleasure and said rapturously, 'I adore Haydn.'

Haddington, who was half awake, murmured approvingly but incoherently. Casey recognized him as the author of a number of difficult philosophical books.

'Mr and Mrs Manpower,' John introduced. 'Meet Mr Casey . . . Mr Ellis.'

'Glad to know you,' Manpower responded heartily.

'Delighted,' Mrs Manpower confirmed, but coolly. She had noted that they were rather shabbily dressed.

'And of course, Professor Haddington.'

Haddington mumbled unintelligibly but with great courtesy and politeness. Casey remembered that he was said to rise at six o'clock every morning and work until noon. At noon, but never before, he opened his first bottle of whiskey. The professor had the reputation of being a man of unshakable habit. No one had ever known him to utter anything intelligible after five o'clock.

'And your friend?' John asked.

There was a noticeable pause.

'They never asked me, mister,' the blind man said triumphantly. 'It's Moore . . . Tom Moore.'

'Our national poet,' Mrs Manpower said sweetly, but to John and Barbara only.

'A shoneen, ma'am,' the blind man contradicted, 'who aped the English gentry because he took them to be his betters.'

There was a pause. John decided to offer drinks. Sara, who was still smiling a little at the Rondo which had just concluded, rose to get glasses.

'Don't fuss, dear,' Barbara said, 'I'll get them.' When she had gone a little while she called out to Casey. He joined her in the dining room.

'Well?' he questioned.

'Everything is beautiful.'

'John is definitely going?'

'Tomorrow, by train. He made no fuss at all about leaving the car when I told him I'd like to spend the weekend with the Burkes. That was the only thing which worried me.'

'What?'

'I thought he might bitch about leaving the car.' She paused.

'Aren't you going to say it's wonderful?'

'Of course,' Casey said. He kissed her. It was all that was required to spark off his desire. But he regretted just a little that such things had to be planned. It would be so much easier if they just happened. They remained in each other's arms for some moments. Barbara said:

'Don't let John delay you tonight by offering you the car. Leave with the Manpowers. They'll drop you home.'

'But why?'

'I don't want you to take the car. I must have it fairly early tomorrow morning.'

'What on earth for?'

'Don't ask so many questions, darling.'

'The Manpowers don't look very musical to me.'

'They're ghastly. Business friends of John. At least he is. She's just a drip. And poor, dear, befuddled Haddington. What a collection.'

'Wait till the blind man gets going.'

'Why on earth did you bring him along?'

Casey held her closer, pressing his face against her hair and reflected why. Love? Because you just could not meet a blind man who was lost without putting him right? Superstition? For some dark primitive reason his infirmity gave him the right to your service? Incompetence? Why not get a policeman to look after everything.

'Love,' Casey said.

'Little Sir Christopher,' Barbara murmured. Casey, knowing she had probably meant to say Saint Christopher, disengaged himself without pointing out the mistake. She handed him glasses.

'Take these in while I get Sara to give you something to eat.'

V

John filled out whiskey and put on another trio. John's measures were liberal. This time it took the blind man two gulps to finish it. When John noticed he filled the glass again. An empty glass in the hands of a guest made him feel restless. His generosity was misguided. The blind man threw it back. Some minutes later, cutting across the music and the reverent silence, he said loudly, 'You're a gentleman.'

Mrs Manpower shot upright. Her husband showed a moment's surprise, then grinned happily.

'Thank you,' John said with a smile. The blind man wiped his lips noisily.

'Don't think I'm trying to scratch your back.'

'Not at all.'

'I'm not that class. There's a lot of our people and when they get thrown in with moneyed people they lose themselves in embarrassment. But I'm an Irish Catholic and I'm not ashamed to be what I am whether I'm in the company of Protestants or Communists.'

Nobody answered, in the hope that in that way their desire to listen to the music might register most forcibly. It worked for some minutes. Then the blind man groped for his stick and made a fumbling attempt to rise.

'I can see I'm not wanted.'

John jumped up and went across. 'Please,' he said, pushing him back gently into the chair.

'Then why does nobody talk to me?'

'We were listening to the music.'

'Can't you listen and talk.'

'Really,' Mrs Manpower observed. 'What a peculiar way to behave.'

'Don't you think because I'm blind that I lack for education. I'd the school of the blind to go to when I was young. And the nuns still come to read to me once a week.'

John, with a grimace of resignation, went over and touched the reject button. The music gave up.

'What a shame,' Mrs Manpower whispered. Mr Manpower looked relieved. Casey felt responsible and consequently embarrassed. He was also a little surprised that anything stupid could happen on a night of such importance to Barbara and himself. In the silence Haddington, registering that something was missing but unable to give it a name, began a vague and incompetent search of his pockets.

'Do have a drink or something,' John invited. He began to fill the glasses and gave an extra large helping to the blind man. Barbara and Sara reappeared with sandwiches. They placed a plate between Ellis and Casey and one on a special table beside the blind man. Barbara arranged herself gracefully and asked for some music. Casey, contemplating her with tenderness, was startled by a half-choked exclamation from the blind man.

'Holy God,' he spluttered.

'Is something wrong?'

'Meat,' the blind man said. 'Meat of a Friday. And I swallowed some of it.'

'Is it meat?' John asked wearily.

'Of course it's meat,' Barbara snapped, 'how was I to know.'

Ellis guffawed, sending a shower of crumbs about the carpet.

'Do you find it so amusing?' Barbara shot at him.

'Gas,' Ellis confirmed. He winked at Mrs Manpower, who

glared. Barbara asked Sara to get some cheese and tomato sandwiches and when they arrived Barbara put them beside the blind man and said, 'Now for goodness' sake let's have some music.'

'I'd like this one from the beginning if nobody minds,' John said to the rest.

Everyone appeared to approve.

While John adjusted the record player the blind man began to eat. He attacked his sandwiches ravenously and not by any means quietly. The task of satisfying his appetite absorbed him. Casey saw Barbara turn away her eyes in disgust, but in a remarkably short time the blind man disposed of the sandwiches and brushed the crumbs from his lap. Then he became abstracted. It was possible at last to attend to the music. Barbara, no longer irritated, smiled at Casey and bowed her head to listen. There was a grace about everything she did, an appositeness of word and gesture which, though studied, was nevertheless quite charming. It had been so a year before, when Casey met her on a road some miles beyond the town of Galway. She had been marooned in her car in the middle of a flock of sheep then, unable to go forwards or backwards. The air was full of the smell of animals and their bleating calls; the sun drew waves of heat from the long stretches of moor and rock. Casey, who was on foot, picked his way slowly through the woolly mass and as he passed her she threw him a grimace of humorous resignation which had the effect of fixing her image pleasantly in his mind for some considerable time. About half an hour later her car drew in beside him.

'You look so dusty,' she invited. 'Hop in.'

He eased the rucksack from his shoulder and accepted. The car, which was roomy and luxurious, smelled in the heat. It was a comfortably expensive smell.

'Clifden any use?'

'That's where I'm going,' he said.

'On foot?'

She sounded surprised.

'It's a hobby of mine.'

'Have you been fishing or shooting somewhere?'

'No. Collecting folk music.'

'Oh. Is that another hobby?'

'No. I'm doing that for a thesis.'

'Any luck?'

'No. In fact I've spent most of my time teaching the people their own folk tunes. I must say they found them quaint and interesting.'

'Too bad for the thesis.'

'Not if you're inventive enough. After all, it isn't difficult to make up a folk tune or two.'

He offered a cigarette.

'Don't the examiners know the difference?'

'Either they don't, or they don't examine them very closely.'

She remained smiling for some time.

Lakes came up to the edge of the road at times and then were left behind, the sheer and desolate mountains lifting steeply on their right accompanied them mile by mile.

'What beautiful country,' she remarked.

They stayed at the same hotel. They went about together for some days. There were the beach and dancing and quiet walks. Some lovemaking too which she made no effort to discourage. One evening when they were sitting in the lounge she was called to the telephone to take a trunk call and when she returned she remained silent for so long that he asked her if it had been bad news.

'No,' she said, 'it was just about my ring.'

'Your ring?'

'My wedding ring. I left it on the dressing table at the Burkes' place. They phoned to tell me it was safe.' Casey found it impossible to say anything. He waited. After a while she said, 'Well . . . now you know.'

Casey noted that for a moment she seemed to have lost her studied elegance. She was hunched, even miserable. This proved an even greater shock than the first, until it occurred to him that this too fitted perfectly. It was both touching and disarming. Next morning she was her sophisticated self and before she left asked him to visit them when he got back to the city. John, she said, adored music.

VI

The look on the blind man's face held Casey's uneasy attention for some time before he realized that anything was going to happen. At first it was unusually pale, with saliva showing at the side of his mouth. His head began to nod from side to side, as though in rhythm with the music. Then his fingers tightened on the arms of his chair as he heaved himself to his feet. He was halfway across the floor before the others realized what was happening, and before Casey could reach him he got violently sick. Mrs Manpower gave a little scream and gazed in horror at the carpet.

'Good God!' Barbara exclaimed.

The blind man, whom Casey had gripped and helped back to his chair, shuddered all over. When he had recovered he said: 'It was the food. Tomatoes and cheese is far too rich for me. You shouldn't have given them to me.'

'Sorry,' John said.

'It's all right,' the blind man said, 'it can't be helped now.'

'I like that,' Barbara exploded, 'what the hell did you eat it for if it wasn't going to agree with you?'

'Why does anybody eat anything that doesn't agree with him,' the blind man snarled back.

'The pleasure principle,' Ellis contributed, addressing Casey exclusively. 'The man is a philosopher.'

'I hear the fellow with the smart talk,' the blind man said.

'Can't you shut up, Ellis,' Casey complained, 'you always manage to make things a good deal worse.'

Sara, who had left the room immediately the incident happened, returned now with a bucket and some cloths.

'Poor Sara,' Barbara sympathized. The rest withdrew, including Haddington, who made his way after them. It required remarkable concentration, but he managed it unaided. The Manpowers, once on their feet, gently declined the invitation to move into another room. They had had a most interesting evening, Mrs Manpower said, but it was quite late and time to go home.

Mr Manpower agreed. He offered lifts. 'We'll take Professor Haddington.'

'Of course,' Mrs Manpower said.

Haddington acknowledged courteously, waved a vague leave-taking, and shuffled out into the night.

'The back seat, Professor,' Mrs Manpower called out after him, with great sweetness. Haddington's unintelligible reply made her smile at the others.

'Such a curious man,' she said, 'but, after all, so brilliant.'

Mr Manpower extended the offer to Casey, Ellis and the blind man.

'But we'd hardly have room, dear.'

'We've managed six before,' Mr Manpower said hospitably.

But the blind man was found to be very unsteady and upset still.

'I think you'd better leave us,' Casey said regretfully.

'Yes, do,' John urged. 'Tom here can take our car. We won't need it.'

'But we do, dear. I wanted it tomorrow morning.'

'Tom can bring it back early.'

Barbara said, 'Never in history has Tom been known to bring back a car early.'

She appealed to Casey, 'Couldn't you manage him?' She looked at him in a way which conveyed the very special nature of her appeal.

'He's not well enough at the moment,' Casey resisted. 'Put him in a car now and he'll be sick all over again.'

'We mustn't keep the professor waiting,' Mrs Manpower said, failing to hide her alarm.

Everybody accompanied them to their car, the gravel crunching under their feet and the night warm about them.

'Hello,' Mr Manpower exclaimed when he had opened the door, 'where's Haddington?'

There was no one in the back seat and no one to be seen anywhere near. A search proved fruitless. They called out several times but got no answer. The night had swallowed Haddington.

'Let's spread out and search the grounds,' John said. It was obvious that he was finding it difficult to remain calm.

VII

In the now silent house Sara bent over her unpleasant task. There was a shadow of suffering on her face but her voice betrayed no note of complaint.

'Who are you?' the blind man asked.

'I am Sara,' she said.

'A foreigner?'

'Yes – a refugee.'

'One of the crowd that gets everything while the poor of Ireland gets nothing. I wonder if you know how lucky you are.'

'I think I do.'

She was mopping the floor, her task half completed.

'From where?'

'I beg your pardon?'

'Where do you come from?'

'From Poland.'

'You're a Catholic so?'

'Yes. I am a Catholic.'

'What do you think of them giving me meat of a Friday. What would you do if it happened to you?'

'Probably I would eat it.'

That brought him to a standstill. But only for a moment. He took it up again.

'No doubt,' he said. 'Foreign Catholics is notorious luke-warmers. They're not a patch on Irish Catholics. The Pope himself said that.'

The girl squeezed the cloth into the bucket and the water slopped about.

'Is there a cigarette handy?'

'Please . . . in one moment.'

'Don't hurry yourself. Irish Catholics didn't get it soft like you. They suffered for the Faith.'

'Please . . . ?'

'Never mind. You're a foreign Catholic. Brought up in indifference. Then taken into good homes where you get the height of good feeding. You never suffered.'

'I think we suffered.'

'No. You've a loose way of living, you foreign Catholics. Not like Irish Catholics. What about that cigarette?'

The girl went out to empty the bucket, washed her hands, and returned with a cigarette. She lit it for him and he rattled on. He talked about the great faith of the Irish and about all they suffered. Some people didn't appreciate how lucky they were, living free in comfortable Irish homes. As she tidied up he asked her questions. She made no answers. For some reason she had begun to weep. But quietly. She did not want him to know.

VIII

The rest failed to find Haddington and after half an hour the Manpowers gave up and drove off. As the wheels crunched on the gravel Barbara waved for a moment and then linked Casey's arm. They moved together towards the house. John and Ellis were still searching. They saw Sara going across to join them.

'We'll search the house,' Barbara shouted.

'He couldn't possibly be in the house,' John shouted back.

'No harm trying,' she answered. 'He must be somewhere.'

Barbara and Casey went from room to room. In the children's room he was about to switch on the light when she stopped him. It would waken them, she said. They passed through into Sara's room, leaving the door open. A small, illuminated cross glowed red in a covering of glass. The air in the room was warm still from the earlier sunshine. It was a small room. On a bed at one side the pillow and sheets looked extraordinarily white.

'You let the Manpowers go,' she accused.

With a shrug he said, 'What could I do?'

'You'll have to take the car now, of course. But you must promise to bring it back early in the morning. It's quite important.'

'Won't it do in the afternoon. We'll have the whole day driving down.'

'The shops close. There are things I want which can't be got just anywhere.'

'Such as?'

She moved into his arms.

'Don't be such a dumb idiot,' she said in a small embarrassed voice.

He realized than what she meant. There were certain preparations; there were the necessary womanly precautions.

'I'm sorry,' he said. 'Put it down to my peasant stupidity.'

After that Casey was silent. He had made a humiliating discovery. He was not as sophisticated as he had believed.

IX

The rest of the night was hardly more successful. They had some more drinks and listened to some more records. But for some reason there was no point of contact between them. The blind man lay back in his chair, looking very pale and breathing heavily. Ellis was unusually subdued. Sara kept her head bowed, her natural gravity emphasized by the lack of communication between the others. Casey looked from Barbara to John and felt the situation keenly. He knew that John had his own infidelities from time to time. He felt, however, that it was not quite the same thing; or rather, that in matters of the kind he himself was not made of quite the same clay. The prospect of the long trip, the excuses, the lies which would inevitably be necessary, began to suggest themselves in a new light. The situation would pass and give way to new situations, but for the moment he saw clearly that it would require a betrayal of his personality which he would have to sustain for many months, perhaps even for life. He felt about such matters at a far deeper level than either Barbara or John, for whom money and well-trained manners had rounded the edges of reality. He saw beyond the situation to its effects. He was not himself pure and he was far from being a prude. But he could not help seeing impurity as a state and not simply as a word. So palpable was it that in a moment of alarming comprehension it had stood before him. It was a brown shroud stiff with the remains which stuck to it, sticky to touch – if one dared. He had seen it a moment before, when the reason why Barbara wanted the car had suddenly become clear to him.

Between his mood and the innocent good humour of the Haydn trio there was a gap which no effort of concentration could close.

Once or twice he smiled across at John, who liked to share their mutual appreciation in that way. He was much relieved when the trio finished and he could rise to take his leave. John gave him the keys of the car.

'What are we to do about Haddington?' he said.

'We've done all we can about Haddington,' Barbara decided. She had had her fill of upsets.

'We really ought to phone the police or something,' John said.

'Perhaps he walked,' Casey offered.

'Or climbed a tree,' Ellis suggested. His effort was not appreciated.

The blind man had to be assisted. When they reached the car they decided to prop him up between them on the front seat. It was difficult in the darkness, but at last they got him fixed. Casey found the switch for the headlights and the half circle of gravel glared back at him suddenly. John waved good-bye. Barbara warned:

'Tomorrow morning early. For God's sake don't oversleep.'

'Don't worry,' Casey shouted, 'you'll have it back.'

The bordering trees spun in a gleaming half circle and they were off. Casey drove. Ellis held the blind man upright. It was a tight squeeze with the three of them in front.

'Not a very successful evening,' Casey said, when they had been driving for some time.

'I got my ten pounds. I wouldn't complain.'

Ellis lit a contented cigarette and looked out of the window to his left, where at regular intervals the beam of a lighthouse traced a golden passage across the calm waters of the bay. The night was heavy and still.

'Light me one of those,' Casey asked. Ellis lit another cigarette and when he had handed it to him he said:

'I met Sara in the garden tonight and she was crying. Something his nibs here said to her.'

'What was it about?'

'She wouldn't say.'

Some minutes later Ellis took up the theme again. He sounded sleepy. But it was obvious that he had been turning it over in his mind.

'I don't think a woman has cried in front of me like that ever before. She's quite an alluring piece of stuff, the fair Sara.'

'Remember your bachelor vows.'

'Ellis will remain single. But not necessarily celibate.'

'Hardchaw,' Casey said.

He knew something of Sara's background, things Barbara had mentioned to him from time to time. It was a topic he did not wish to pursue. They made the circuit in silence and swung away from the coast road, encountering a long, hedge-lined suburban avenue and then, quite suddenly it seemed, a wide street, closed and shuttered shops, the first traffic lights.

'You're very subdued,' Casey remarked.

'I'm trying to keep Father Rabelais here from falling off the bloody seat. He has me half strangled.'

'How is he?'

'Still breathing – I think.'

'We didn't ask him where he lived.'

'No.'

'I suppose you wouldn't have room . . .'

'No.'

'That's what I thought. No harm asking.'

'Divil the bit. You're welcome.'

That was that. Casey took responsibility for furnishing accommodation for the blind man. They had a job wakening him when Ellis was being dropped, but after a good deal of rough treatment he opened his eyes.

'Where am I?' he asked.

'Back in the city,' Ellis said. 'You'd better lean on your own shoulder from now on. I'm getting out.'

X

There was a hint of greyness in the air when Casey got home. He brought the blind man up the steps and into his bedroom. He led him over to the bed.

'Where are you going to sleep yourself?' the blind man asked.

'In the car.'

'That'll be cold enough.'

'I'll take a blanket.'

The blind man removed his boots and began to undress.

'Where do you keep the yoke?' he asked.

Casey was puzzled. The blind man got annoyed.

'Don't tell me you don't use a yoke. Everyone has a yoke in the bedroom.'

Light dawned on Casey. 'I use the toilet in the bathroom,' he said.

'You can't expect me to be able to find that.'

It was, Casey supposed, a reasonable point of view. He looked around. In an ornamental bowl by the window Mrs O'Keeffe kept a depressing geranium. Casey removed the plant and handed the bowl to the blind man. It was a fancy bowl with teethed edges which were meant to represent the opening bud of a flower. The blind man ran his hands around it and began to criticize it.

'This is a highly dangerous contraption . . .' he began.

Casey cut him short.

'It's the only yoke available,' he said. 'You'll have to do your best with it.'

He closed the hall door softly and realized that morning had come. He could see the houses opposite and below him the car, its shape misty with dew, black-skinned and moist like a large slug. He walked down past it and up the road, past the railings of the church, past the notice board with its aggressive message and its unkept plot of graves and dandelions. They smelled sweetly and damply now in the early morning air. Then he turned back and as he did so he arrived at a decision. He was not going to Galway with Barbara. She would feel badly about it, he knew, but in the long run it would be better. It had been more than exciting, the whole prospect. She was beautiful, she was rich, so much so that her interest in him had always been something of a mystery to Casey. He was humble enough most of the time to wonder what she could see in him. She would suffer, of course. How much Casey could not venture to guess. Not very much he thought. In her world there were plenty of distractions. Besides, it would do her no harm. Out of some nightmare background of suffering, at some awakened memory of a family scattered and murdered, Sara had wept in front of Ellis. He had been touched to the extent that he desired to seduce her. And that was all. As for himself, he would retire once again to Mrs O'Keeffe's room and the companionship of her favourite geranium, thinking now and then of the indignity to which circumstances had subjected its fancy container; thinking now and then also of a sunlit road, animal cries and the huddled, white gleaming of fleece.

Casey opened the door of the car and froze. Someone was sitting on the back seat.

'You,' he exclaimed.

'You took a devilish long time,' Haddington complained. 'What on earth kept you?'

'How did you get here?' Casey asked.

'Come, come,' Haddington said. 'I was told to sit in the back seat.'

Quite suddenly Casey saw that there was a simple explanation.

'My God!' he said. 'You got into the wrong car.'

'I waited quite a long time, then fell asleep. I appear to have slipped off the seat at some stage. When I woke up a while ago I was lying on the floor.'

'We searched for you for hours.'

'You mustn't blame me. After all, you knew there were two cars. I didn't.'

'It never occurred to us.'

'I have noticed myself,' Haddington observed, 'that the simple and obvious never really does. However, what are we going to do?'

'I don't know what you intend to do,' Casey said, 'but I'm going to sleep.'

'Here in the car?'

'Yes, I have a blanket.'

Haddington considered the matter while Casey settled down. Then he said:

'Could you spare me a corner of the blanket?'

'Certainly,' Casey said. He rearranged it so that it covered both of them. He felt Haddington's head on his shoulder, a bony casket, which housed a rich store of erudition, a mind capable of fine distinctions which, in its time too, had probably differentiated between happiness and pleasure.

'I had a drink or two last night,' Haddington confessed. Casey smiled quietly. Along the garden of the house outside a line of sunshine had appeared, the first thin manifestation.

'The sun has risen,' Casey said.

Haddington gave careful thought to this latest intelligence.

'Alleluia,' he murmured at last. Then they both slept – more or less.

from *The Trusting and the Maimed*, 1959

A Change of Management

JOHN MONTAGUE

9.50 a.m.

John O'Shea groaned as he lifted the morning paper from the front of his desk, where his secretary, Nan Connor, had left it. He was already in a bad temper (for the second time that week he had got snarled in a traffic jam on his way in from Clontarf) but what he saw on the front page did not help. That bastard Clohessy was in the news again; chubby and smiling, an assuring blend of episcopal dignity and *bon viveur's* charm, his face seemed to start out from the lead photograph with the immediacy of a film star's. Among the dignitaries at the blessing of the dried-vegetable factory were the Most Rev. Dr Martin, Bishop of Avoca, the Most Rev. Dr Nkomo, Vicar Apostolic of Katanga (a fine tall African, nurtured by Irish nuns) and Dr William Pearse Clohessy. At a dinner in the Leinster Hotel afterwards, Dr Clohessy, chairman of *Bord na h-Ath Breithe*, the National Renaissance Board, said that this new factory, for which they had all worked so hard, represented another beam in the scaffolding of Ireland's future.

Another nail in its coffin, more likely, thought O'Shea, nearly disintegrating with rage as he gazed at the picture of the new factory which headed the Advertising Supplement. A long low building, it seemed to consist mainly of glass, acres of it, with intersecting ridges of concrete creating a pattern grid. Surely normal people would not be expected to work in a chilly barracks like that, which looked as if it were designed for Martians. He looked to the side for space vehicles, but all he could see was a car park, with the Tricolour flying, against a background of mountains. We congratulate the architect, said Dr Clohessy, on his revolutionary conception, which liberates the forces implicit in the building's environment, so that employees will have the sensation of working close to nature, without its disadvantages. The stark beauty of its outline challenges nature's ruggedness in the granite majesty of the Wicklow Mountains.

As O'Shea was dwelling with tortured relish on the idea of granite majesty, and wondering which of Clohessy's team of ghost-writers had dreamt it up, the door of his office opened and his secretary came in. 'Here are the letters, Mr O'Shea,' she said, placing a small pile of opened envelopes on the IN tray to the right of his desk. She stood back, smoothing her skirt with a broad hand, as he ruffled through them. 'Will you be wanting me?' she asked, at last, with unconscious generosity, gazing over his head through the window.

'Is there anything urgent?'

'The chairman wants to see you at eleven; his secretary rang to confirm the appointment. I believe the Efficiency Experts are due soon.'

'Anything else?'

She hesitated. 'Mr Cronin called.'

'What did he want?'

'He said you were to meet him for lunch in the Anchor.'

As always she delivered the message with a disapproving air, as if she felt that he should not be going to places like the Anchor, especially with people like Tadgh Cronin. Nan Connor was a decent, middle-class Dublin woman, and there were certain classes of behaviour which she could not admire. Once when she had tried to stall Cronin, saying that Mr O'Shea was engaged, he had broken into a torrent of bad language. 'Will you get that bastard for me, or I'll come and wrap your guts around a lamppost,' he finished. The girls at the switchboard had laughed, but she had not found it amusing; and she never would.

John O'Shea smiled affectionately after her, as her masculine shoulders disappeared through the door. Whoever had dreamt up granite majesty should have known Nan Connor; there was something heart-warming about people who behaved according to form. He reached for the first file on his desk and began to turn its pages thoughtfully. It was ten-fifteen, and all across Claddagh House the typewriters took up their morning song.

MEMORANDUM: ON THE HISTORY OF CLADDAGH HOUSE

Claddagh House was a handsome building, of port-wine brick, standing on the South Side of Dublin, near the river Dodder. Formerly known as Kashmir House, it had been built by a retired Army Officer at the turn of the century. But the family had left after the Revolution, no longer finding life comfortable in Ireland, and the house had changed hands several times. After a period as divisional headquarters of the Boys Scouts (Dublin Brigade) it had caught the eye of a government minister, who was looking for somewhere to house an off-shoot of his department. Since money was scarce, no effort was made to remodel it: the stuffed tiger heads of the original owner still lined the entrance hall, and in the chairman's room hung two crossed assegais, with the head of an eland between them.

What pleased John O'Shea about Claddagh House was its Victorian spaciousness; it was unashamedly designed to be lived in. A militant laurel hedge protected it from the road, too high for the curious, but just enough for the occupants to command both directions. There were two pillared entrances, through which one could sweep, the car coming to a halt before the door with a satisfying spurt of gravel. A well-tended lawn began at the side of the house, coming to a climax in the tree-shadowed expanse at the back.

The front was dominated by two enormous bay windows, a flight of steps between them mounting to the door, with its well Brassoed-knocker and official plaque. John O'Shea still remembered the first day he had penetrated the grave dignity of that façade. A junior civil servant, he had just been seconded to Claddagh House, and did not know what to expect. He stood at the empty reception desk in the hall, under the stuffed animals, with their bared teeth and eyeballs. The only sound in the building seemed to be coming from underneath the stairs.

When he opened the door and saw the crowd around a table he nearly backed out, thinking he had interrupted a conference. Then he recognized the object in the middle of the table: from a battered looking radio rose the florid accents of a racing commentator.

They're coming into the bend now, King's Pin in front, Whistling Nun second, Richards nursing Champagne Paddy on the rails. AND here we come into the straight. It's still King's Pin; but Whistling Nun is challenging. I say, this is something; King's Pin, Whistling Nun and Champagne Paddy neck and neck. TWO furlongs to go and King's Pin is falling back; it's between Whistling Nun and Champagne Paddy. ONE furlong and Richard's mount is beginning to flag; it's Whistling Nun all the way now – WHISTLING NUN BY A LENGTH!

11 a.m.

After ten years, John O'Shea still found that first view of Claddagh House prophetic. It was not that work did not get done, but that it took its own sweet pace, without the panic of a central department. Files accumulated and were dealt with as they simmered into urgency. Then they were tied in red folders and buried in cupboards as large as bank-vaults.

And there was always time for relaxation. Twice daily they assembled in the old kitchen under the stairs for tea. In the summer they could take their work out onto the lawn; O'Shea had been sitting under a lilac tree when a swallow dunged on a letter from the Department of Finance. Everyone contributed to the typists' Black Babies Fund; everyone went off sugar and milk during Lent; everyone joined in the Staff Dance and Annual Outing.

Which was why he found the timing of his appointment with the chairman curious: if he was holding it during the tea-break, it was because he wanted no one to interrupt them. And that was unlike Jack Donovan, who gave the impression of conducting his business in public. His gregarious vagueness masked a veteran shrewdness; he might be late but he was rarely wrong in a decision. From ten-thirty when he rolled in to consult the rain gauge, until he left for his game of golf in the afternoon, he refused to be hustled by or for anything.

As John O'Shea opened the door (after a polite knock) he caught the sharp odour of the cigars Donovan favoured. On one of the eland's horns a hat was hanging: it gave the animal a querulous, lopside look. Donovan himself was at his desk, a plump tweed-suited man, who raised his head cordially to indicate a chair.

Rejecting the open box of Will's cheroots which his chairman pushed towards him, O'Shea settled himself expectantly.

'You wanted to see me, sir?'

As usual, Donovan took his time to answer, tidying the papers on his desk before leaning back, his fingers joined.

'Yes, indeed,' he said. 'I have a job for you. Rather, I have two jobs; or one job with two aspects.'

O'Shea waited politely for clarification.

'There's a dinner tonight in' – he pulled a piece of paper towards him – 'the Royal Hotel, Carricklone, which I am supposed to attend: they're launching a local development plan. But . . .'

'You would rather I did.' Which was it, this time, yachting or golf? Since it was mid-week, it was probably golf, at his favourite seaside course, near Bray.

Donovan smiled. 'That's right. But not for the reason you think, though I do have a previous engagement. In any case, even if I was free, I think you should go. You see, Clohessy will be there.'

John O'Shea started. 'That . . .' he began automatically.

'I'm not sure that I don't share your impatience with Mr – Dr! – Clohessy: he seems a rather pushing fellow,' said Donovan judiciously. 'But one mustn't rely on spot judgements; he has the reputation of being very capable. Which brings me to the second part . . .'

'I hope it has nothing to do with Clohessy,' O'Shea burst in.

'Well, as a matter of fact, in a sort of a roundabout way, it has. You know that the Minister feels that perhaps we should be reorganized. It's partly a political thing, of course – we were founded by the previous government – but they also feel that perhaps we are a little old-fashioned. You've heard the efficiency experts are coming in . . .'

'Miss Connor said they were due next week.'

'They're only a front, of course. I don't mean that they won't do their – whatever they do – conscientiously, but their report will give an official reason for pointing out something that we all know already: that this is not a very modern organization, and that I'm not a very modern manager.'

'I don't think that's so important, sir,' said O'Shea loyally.

Donovan wheeled his chair slightly, so that he was gazing

through the window. On the green pelt of the lawn, a solitary blackbird was trying to extricate a worm; when it succeeded, it nearly fell backwards, the worm projecting like a typewriter ribbon from its beak.

'I'm a bumbler,' he said quietly, 'and the age of bumblers is past. But I was lucky; I managed to last until nearly retiring age. I'll be able to disappear without undue fuss.'

'Have you any idea of who might be replacing you?' asked O'Shea nervously.

It was a minute or two before Donovan answered. 'Yes,' he said heavily, 'I think I do. It's mainly guesswork on my part, coupled with one or two fairly obvious straws in the wind. But I think that not merely me, but also Claddagh House, are to be retired. There's going to be what the English papers call, I believe, a takeover bid.'

'By whom?'

'By Bord na h-Ath Breithe. They plan to pull down the house and set up a new joint building.'

'Under Clohessy?' breathed O'Shea.

'Under Clohessy.' Donovan swung the chair round so that he was facing O'Shea directly. 'That's why I want you to go to Carricklone. So that you can get a closer look at the man you may soon be working under.'

1 p.m.

Why did Tadgh Cronin always spend his lunch hour in the Anchor? As John O'Shea pushed open the heavy mahogany door, a hollow sound rose to greet him, like the sea booming in a cave. They were standing six deep at the bar, with waiters threading through the mass, carrying platters to the tables at the back. It was certainly not the food, because it was always cold, pallid thighs of chicken or rough cuts of ham and beef. It was certainly not the women because, although there were several presentable girls present, they seemed to accept that they were on sufferance and did their best to pass muster as men, sucking their pints slowly. A lecher would have had a field-day, provided he remained sober enough to remember his priorities.

No, the sole purpose of this draughty, uncomfortable high-ceilinged place was drink. And with that O'Shea caught sight of

Tadgh Cronin, ensconsed (his brooding posture demanded the word) in a corner, under a vine-leaved mirror advertising Guinness. His black steeple hat was on the chair beside him, flanked by a crumpled *Irish Times*. As O'Shea sat down opposite, he saw that his face looked heavy and flushed, and that the hand that reached out for the pint was shaking.

'Hard night?' he asked sympathetically.

Cronin turned an imploring eye towards heaven. 'Christ!'

Then, step by step, he began to piece together (as much for his own sake as O'Shea's) the events of the previous night. They had all been having a quiet jar in the Anchor when that bastard Tomkins, the sculptor, barged in. A row had developed between him and Parsons, the stained-glass artist, and they had all been thrown out. When they moved to some girl's flat in Rathmines he, Cronin, had tried to make peace between Tomkins and Parsons, with the result that they both turned on him. A window had been broken, and when he got home at four o'clock, he found he had been cheated by the taxi man.

O'Shea made another sympathetic noise; he had heard the same story before but he had a connoisseur's taste for the gruesome detail. How much had the fare been from Rathmines to Ballsbridge?

'I got half a dollar back: that makes nearly a quid for two miles. Over eight bob a fecking mile – you could fly cheaper!'

Together, in gloomy silence, they surveyed the bar and its customers. A well-known actor was leaning at the counter, surrounded by a circle of admiring young men. When he saw Cronin, he bowed gracefully so that they could see the dark, corrugated lines of his wig. 'Did you make it to the office, at least?'

'I'm going in this afternoon. Old Brennan's beginning to get a bit narky.'

Brennan was Cronin's immediate superior in the Department of Woods and Lakes. A harmless, long-suffering man, he not merely overlooked the fact that Cronin spent most of his time in the office studying form, or writing reviews for the daily papers, but even countenanced his long absences, periods when he disappeared underground, only to turn up looking as if he had been passed through a mangle. It was a combination of old-fashioned fidelity and the respect still paid in the community to the idea of the poet, half sure spirit, half biting satirist. But the latter excuse was beginning to wear thin; Cronin had not published a book of poems since his flamboyant post-university days.

'That reminds me,' said O'Shea, 'did you see Clohessy in the paper?'

Cronin's gesture combined dismissal and disgust. 'That smooth bastard!'

'He seems to be getting on,' said O'Shea carefully.

For a split second Cronin's lethargic eyes ignited with hatred.

'*On!*' he growled. 'Of course he's getting on. Hasn't he got what you need to get on in this country?'

'You mean energy?'

'I mean neck; pure, unadulterated, armour-plated, insensitive *neck*. The countryman's recipe for all occasions.'

O'Shea forbore from pointing out that like himself Cronin had been born in the country: having taken root in Dublin during his student days, he now saw himself as a city father, defending civilization against the barbarian.

'Still, he's a fine-looking fellow,' he insinuated.

A snort was regarded as sufficient answer to that remark. But Cronin seemed to turn the matter over, for a few minutes later he raised his pint and looked across it at O'Shea. 'I'll tell you what's really wrong with Clohessy.'

O'Shea waited expectantly. 'What?'

'It was one of the boys in his office put me on to it. He said that Clohessy whipped over to him at one of their new Press Conference do's and took the glass from his hand telling him he had had enough.'

'Well?'

'It's the old De Valera trick brought up to date: no one ever saw that sacerdotal heron under the influence. There is something fundamentally wrong with someone who has never been seen drunk. *They can't be trusted.*'

5.15 p.m.

South of the Liffey, on a late autumn evening. People are beginning to pour from offices, Government Buildings in Kildare and

Upper Merrion Street, The Tourist Board along the canal, the Electricity Supply Board on Lower Fitzwilliam Street. The stone fronts of the Georgian houses look mournful, with bulbs already lit in ground floor and basement rooms. Above the shiny, wet rows of parked cars a light mist is gathering on the trees; a plume of smoke shows where leaves are being burned in a black-railed square. At the end of a wide street rises a blue shoulder of the Dublin Mountains. . . .

The curious thing, O'Shea reflected, as he swung his Volkswagen along the canal leading towards the main Cork-Limerick road, was that he actually knew Clohessy. Or rather he had known him briefly years ago, when they were both students. But why had he never mentioned the incident to anyone, not even to Cronin or Brennan? Especially when it would have made ideal material for pub gossip!

It had been a seaside resort in Donegal where O'Shea was in the habit of going for his holidays. Generally he went with a gang from the University who, to save money, camped in a field overlooking the bay. For a fortnight they racketed through the town, drinking, dancing, swimming. One year Clohessy had joined them for a few days, brought by one of O'Shea's friends. Although he moved in different circles from the rest at college (he was a member of the fencing team and secretary of something new called the Political Society), he seemed a decent enough chap, fresh-faced, rather silent. When they splashed in the diving pool or chased girls in the smoky dance hall, he tagged along though somehow a little distant and separate.

Then, one evening, a group of them were sitting out on the cliffs. The air was cool, and they felt full of youthful idealism and sadness, watching the sun go down on the Atlantic. They were discussing what they would be after they left the University. One had said he just wanted to be a good doctor, if he could get a practice. Carmody, O'Shea's bosom pal, had said (his arm looped around a girl as usual) that he wanted to see a bit of the world first: poor bastard, he had joined the Air Force and been shot down in a dog-fight over Benghazi. Another wanted to go back to teach in his home town in Tipperary. Then someone asked Clohessy what he wanted. He did not answer immediately and O'Shea remembered watching the fishing fleet sail slowly back towards the harbour. They seemed so frail and motionless and yet they kept edging imperceptibly towards their goal.

Then, in clear and precise tones, Clohessy outlined for them the shape he wished his career to follow. By twenty, he hoped to graduate with First Class Honours in Legal and Political Science; he would then enter a well-known Dublin firm as a Junior executive. By twenty-two, he would be Fencing Champion of Ireland, but would give it up afterwards: it took too much time. By twenty-five, he should be Assistant Manager and have his Doctorate in Economics. By thirty, he would certainly be a section head, but since he could hearly hope to rise any further in Ireland for the moment, he would probably go abroad and work for one of the big economic organizations, to gain top managerial experience. It was difficult to get a proper salary in Ireland at that level, but he felt sure that the government would ask him back before he was forty, to take charge of a national or semi-state organization. Perhaps they would even create a new one, some man-sized job commensurate with his training and abilities.

O'Shea heard Carmody suck in his breath sharply, whether in astonishment or in anger he did not know. The others seemed struck numb: coming from farms and country pubs, they had probably never heard anyone reveal such ambition before. Perhaps it was meant to be a joke? Clohessy, unaware of the effect he had made, was squatting like a Buddha on the esparto grass, throwing pebbles over the edge. They could hear them fall from ledge to ledge, before striking the pool at the base of the cliff. It was getting cold: one of the girls suggested they should be going in. As they left, O'Shea saw that the others avoided Clohessy.

That scene had remained in O'Shea's mind ever since, a secret source of contemptuous amazement as, year by year, he saw Clohessy's career trace the rising arc of its fulfilment, less like a human than some natural phenomenon. Would the great man remember their earlier meeting? He doubted it: he was hardly the type to bother with those who had not kept pace with him in the world. Nor was O'Shea the sort to remind him. Catching sight of the flat spaces of the Curragh, he accelerated: he still had a good distance to travel before Carricklone.

9.50 p.m.

It was the brandy and Irish coffee stage; wreaths of cigar smoke drifted slowly upwards in the dining-room of the Royal Arms Hotel, Carricklone. In the foreground, balloon glasses caught and reflected light: in the background waiters were grouped in stylish impassivity. His Lordship the Bishop of Carricklone was speaking and he was well known to detest interruption. A small man, with bushy eyebrows incongruously grafted on an old woman's face, he was launched onto one of his favourite subjects – the impurity of modern life. It had nothing to do with the problems of local development but, somehow, it always seemed to crop up in His Lordship's speeches. His pectoral cross danced as he thundered into the home stretch of his peroration.

'Gentlemen, we must never betray this pearl! In this modern world of drinks and dance halls, of so-called progress and speed, our country should remain a solitary oasis. On all sides we are wooed by the sirens of lax living, but – remember this – if Ireland holds a special place in God's plan it will be due to the purity of her men and the modesty of her women.'

The bishop blew his nose with a large white handkerchief and sat down abruptly. As polite applause rippled down the table, John O'Shea looked at the faces of his companions for any response to this stirring call to arms. A dozen well fed (Galway Oysters, Roast Kerry Lamb, Carrageen Moss) and well wined (Chateauneuf Saint Patrice) faces reflected nothing but sensuous contentment. At least it was an audience of adults: the last time His Lordship had spoken it was to warn a Confirmation class in a remote Kerry parish against the dangers of Communism.

As O'Shea's gaze reached the end of the table, it encountered the smooth full moon of Clohessy's face, sailing above an immaculate shirt front. Why did so many public figures come to look like that, as though moulded in wax? To O'Shea's surprise the left eyebrow appeared to flicker slightly in his direction, in a kind of conspiratorial schoolboy's wink. But before he could decide whether he was mistaken or not, a brandy glass rang, and he saw that Clohessy was getting to his feet to reply to the Bishop.

The voice was clear, but it took some time before O'Shea grasped the substance of the argument. It was not a dramatic speech, compared to the Bishop's, but it seemed an unobjectionable one, its points neatly tied together every now and then by a mild joke. What His Lordship had said showed his deep concern for the community, a concern they all echoed. There was often a bleakness about village life in Ireland due, not of course to our own faults, but to our sad history. The absence of trees and adjoining woods, the fact that the church was generally towards the outside of the town, the grimness of the public houses – all this made for a certain gloom. He did not mean to say that Carricklone was not a wonderful place, all Munster knew it was (this reference to the Hurling Championship brought cheers) but its charm was a trifle obscured by decayed houses and concrete run-ups. Hc looked forward to the day when the people of Carricklone would have the model town they obviously deserved. It was a pity that the factory that was coming was a foreign one, but we were a little retarded in these matters, and besides it would restore Carricklone's ancient links with the Continent! After that, there should be a crafts and recreation centre: it was important, as the Bishop had said, to train the young for their place in modern life. And for the summer, a swimming pool, so that they could meet in the open air. These new buildings could form the nucleus of a true community; before long the people of Carricklone might be strolling around their piazza or village square in the evenings, while from the open door of every pub came the sound of colourful music and dancing warm as Italy or Spain, our fellow Catholic countries.

As Clohessy sat down, to a thunder of applause, O'Shea turned to look at the other end of the table. Most of what Clohessy said, it had slowly dawned on him, was an inversion of the Bishop's speech, using its emotional power as a springboard. On paper, it would have seemed the usual parade of clichés, but in its context, it was almost revolutionary; yet to O'Shea's surprise, His Lordship the Bishop of Carricklone was not merely smiling broadly, he was leading the applause.

After Clohessy, nearly everyone spoke. The Mayor of Carricklone promised his warm support for every worthwhile endeavour. Several local merchants pledged not merely moral but financial assistance. The local architect and town clerk began to compare sites for the crafts and recreation centre. As the speeches gradually crumbled into specific discussion people changed places to keep up with them. In this excited buzz of proposal and counter-proposal the bland mask seemed to have settled again over Clohessy's face. He was sitting between the Lord Mayor and the Bishop's Secretary, and the inclined head of the priest, redolent of discreet satisfaction, the way Clohessy curled his finger round his glass or raised his head briefly to smell his cigar before leaning confidentially towards his companions, seemed a paradigm of worldliness.

And then the dinner was breaking up, people rising and moving towards the door in little groups. O'Shea saw that, with the swiftness of long training, Clohessy had already shaken off the Lord Mayor and the Bishop's Secretary. Now he was cruising across the room, shaking hands as he went. Having worked his way almost to the door, he came level with O'Shea, who was still standing awkwardly behind his chair. There was an instant's delay, and then his face creased into its famous smile:

'John O'Shea!' he said. 'After all these years.'

11 p.m.

'Well, what did you think of the speeches?' asked Clohessy. He and O'Shea were sitting together in the comfortable, club-like atmosphere of the hotel lounge, with the two Martels that Clohessy had ordered before them.

'Do you mean yours or the Bishop's?' asked O'Shea carefully. Clohessy burst out laughing. 'Wasn't he wonderful! John of Carricklone is one of the last of the Old Guard: he ought to be in a museum. I heard him give the same speech two years ago in Mullingar; only there it was a sermon. I suppose,' his face became suddenly serious, 'he believes it's expected of him.'

'What do you mean?' demanded O'Shea. He was not used to this class of talk about bishops: satire, yes, he could appreciate, but friendly familiarity was a rather unsettling note.

'It's one of the troubles of being a public figure. What is the average bishop but an elderly man closed up in a palace, surrounded by people who tell him what he wants to know. Which he then tells back to them; there is nothing more corrupting than a captive audience.'

He spoke with some passion and O'Shea could not resist a probe.

'Is that how you feel?' he inserted quietly.

Clohessy started slightly and gave O'Shea a cautious side-long glance. But, though repenting of his outburst, he seemed willing to continue.

'Yes, a bit,' he admitted. 'But of course it's different for us.' The 'us' was so unconsciously patronizing that O'Shea stung back before realizing it.

'You don't mean to say you don't like it?' he said with heavy sarcasm.

'Like what?' demanded Clohessy.

'You know – the fuss, the dinners, the photographs – what people call fame. Surely – '

Clohessy gave a controlled sigh. 'Oh yes, I know what people think: that I do all this for personal gain and glory. Clohessy the big-time executive, his right hand greeting a bishop, while his left robs the nation's till. And I know I do fairly well out of it, but I regard that as a reward –'

'Reward for what?' O'Shea burst out involuntarily. Then, catching himself in time: 'What do you mean, sir?'

'You know bloody well what I mean. It's not the board meetings that kill. It's going from cocktail party to cocktail party every evening; eating chicken and ham at public banquets three times a week; never once getting angry or dropping a wrong word. How much stamina do you think that takes?'

There was such a note of sincerity, almost of agony in his voice that O'Shea was embarrassed into silence.

'And that's not the worst. Going down the country to try and put across the merit of some project – the county councillors – you saw, Christ, man, it's like being thrown to wild animals.'

'So you mean to say you don't enjoy it!' repeated O'Shea incredulously.

'Enjoy it! There's nothing I loathe more. Nowhere else in the world is a top executive at the mercy of every self-important little fart with a grievance.'

'Then, why do you do it?'

Clohessy revolved the brandy glass slowly between his podgy, well-manicured hands.

'I suppose you'd call it patriotism,' he said, with some sadness.

'Patriotism!'

'Look, Sean.' At the lapse into the vernacular, O'Shea felt his spine stiffen, but Clohessy was only leaning forward with confidential eagerness.

'When I came back to this country after the war, I saw that it had no future. My first instinct was to clear out again, and to hell with it: with my background and training I could have a comfortable life anywhere in the world. You'll admit that. . . .'

O'Shea nodded. There was no denying that just as some men bore the marks of sanctity, so Clohessy had the credentials for worldly success stamped on his brow.

'Then I thought that was a bit cowardly. Why not come back and try and create a future for the country at the same time as I was creating my own? As you know, we've had a lot of patriots.'

'You can say that again,' said O'Shea fervently.

'But what it has never had are a group of practical, hard-headed people who would try to put it back on its feet, like any business. People not afraid to face the priests, the politicians, the whole vast bog of the Irish middle-class, and woo something positive out of it. One would have to give up a lot, of course. . . .'

'Like what?'

'Oh,' said Clohessy expansively, waving his hand in the air, 'it's not easy to define; the fleshpots of high commerce – the knighthood, the Tour d'Argent and Claridge's, the yacht at Cannes. The mistresses, even, if you like. A salesman of silk stockings could do better. The really big stuff never comes to Ireland. I know: I've seen it.'

O'Shea was silent.

'But there would be the satisfaction of being one of the first in a new line of well-trained – eh –'

'Patriots,' finished O'Shea.

'Yes.'

There was the awkwardness which often follows an unexpected burst of intimacy: the two men sat side by side, without speaking, in the curved leather armchairs. O'Shea glanced covertly once or twice at his companion, but now that urgency had left it, his face had resumed its usual bland, immobile expression. The skull was full and round, with a light fringe of silver hair on the edge of the Roman brow. The cheeks, in particular, were smooth and ruddy as though he had only been born that morning. Ten thousand mornings of close shaving, and Yardley's Lotion, had left the skin as polished as wood; even the wrinkles seemed deliberate, the necessary fine grain of maturity. It only required a Papal Cross or the panoply of an honorary degree to complete the picture of what Cronin had once called 'His Royal Emptiness'. Could such a man be sincere?

'Do you see Cronin much now?' asked Clohessy suddenly, as though divining O'Shea's thoughts.

'Now and again.'

'God, poor Cronin! The original Stone-Age Bohemian; in any other country he would have been remaindered years ago. I wouldn't mind if he did his own work, but as it is, he just mucks up both jobs. And to think that we all admired him so much at College! The pity is . . .' (thoughtfully).

'What?' asked O'Shea with some wariness.

'We could still use a man like that. Business has broadened, you know, become more intellectual, more of a science.'

'He would probably think Public Relations corrupting,' said O'Shea feebly.

Clohessy's nostrils flared. 'I hate irresponsibility like that! People like Cronin think they are the salt of the country, but what did they ever do for it? This is not Dark Rosaleen, the Silk of the Kine, but a little country trying to make its way in the world: why can't Cronin get down and push like the rest of us?'

There was an answer to that, but O'Shea couldn't think of it at the moment. Instead he finally asked the question that had been bothering him all night.

'Tell me, sir, why did you tell me all this?'

There was a pause during which O'Shea was made to feel his tactlessness. Then Clohessy rose to his feet, buttoning his short coat briskly.

'Well, you know,' he said slowly, 'there aren't really very many people one can talk to. And we are old school chums, in a manner of speaking. Besides' – O'Shea had never encountered a glance which combined affability and threat in such proportions before – 'we'll soon be working together, and I felt we should have a little talk first; on neutral ground.'

After Clohessy had gone (his chauffeur stepping smartly from the corner of the bar, where he had been waiting over a bottle of stout, to open the door for him), O'Shea remained sitting for several minutes. What Clohessy told him differed very little from what he remembered of their boyhood meeting, except for the note of idealism. Was the latter only an afterthought, to disguise the thrust of naked ambition? The fact that their talk had been planned, not spontaneous, argued as much, but he couldn't be sure. For the first time, O'Shea realized why he had never retold that original encounter: despite his surface scorn, he had never really made his mind up about Clohessy. Now he would have to make it up pretty soon.

9.50 a.m.

'Can he not wait?' asked O'Shea fretfully.

The hysteria in Nan Connor's voice came through the intercom as a sort of flat shriek. 'He just won't. He says he must speak to you. And he's beginning to use bad language.'

O'Shea looked despairingly at the litter of papers on his desk. 'All right, put him through.'

There was a crackle, a silence and then he heard Tadgh Cronin's voice intoning angrily: '*Will you for Christ's sake put me through to John O'Shea or I'll –*'

'O'Shea here.'

'Jesus, John, is that you, at last. I had a hell of a job trying to get past that female full-back you call your secretary.'

O'Shea was going to remark that after all she was only doing her duty, but all he said was: 'Well, what's on your mind?'

'I'm going to resign.'

'You're what?'

'I'm going to resign. Old Brennan told me yesterday afternoon that the Secretary had informed him that my behaviour was a disgrace to the Department and that if I didn't pull my socks up drastic action would have to be taken. Very well, says I, if it's a case of pushing or being pushed, I know my position. I'll resign!'

There was a dramatic pause, but before O'Shea could venture a comment, Cronin was away again.

'Of course, I told Brennan that it wasn't his fault, he isn't a bad old bugger. But do you know what they introduced last week: *all latecomers to sign the book in the boss's room*. No man with any pride could stand for that class of nonsense. Next thing they'll be having management classes during the tea break. Still, old Brennan looked surprised: you shoulda seen his gob drop.'

'I'll bet he was,' muttered O'Shea fervently. He would have said more, but there was a peculiar note in his friend's voice, a kind of forced complacency that warned him.

'Well, there you are, I showed them. I'd have told you last night but I couldn't find you. Where were you, by the way?'

'In Carricklone. With Clohessy,' he could not help adding.

'With Clohessy!'

Gratified by Cronin's surprise, O'Shea found himself, almost without thinking, giving an account of the previous night. At first he only described the dinner and Clohessy's speech but as he warmed up to his subject, he could not help including a (discreetly garbled) version of their interview as well. It was partly that he wanted to speak of it, partly also because he could not resist rubbing in that he had news of his own.

'You don't mean to say you swallowed that?' said Cronin incredulously.

'I don't know,' said O'Shea uneasily. 'What do you think?'

There was a pause at the other end of the line and then Cronin's voice came through, triumphant, low, almost a snarl.

'I was fucking well right!'

'What do you mean you were right?'

'To resign. The hour has come. *The bastards are on the march.*'

'What?'

'Listen.' O'Shea could nearly see Cronin grasping the receiver at the other end, in his excitement. 'Since this country was founded we've had two waves of chancers. The first were easy to spot; the gunmen turned gombeen: they were so ignorant that they practically ruined themselves. But this second lot are a tougher proposition. In fifty years they'll have made this country just like every place else.'

'And what's so wrong with that?'

'You know damn well what's wrong with that: they'll murder us with activity! Factories owned by Germans, posh hotels catering to the international set, computers instead of dacent pen-pushers, a typists pool: do you call that progress? Well, by Jesus, I don't, and I'll fight it tooth and nail. If this country becomes a chancer's paradise, it will be over my dead body. *Over my dead body, do you hear?*'

And that (repeated several times with increasing vehemence) was Cronin's parting shot. After vaguely agreeing to meet him for lunch in the Anchor sometime during the week, John O'Shea put down the phone, and turned to pick up the uppermost of his files. But he found it hard to concentrate, Cronin's words ringing in his ears. They had been friends for years, drawing an odd comfort from their differences of temperament, but of late O'Shea had begun to feel the strain. It was all right for Cronin to feel so defiantly about things; if the rhythm of drinking had not already corroded his faculties, his resignation might be the spur his talent needed. But for people like himself, there was no real escape: the most they could hope to find was someone under whose direction they might give of their best. Besides, was it such a criminal thing to wish to lead an ordinary life?

Somewhere, on the banks of the Liffey, or overlooking a Georgian square, a great new building would rise, a glass house against which the world might, at first, throw stones, but would gradually accept. Inside, in a large, discreetly lighted room, with Tintawn carpeting and an abstract on the wall, would be Clohessy. And in one of the adjoining cubicles, perhaps a file open before him, just as it was now. . . . Half-surprised, as though looking into a mirror, John O'Shea greeted his own future.

from *Death of a Chieftain*, 1964

Charlie's Greek

SEAN O'FAOLAIN

It was twenty-odd years before I saw Rika Prevelakis again, encouraged to visit her by, of all people Charlie, for, of all things fun, in, of all places Athens. 'You will have no trouble in finding her,' he assured me. 'Everybody in the university knows her well.'

She did not look her forty-five years, though she had grown stout, motherly and quizzical. Her hair was still black but not so oily. Her skin looked so delicately soft and pink that I at once remembered our old Dublin joke: 'Charlie, does her face-powder taste of Turkish Delight?', and his cheerful wink in reply. Nothing really betrayed her age except those Swiss rings she wore, too tight on her plump fingers, the faint necklace of Venus on her throat, and the hard ball of her calf. I gathered that her husband, whom I did not meet, was an exporter of fruit, and judging by her charming house, with its modern paintings and pieces of modern sculpture, he was a highly successful one. She told me that her eldest son – she had three – was nineteen, a figure that startled me by taking me back directly to the year after her famous visit to Dublin. So she had made up her mind about Charlie as rapidly as that!

She was delighted to get first-hand news of him, asked many questions about him, and although she now clearly thought of him with a certain good-humoured self-mockery it was plain that she still remembered him with a warm and grateful affection.

'He made me come alive,' she said so simply that the hackneyed words sounded as fresh as truth.

We chatted for nearly an hour; at the end, just as I was leaving her, I said:

'I'd be interested to know how you would sum up Charlie at the end of it all?'

She laughed and put on a stage Anglo–Greek accent:

'My husband always say, and my husband ees a wise man, that

whenever he ees asked hees opinion of any man he avoids the opeenion and sketches the leetle portrait.'

Wise man, indeed I thought as I walked away from her delightful house whose garden overlooked the winking blue of the Piraeus. 'Opeenions?' If I asked any dozen men who knew Charlie in his heyday I could guess the sort of juryman's anthology I would collect:

1. Charlie Carton? I'd trust him with my wife! For five minutes.

2. You know, I honestly and truly believe that he was the most outgoing, warmhearted, affectionate young fellow I ever met.

3. A cold, self-indulgent, self-centred, unprincipled hedonist!

4. A genuine lover of mankind, a born reformer and a natural revolutionary. Damn few people like him left in Ireland today.

5. What an orator! Brilliant! And so gay. A most amusing chap. A dreamer and a rebel. The essence of everything that is fine in the Irish nature.

6. Charlie Carton? That Big Mouth!

7. Would you not agree with me that he was rather a nice blend of Don Juan and Saint Francis? I mean, it was a toss of a coin which side of him would win out in the end. By the way, which has won out?

8. Had he any principles at all? I've seen him weep over a sick child in the slums one minute and the next minute deceive a woman, pitilessly.

9. No, I don't think I'd say that Charlie ever had many principles. A few? Perhaps? They certainly didn't lie too heavily on him. Do you remember what Aristide Briand said one time about principles? *Il faut toujours s'appuyer sur les principes; ils finissent par en céder.* Always lean hard on your principles – sooner or later they will give way. One thing about Charlie, though – he was a damn good sport. A real man's man. I liked him.

10. If you want my frank opinion of him he was a flaming bloody humbug.

11. I only knew him in his college days. He'd give you the shirt off his back. You have to forgive a lot to a youngster like that.

12. Soft. To the marrow of his bones. Mush. Incapable of tenderness because incapable of fierceness. Ask any woman. The only good thing they could all say for him would be that if he deceived them he damn soon undeceived them.

There was that night he loaned me his bed-sitter in London. The telephone rang every half-hour from midnight on. Always the same woman or girl.

'No,' I would reply. 'Mr Carton isn't here. I'm only a guest, occupying his room for the night.' Or: 'I assure you Charlie isn't here. For God's sake do you realize it's one o'clock in the morning, and I'm trying to sleep!' Each time she said the same forlorn thing: 'Well, just tell him I just rang up just to say goodbye.' After half an hour back she would come again, and again, and again, until, between fury and pity, I began to wonder whether he had not been expecting exactly this when he so generously offered me the loan of his room. In the end I appealed to the operator. In a tired, polite, English, three-o'clock-in-the-morning voice he said: 'I'm very sorry, sir, I've explained to the lady that Mr Carton isn't there. It does no good, poor thing. Besides, I'm obliged to put the calls through. And mark you, this is costing her a pretty penny – she's on long distance from Strasbourg.'

A Salvador Dali would have painted him with a woman looking out of each eye. His handsome boyish face would have delighted any painter of the high Renaissance in search of the epitome of the power and prime of youth; though it would have been a Florentine painter rather than a Venetian, because of his colourless skin, his buttercup hair, his teeth so small and perfect, his heavy-lidded eyes and because in spite of his bulk he suggested surface rather than roundness, depth or solidity. Neither his face nor his body ever made you conscious of his bones. Stripped for the boxing ring his body looked so soft, almost so feminine that nobody who had not already seen him box would have taken him for a stayer. But he was a stayer, and a frequent winner, obstinate, agile as a boy, a fender rather than a fighter, winning always on points of skill, He outboxed his men and outflirted his women. His boyishness was a fake. At forty-one he was still eager, laughing, garrulous, completely indifferent to appearance, uncombed, almost unkempt, genuinely feckless – he never gave a tuppenny damn about money or possessions and he was generally broke; which may have been the main reason why, even in his schooldays, women wanted to mother him and love him. It must have come as a shock to them to discover that his fecklessness was all-embracing, in every sense of the word. Their pretty boy was as hard as nails. I thought of him the first time I saw that well-known portrait of Lodovico Capponi by Bronzino in the Frick museum – an elegant young ephebe as you might think until you looked into his cool, grey X-ray eyes, and they make you jump like a drop of boiling water on your hand.

One of our jurymen remembers him as a natural revolutionary; another as a rebel. He was born in the wrong place and the wrong age to be either, to the full – in Ireland after the Troubles. How happy he would have been in the thick of them! If he had been shot then (though I have the feeling that he would have outboxed them too) he would now be one of our best-loved boy-heroes. He was born too soon for the war against the Nazis, and the Spanish Civil War was almost over when he was leaving school – together with the not-all-that-young school-mother who took him camping in a pup-tent all around England for the whole of that summer.

'She completed my education,' he used to say, with his usual happy grin. 'What happened to her? I don't know. She got sacked, of course. Oh, yes, she wrote to me. But,' with a graceful circle of his slender strong hand, 'we had completed the medallion of our love.'

That was the way he always talked, romantically; and behaved, ruthlessly. He used to say:

'I'm not really all that Irish, you know! The Cartons were always Cromwellian settlers. And you know how it is with these colonials. One moves on.'

'Would you,' I asked Rika Prevelakis, 'say he was ruthless?'

By way of reply she recalled their last encounter. I already knew (we all knew) something about it. She frankly filled in the details.

It happened at the time of his famous Monster Public Protest Meeting in Forty-one. He was then one of Ireland's active Communists (had we twelve?); in public calling himself a member of the Irish Labour Party which, as everybody knows, was and is about as left as my right foot; calling himself a socialist in private; and (his

own confession) in his bed or his bath loudly declaring himself a
Marxist. The date is vital, Forty-one was a tough time anywhere in
these islands for anyone to be a Communist. The Russians were
still holding to their non-aggression pact with Hitler. The many
thousands of Irish in the British army felt they were there to fight
Communism as well as Nazism. Dunkirk was over. So was the
Battle of Britain. But when Spain invaded Tangier, which reminded us all of the existence of General Franco, and the Germans
entered Athens, which reminded Charlie of Lord Byron, it seemed
the perfect moment to appeal to Ireland about the rights of small
nations. Accordingly, Charlie and his friends boldly announced a
Monster Public Meeting 'in honour of Greece' for the night of May
4th. The timing could not have been more awkward for all
concerned. Had they waited until June Russia would by then be
fighting Germany. And four days before the meeting this old flame
of Charlie's turned up in Dublin.

She was about twenty-five then; small, dark, reasonably pretty,
and so enchanted to find Charlie up in arms in defence of her
country that her prettiness bloomed out in a sort of fiery beauty. In
every way but one she was a most appealing young woman, as all
who met her agreed; and most of us did meet her because from the
minute she arrived he was madly trying to fob her off on his friends.
(With her, also, it appeared, he had completed the medallion of
their love – anyway of his love.) Her one unappealing characteristic
was that although she was highly educated – she was then teaching
Greek and Greek history in London to Foreign Office chaps – and
well informed about most things, shrewd, hard-headed and clear-
eyed, she was pathetically unable to perceive that Charlie detested
her in proportion as her pursuit of him and his flight from her made
them both look ridiculous.

'It's awful!' he sweated. 'It's like a blooming honeymoon! She
never lets up for one minute. Can we have breakfast together?
What am I doing for lunch? Where am I going for dinner? What
about tonight, tomorrow night, the day after tomorrow! Listen –
be a sport for God's sake; take her out to lunch for me and lose her
somewhere in the mountains.'

One immediate result during those days before the Meeting was
that we all had her on the telephone:

'Can I speak to Mr Carton, please?'

'Hello! Is that Rika? I'm afraid Charlie isn't here. He's never here. He doesn't live here, you know.'

'But he must be there! He told me to ring this number if he didn't turn up!'

'Turn up where?'

'In Stephen's Green. At three o'clock. Beside the bust of James Clarence Mangan.'

In the soft Spring rain? Now four o'clock! With a drop on the tip of James Clarence Mangan's green nose? What a good idea for getting shut of a girl! But it was not good enough for Rika.

'Well, he just isn't here.'

'I will ring again.'

'It isn't any good. He never is here.'

'I will ring again. He told me to keep on trying. When he comes please tell him to wait until I ring again.'

We kept asking ourselves, and asking one another why he was so devious with her. Why, if only in sheer kindness of heart didn't he give her the straight uppercut? Was this the soft streak in him? She revealed that whenever he could not avoid meeting her he would sit by her side, hold her hand, gaze into her eyes and in his rich Irish voice recite poetry to her, Byron for preference:

> *Eternal spirit of the chainless Mind!*
> *Brightest in dungeons, Liberty, thou art,*
> *For there thy habitation is the heart –*
> *The heart which love of thee alone can bind* . . .

If she raged at him he would say, soothingly and softly, 'Let the doves settle, Rika! Let the doves settle on your looovely head!' Once, being still as tempestuous as (in his admiring phrase) the stormy Aegean she found him gripping her hand and asking, 'Do I hold the hand of Queen Maeve?' to which she unwisely replied, 'Who is Queen Maeve?' only to find herself at once bewildered, delighted, infuriated and irrecoverably lost in a golden-and-purple tapestry of Celtic myth and legend:

'Our past, Rika, is so old and rich, like your great past, out of which you have come to us, so filled with wonder and mystery that it surrounds us like the murmuring night-sea, crowded with the dim faces and the lost voices of our dead, whose whispering words we never cease to hear and can never hope to understand. In that dark night of the Irish memory there looms always our bull-goddess Queen Maeve, surrounded by the tossing heads of the eternal sea, her herd of white bulls, up to their bellies in the green pastures of the ocean, her spear aloft, her great eyes roolling . . .'

She was never to know how that story ended. Dazed and mesmerised, in the very heat, heart and height of it, she saw him leap up and cry: 'My comrades await me! The battle approaches. Meet me in Davy Byrne's back in an hour's time.'

And there he was pounding down the stairs with her shouting over the banisters, 'But if you aren't there?', and him shouting up from the bottom of the well 'Ring 707070!' She had waited for the length of four whiskeys in Davy Byrne's. She had then found that there is no such telephone number as 707070, and decided that she had misunderstood him: until she saw it the next day in a bookshop window. *I Did Penal Servitude*. By 707070.

By the morning of the Meeting she was beside herself. Up to then she had grudgingly accepted that his secret preparations for the Meeting were a reasonable explanation for his disappearances and non-appearances. But when the Meeting would be over and done with? She knew that that would be either the end or the beginning of everything. Early that morning, so early that the gulls were still screaming down on the garbage bins, she found herself awakened by a knocking on the door of her hotel bedroom. He was standing in the corridor carrying a suitcase, his collar up, his buttercup hair in his eyes, and his eyes staring. He laid the suitcase at her feet and said with a terrible earnestness:

'Rika, when, perhaps even before, the Meeting ends tonight the whole city will be a cauldron of excitement. There may be riots. Blood may flow in the streets. Unless I am in jail, or dead, I will come to this hotel at twelve o'clock tonight with a motor-car. I know the night porter. A grand young fellow from Kerry. One of us. Absolutely reliable. He will let me in by the back door. We will fly together into the mountains where a friend of mine has a lime-white cottage with a roof of golden thatch beside a dark lake where the ripples are for ever washing in the reeds and the wild water for ever lapping on the crags, and there at last we will be alone.'

'But,' she had asked, clutching her dressing-gown to her neck, 'how do I really know that I can really trust you to come?'

He had glared at her.

'Trust? It is I who trust you. This case,' down-pointing, 'contains everything I possess – papers, books, letters, plans, maps. Enough to ruin me for life! Is this hand I grasp the hand of a weakling or the hand of Queen Maeve?'

('Idiot that I was,' she sighed, 'I said "Queen Maeve".')

'At midnight! Be ready! Be waiting! My Grecian bride!'

(Throwing out her arms like a pope she cried: 'And he was gone!')

She went to the Monster Meeting. ('I *attended* it,' she said mockingly.) The evening was a trifle damp. Charlie had said that College Green would be thronged from end to end. Rika found a gathering of about three hundred people most of whom looked like evening strollers, invited by a loudspeaker – and gently shepherded by an Inspector and six guards – off the main thoroughfare of College Green into a piazzetta called Foster Place. This broad brief cul-de-sac, mainly occupied by banks, is used during the day as a parking space, and commonly used by night for smaller public gatherings such as this. She soon observed that the organizers of the Meeting (old campaigners), having placed their decoy speaker at the farther or inner end of the cul-de-sac, then drew up a convertible motor-car at the other or open end for their main speakers, with the evident intention of leaving themselves a ready line of retreat into College Green if things turned nasty. Across the backs of the convertible's seats they had laid the kind of shallow packing-case which is used for transporting such flat objects as sheets of glass, wall-boards or pictures, a platform just wide enough to support and display one speaker at a time.

The pilot-speaker – a young Trinity College student named Phil Clune, who was later to become chief financial adviser to one of the new African nations – was both careful and lucky enough not to provoke his audience to anything more serious than a few sarcastic interruptions on the lines of 'Lord Byron was a dirty scut!', or 'And what did Greece do for us when we wor fightin' the Black and Tans?', or, in bland disregard for Phil's age, 'And where wor you in Nineteen Sixteen?' She found it all deflating and confusing until the crowd had to turn right around to face the main speakers. Then things began to warm up a bit while still remaining confusing, especially when what she called 'a butchy-looking woman with cropped grey hair like Gertrude Stein' started to speak of the Greek church as a citadel of truth, liberty and outstanding moral courage. This produced shouts of 'What Greek church?', and 'We don't recognize no Greek Church', which made her feel that it was her duty to explain to those near her what the Greek church really was; the main effect of which was to break up the opposition into small growling groups arguing among themselves about which Greek church recognized Rome and which recognized Constantinople. These arguments subsided when the butchy woman started talking about 'the deplorable silence of the Prisoner of the Vatican', whom she referred to, rather over-familiarly, as 'Papa Pacelli'. The result was such angry cries as, 'His Holiness the Pope to you, ma'am!' and, 'Hey! Are you from Belfast?'

At this point, if Rika had known her Dublin properly she would have realized that it would only be a matter of minutes before somebody would start singing *Faith of Our Fathers*, and then it would be high time for all prudent men and women to start edging off to the shelter of the nearest bank-doorway. Instead she started elbowing to the front where she saw Charlie insistently plucking at the tail of Gertrude Stein's skirt and madly whispering something to her that made her quickly wind up whatever she was saying about the Red Dean of Saint Paul's and lumber down off the packing-case.

Charlie at once leaped to the rostrum, his arms spread, his yellow hair blowing in the wet wind, his splendid voice ringing out:

> '"*Eternal spirit of the chainless mind!*
> *Brightest in dungeons, Liberty, thou art,*
> *For there thy habitation is the heart –*
> *The heart which love of thee alone can bind . . .*"'

'My friends! I give you a clarion-call that I believe no man or woman listening to me can fail to answer. Up the Republic!'

The crowd did not say a word in answer to this clarion call – which was probably exactly what he wanted since they at once fell silent to listen, though possibly more dominated by his fine orator's voice and his burly lithe boxer's body than by the actual words he said:

('Oh!' she recalled. 'He looked superb. I fell in love with him all over again. Say what you like about him, he had presence. He had guts.')

'My friends!' he shouted. 'We are an old and ancient race whose past is so old and so rich, so filled with wonder and mystery that it surrounds us like the murmuring night-sea that defends our green shores, like the whispering Aegean whose antique memories for every ripple among the reeds and lap upon the crags of ancient Greece. That darkness of Ireland's primordial memories is crowded tonight with the dim faces and the murmuring voices of our beloved and rebellious dead, whose words we never cease to hear and every syllable of which we fully and clearly understand – whether it be Queen Maeve of Connaught among her herds of milk-white bulls, the tossing foam of the sea, her great spear aloft, her thunderous voice calling to us to remember our birthright, or the quiet, sad figure of Cathleen the daughter of Houlihan passing through the shadows like an uncrowned queen.'

(Rika shrugged. 'Yes! He had only been practising on me. But I felt it made me his colleague! And I was proud of it!')

'My friends!' Charlie was bellowing. 'What do those voices say to us tonight? They say to us: "As we are free and as we will remain free, so must all mankind be free and for ever so remain."'

At which point he whipped a small tricolour from his left-hand inside pocket and waved it over his head – a gesture that actually produced a few approving cheers.

'But, my friends, I said "*all* mankind!"'

At which he whipped from his right-hand inside pocket the blue and white flag of Greece.

'This is the flag of fighting Greece! Tonight we fight under two flags in Freedom's name. Long live Liberty!'

He got a few more cheers. He now produced from his left-hand outside pocket the black swastika on a red ground.

'Does this flag stand for that Liberty? For your liberty, or for the liberty of your children? What can you say, what think, what feel? I will tell you what I think of it.'

And like a conjurer he produced half a dozen matches from his vest pocket, struck them alight on the seat of his trousers, and the Nazi emblem burst into flames. ('I had it well soaked in petrol!' he explained to us afterwards.)

'A sign!' he roared, as the emblem flamed and fell. 'A sign as black as treachery and as red as blood. And only in blood can all its cruelties be avenged!'

At this the Inspector and his six guards began to edge forward. After all, Ireland was officially a neutral country, even if we were more neutral against Germany than for it, and he had issued stern warnings before the meeting began that no word should be said that night contrary to Irish neutrality. But Charlie's next words made him pause, indecisively:

'I mean, my friends, the blood coursing through your veins, pulsing in your hearts with pity for the children in our slums, our unemployed wailing for bread, our aged sick neglected and dying all about us, the thousands of our young men, aye and our young maidens, mounting the gangways day and night to emigrate to foreign shores. Your warm Irish blood can remind you only of the triple cry of Liberty, Equality and Fraternity that led so many of our young men in every age to die for the Republic. That blood is the Rights of Man! That blood is the colour of universal brother-hood!'

Reaching behind him he received, unfurled and waved, blazing in the electric light of the street lamps, the red flag.

At one and the same moment a collective howl of rage burst from the crowd, a female voice began to sing *Faith of Our Fathers*, the Inspector and the guards breasted towards the car, the mob surged forwards, the car rocked and Charlie, to prevent himself from being thrown down among the lions, grasped the lamp-post beside him, and clambered up it like a monkey, still waving the red flag, still shouting 'Long live Liberty!'

(I could see it all in Rika's eyes, immense as two coloured television screens.)

'You know, those Irish policemen were marvellous! They got in a circle around the car and the lamp-post. One of them climbed up and pulled Charlie down by the legs, and the Inspector said, "Run, you bastard!" And, my God, how he ran! Some of the crowd ran after him, but he was too fast for them. I kept clawing at the Inspector and shouting, "I am a Greek girl!" He caught me and threw me head first into the car, my legs up in the air, just as the car started and ran away with me, the butchy woman, four or five men, and the red flag streaming behind them. They stopped in a long, quiet street, pulled me out and dumped me on the pavement, and drove away off down that long street into the fog.

'My face was bleeding. My stockings were torn. I was a sight. When I got up I saw I was opposite the Abbey Theatre and I will always remember the play they were playing that night. It was called *The Whiteheaded boy*. When I saw it I thought of Charlie. My God! I said to myself. He may want to hide in my hotel, and I ran all the way to it. I cleaned myself up to look my best for him when he would come at twelve o'clock. I packed my bags though I was shaking so much I could hardly do it, and then I threw myself on the bed and I cried for my whiteheaded boy. I cried that he knew I had seen him run, that he had been shamed into running for his life, that he was homeless and an outcast. Then suddenly I saw his suitcase and I thought, my God, the police may come here searching for him and find all his papers, and letters, and plans. I managed to lug it to the window-sill – it was very heavy – and I stood it up there outside the window and I drew the blind and the curtains, and I lay down again to cry and to wait.'

'I woke up at half-past one. I ran down to consult with the night porter, Charlie's friend. He was a nice, sweet boy, about seventeen or eighteen. He told me he had never heard of Charlie Carton. I knew then that Charlie would never come. But what was I to do with the suitcase? I decided to take this boy into my confidence. I told him that Charlie was a patriot and a hunted man. I shall never forget what he said to me. He said, "Miss, if he's for Ireland, I'll do anything for him." I cried when he said that, it was so warm, so Greek. When I told him about the suitcase that I must protect with my life, he got a bunch of keys and a screwdriver and we went upstairs together to see what we should do with this terrible suitcase. Between us, this boy and me, we dragged it in from the window-sill – it was by this time soaked with the rain – and we laid it on the ground and we worked on it and at last we managed to open it.'

(I shook my head. Not because I did not know what was in it –

Charlie had told me – but in pity for her. Rika looked out of her window down at the waters of the port.)

'I suppose,' she said, 'in everybody's life there is one moment of shame that he never forgets. This was my moment – when that boy opened that suitcase, that nice boy who would have done anything for Ireland. It contained two bags of sand. Nothing else.' She laughed merrily. 'He really was a rascal! I told the boy, "This is probably dynamite." All he said was, "Yes, miss." I stayed in my room until the morning broke. Then I took the boat for London.'

I think if Charlie were with us at that moment I would have struck him. I said:

'Some people would be less kind about him than you. They would say he was a poseur, a sham, an actor.'

'Oh, no! He was much more than that! Much more! He was actor, dramatist, producer and play all in one. And we were his audience. He was always trying to play out some play of life that was real to him for as long as he imagined it, though it was always only real in the way a child's soap bubble is real. A dream full of swirling colours, in the end floating away, exploding silently.'

'Wasn't that a bit hard on the people who had to be his co-actors?'

'You mean people like me? Very hard. If we were foolish enough to think that any of his plays would last. Not hard if we knew that at any moment he would ring down the curtain and start another romantic play in some other theatre, in some other city, in some other country. Even then, of course, it was hard on his fellow-actors whom he left behind out of a job. He was inexpressibly selfish because he was so hopelessly romantic. Always dashing away. An artist whose only art was his life. Not a very good artist, I grant you, but, still, an artist.'

'Some people would say he was just a Don Juan.'

'I hope not! That most unhappy race of men. Always chasing shadows. Always hoping. Never sure. He is married.'

Was it a statement or a question?

'How did you know?'

She smiled:

'We all marry. If it comes to that Don Juans – and Donna Juanitas too – are of all people the most certain to marry, in order to be sure at least once before they die, or become impotent. To feel sure that their search was . . . Oh, well, it's too difficult. It took me a long time to work it out. Until I did I hated him more than I have hated anyone else in my whole life. And,' she grinned, 'I'm very good at hating. When I realized that he just had to be what he is I no longer cared.'

'Have you ever written to him?'

She looked at me coldly.

'I am a happily married woman, with three sons. I am a professor. I have an adoring husband. I have a lovely home. Why should I write to him?'

'He has not forgotten you.'

She smiled a gratified smile and we shook hands.

'Give him my affectionate greetings. And all my sympathy.'

I glanced at her, startled until I saw that she did not mean it derisively. Her last question was to ask what he was doing now. I told her: a salesman for sanitary equipment. She was still laughing as she closed the door.

As I walked down through the narrow streets about the port I wondered for a long time what I would say if somebody asked me for my opinion of her. Like all experienced women, sensible, practical, and absolutely without illusions, despising above all those fantasies of which even the older men are never entirely free? Or would even she sometimes remember, with a tiny, secret, happy smile, certain earlier days when she had been a little otherwise?

I was amused when I told Charlie of our meeting in Athens, and he at once asked, eagerly, if she remembered him.

'Indelibly!'

'And is she still beautiful?'

'More so than ever!'

I watched his blue X-ray eyes narrow with penetration, widen with the lovely image they received, and then, ever so slowly, relinquish another dream. He had little bags under his eyes. His hair was thin as dust. He said, 'Oh, well! We had completed the medallion of our love!' – and made a graceful circle with his slender hand.

from *The Heat of the Sun*, 1966

A Memory

MARY LAVIN

James did all right for a man on his own. An old woman from the village came in for a few hours a day and gave him a hot meal before she went home. She also got ready an evening meal needing only to be heated up. As well, she put his breakfast egg in a saucepan of water beside the paraffin stove, with a box of matches beside it in case he mislaid his own. She took care of all but one of the menial jobs of living. The one she couldn't do for him was one James hated most – cleaning out ashes from the grate in his study and lighting up the new fire for the day.

James was an early riser and firmly believed in giving the best of his brain to his work. So, the minute he was dressed he went out to the kitchen and lit the stove under the coffee pot. Then he got the ash bucket and went at the grate. When the ashes were out the rest wasn't too bad. There was kindling in the hot press and the old woman left a few split logs for getting up a quick blaze. He had the room well warmed by the time he had eaten his breakfast. His main objection to doing the grate was that he got his suit covered with ashes. He knew he ought to wear tweeds now that he was living full-time at the cottage, but he stuck obstinately to his dark suit and white collar, feeling as committed to this attire as to his single state. Both were part and parcel of his academic dedication. His work filled his life as it filled his day. He seldom had occasion to go up to the University. When he went up it was to see Myra, and then only on impulse if for some reason work went against him. This did happen periodically in spite of his devotion to it. Without warning a day would come when he'd wake up in a queer, unsettled mood that would send him prowling around the cottage, lighting up cigarette after cigarette and looking out of the window until he'd have to face the fact that he was not going to do a stroke. Inevitably the afternoon would see him with his hat and coat on, going down the road to catch the bus for Dublin – and an evening with Myra.

This morning he was in fine fettle though, when he dug the shovel into the mound of grey ash. But he was annoyed to see a volley of sparks go up the black chimney. The hearth would be hot, and the paper would catch fire before he'd have time to build his little pyre. There was more kindling in the kitchen press, but he'd have felt guilty using more than the allotted amount, thinking of the poor old creature wielding that heavy axe. He really ought to split those logs himself.

When he first got the cottage he used to enjoy that kind of thing. But after he'd been made a research professor and able to live down there all year round he came to have less and less zest for manual work. He sort of lost the knack of it. Ah well, his energies were totally expected in mental work. It would not be surprising if muscularly he got a bit soft.

James got up off his knees and brushed himself down. The fire was taking hold. The nimble flames played in and out through the dead twigs as sunlight must once have done when the sap was green. Standing watching them, James flexed his fingers. He wouldn't like to think he was no longer fit. Could his increasing aversion to physical labour be a sign of decreasing vigour? He frowned. He would not consider himself a vain man, it was simply that he'd got used to the look of himself; was accustomed to his slight, spare figure. But surely by mental activity he burned up as much fuel as any navvy or stevedore? Lunatics never had to worry about exercise either! Who ever saw a corpulent madman? He smiled. He must remember to tell that to Myra. Her laugh was always so quick and responsive although even if a second or two later she might seize on some inherently serious point in what had at first amused her. It was Myra who had first drawn his attention to this curious transference – this drawing off of energies – from the body to the brain. She herself had lost a lot of the skill in her fingers. When she was younger – or so she claimed – she'd been quite a good cook, and could sew, and that kind of thing, although frankly James couldn't imagine her being much good about the house. But when she gave up teaching and went into free-lance translation her work began to make heavy demands on her, and she too, like him, lost all inclination for physical chores. Now – or so she said – she could not bake a cake to save her life. As for sewing –

well here again frankly – to him the sight of a needle in her hand
would be ludicrous. In fact he knew – they both knew – that when
they first met, it was her lack of domesticity that had been the
essence of her appeal for him. For a woman, it was quite remarkable how strong was the intellectual climate of thought in which she
lived. She had concocted a sort of cocoon of thought and wrapped
herself up in it. One became aware of it immediately one stepped
inside her little flat. There was another thing! The way she used the
word flat to designate what was really a charming little mews house.
It was behind one of the Georgian squares, and it had a beautiful
little garden at the back and courtyard in front. He hadn't been
calling there for very long until he understood why she referred to it
as her flat. It was a word that did not have unpleasant connotations
of domesticity.

Her little place had a marvellously masculine air, and yet,
miraculously, Myra herself remained very feminine. She was, of
course, a pretty woman, although she hated him to say this – and
she didn't smoke, or drink more than a dutiful pre-dinner sherry
with him, which she often forgot to finish. And there was a nice
scent from her clothes, a scent at times quite disturbing. It often
bothered him and was occasionally the cause of giving her the
victory in one of the really brilliant arguments that erupted so
spontaneously the moment he stepped inside the door.

Yes, it was hard to believe Myra could ever have been a
homebody. But if she said it was so, then it *was* so. Truth could
have been her second name. With regard to her domestic failure,
she had recently told him a most amusing story. He couldn't recall
the actual incident, but it had certainly corroborated her theory of
the transference of skill. It was – she said – as if part of her had
become palsied, although at the time her choice of that word had
made him wince, it was so altogether unsuitable for a woman like
her, obviously now in her real prime. He'd pulled her up on that.
Verbal exactitude was something they both knew to be of the
utmost importance, although admittedly rarer to find in a woman
than a man.

'It is a quality I'd never have looked to find in a woman, Myra,'
he'd said to her on one of his first visits to the flat – perhaps his very
first.

He never forgot her answer.

'It's not something I'd ever expect a man to look for in a woman,' she said. 'Thank you, James, for not jumping to the conclusion that I could not possibly possess it.'

Yes – that must have been on his first visit because he'd been startled by such quick-fire volley in reply to what had been only a casual compliment. No wonder their friendship got off to a flying start!

Thinking of the solid phalanx of years that had been built up since that evening, James felt a glow of satisfaction, and for a moment he didn't realize that the fire he was supposed to be tending had got off to a good start, and part at least of his sense of well-being was coming from its warmth stealing over him.

The flames were going up the chimney with soft nervous rushes and the edges of the logs were deckled with small sharp flames, like the teeth of a saw. He could safely leave it now and have breakfast. But just then he did remember what it was Myra had been good at when she was young. Embroidery! She had once made herself an evening dress with the bodice embroidered all over in beads. And she'd worn it! So it must have been well made. Even his sister Kay, who disliked Myra, had to concede she dressed well. Yes, she must indeed have been fairly good at sewing in her young days. Yet one day recently when she ripped her skirt in the National Library she hadn't been able to mend it.

'It wasn't funny, James,' she chided when he laughed. 'The whole front pleat was ripped. I had to borrow a needle and thread from the lavatory attendant. Fortunately I had plenty of time – so when I'd taken it off and sewed it up I decided to give it a professional touch – a finish – with a tailor's arrow. It took time but it was well done and the lavatory attendant was very impressed when I held the skirt up! But next minute when I tried to step into it I found I'd sewn the back to the front. I'd formed a sort of gusset. Can you picture it. I'd turned it into trousers!'

Poor Myra! He laughed still more.

'I tell you, it's not funny, James. And it's the same with cooking. I used at least to be able to boil an egg, whereas now –' she shrugged her shoulders. 'You know how useless I am in the kitchen.'

She had certainly never attempted to cook a meal for him. They always went out to eat. There was a small café near the flat and they ate there. Or at least they did at the start. But when one evening they decided they didn't really want to go out – perhaps he'd had a headache, or perhaps it was a really wet night, but anyway whatever it was, Myra made no effort to – as she put it – slop up some unappetizing smather. Instead she lifted the phone, and got on to the proprietor of their little café and – as she put it – administered such a dose of coaxy-orum – she really had very amusing ways of expressing herself – that he sent around two trays of food. Two trays, mind you. That was so like her – so quick, so clever. And tactful, too. That night marked a new stage in their relationship.

They'd been seeing a lot of each other by then. He'd been calling to the flat pretty frequently and when they went out for a meal, although the little café was always nearly empty, he had naturally paid the bill each time.

'We couldn't go on like that though, James!' she'd said firmly when he'd tried to pay for the trays of food that night. And she did finally succeed in making him see that if he were to come to the flat as often as she hoped he would – and as he himself certainly hoped – it would put her under too great an obligation to have him pay for the food every time.

'Another woman would be able to run up some tasty little dish that wouldn't cost tuppence,' she said, 'but –' she made a face ' – that's out. All the same I can't let you put me under too great a compliment to you. Not every time.'

In the end they'd settled on a good compromise. They each paid for a tray.

He had had misgivings, but she rid him of them.

'What would you eat if I wasn't here, Myra?' he asked.

'I wouldn't have *cooked* anything, that's certain,' she said, and he didn't pursue the topic, permitting himself just one other brief inquiry.

'What do other people do, I wonder?'

This Myra dismissed with a deprecating laugh.

'I'm afraid I don't know,' she said. 'Or care! Do you?'

'Oh Myra!' In that moment he felt she elevated them both to such pure heights of integrity. 'You know I don't,' he said, and he'd laid his hand over hers as she sat beside him on the sofa.

'That makes two of us!' she said, and she drew a deep breath of contentment.

It was a rich moment. It was probably at that moment he first realized the uniquely undemanding quality of her feeling for him.

But now James saw that the fire was blazing madly. He had to put on another log or it would burn out too fast. He threw on a log and was about to leave the study when, as he passed his desk, a nervous impulse made him look to see that his papers were not disarranged, although there was no one to disturb them.

The papers, of course, were as he had left them. But then the same diabolical nervousness made him go over and pick up the manuscript. Why? He couldn't explain, except that he'd worked late the previous night and, when he did that, he was always idiotically nervous next day, as if he half expected to find the words had been mysteriously erased during the night. That had happened once! He'd got up one morning as usual, full of eagerness to take up where he thought he'd left off only to find he'd stopped in the middle of a sentence – had gone to bed defeated, leaving a most involved and complicated sentence unfinished. He'd only dreamed that he'd finished it off.

This morning, thank heavens, it was no dream. He'd finished the sentence – the whole chapter. It was the last chapter too. A little rephrasing, perhaps some rewording, and the whole thing would be ready for the typist.

Standing in the warm study with the pages of his manuscript in his hand James was further warmed by a self-congratulatory glow. This was the most ambitious thing he'd attempted so far – it was no less than an effort to trace the creative process itself back, as it were, to its source-bed. How glad he was that he'd stuck at it last night. He'd paid heavily for it by tossing around in the sheets until nearly morning. But it was worth it. His intuitions had never yielded up their meanings so fast or so easily. But suddenly his nervousness returned. He hoped to God his writing wasn't illegible? No. It was readable. And although his eye did not immediately pick up any of the particularly lucid – even felicitous –

phrases that he vaguely remembered having hit upon, he'd come
on them later when he was re-reading more carefully.

Pleased, James was putting down the manuscript, but on an
impulse he took up the last section again. He'd bring it out to the
kitchen and begin his re-reading of it while he was having his
breakfast, something he never did, having a horror of foodstains on
paper. It might, as it were, recharge his batteries, because in spite
of his satisfaction with the way the work was going, he had to admit
to a certain amount of physical lethargy, due to having gone to bed
so late.

It was probably wiser in the long run to do like Myra and confine
oneself to a fixed amount of work per day. Nothing would induce
Myra to go beyond her pre-determined limit of two thousand
words a day. Even when things were going well! It was when they
were going well that paradoxically she often stopped work. Really
her method of working amazed him. When she encountered
difficulty she went doggedly on, worrying at a word like a dog with
a bone – as she put it – in order, she explained, to avoid carrying
over her frustration with it to the next day. On the other hand,
when things were going well and her mind was leaping forward like
a flat stone skimming the surface of a lake (her image again, not his,
but good, good) *then* sometimes she stopped.

'Because then, James, I have a residue of enthusiasm to start me
off next day! I'm not really a dedicated scholar like you – I need
stimulus.'

She had a point. But her method wouldn't work for him. It
would be mental suicide for him to tear himself away when he was
excited. It was only when things got sticky he stopped. When an
idea sort of seized up in his mind and he couldn't go on.

There was nothing sticky about last night though. Last night his
brain buzzed with ideas. Yet now, sitting down to his egg, the page
in his hand seemed oddly dull – a great hunk of abstraction. He
took the top off the egg before reading on. But after a few
paragraphs he looked at the numbering of the pages. Had the pages
got mixed up? Here was a sentence that seemed to be in the wrong
place. The whole passage made no impact. And what was this?
He'd come on a line that was meaningless, absolutely meaningless –
gibberish. With a sickening feeling James put down the

manuscript and took a gulp of coffee. Then, by concentrating hard he could perceive – could at least form a vague idea of – what he'd been trying to get at in this clumsy passage. At one point indeed he had more or less got it, but the chapter as a whole –? He sat there stunned.

What had happened? Could it be that what he'd taken for creative intensity had been only nervous exhaustion? Was that it? Was Myra right? Should he have stopped earlier? Out of the question. In the excited state he'd been in, he wouldn't have slept a wink at all – even in the early hours. And what else could he have done but go to bed? A walk, perhaps? At that time of night? On a country road in the pitch dark? It was all very well for Myra – the city streets were full of people at all hours, brightly lit, and safe underfoot.

Anyway Myra probably did most of her work in the morning. He didn't really know for sure of course, except that whenever he turned up at the flat there was never any sign of papers about the place. The thought of that neat and orderly flat made him look around the cottage and suddenly he felt depressed. The old woman did her best, but she wasn't up to very much. The place could do with a rub of paint, the woodwork at least, but he certainly wasn't going to do it. He wouldn't be able. James frowned again. Why was his mind harping on this theme of fitness? He straightened up as if in protest at some accusation, but almost at once he slumped down, not caring.

He got his exercise enough on the days he went to Dublin. First the walk to the bus. Then the walk at the other end, because no matter what the weather, he always walked from the bus to the flat. It was a good distance too, but it prolonged his anticipation of the evening ahead.

Ah well! He wouldn't be going today. That was certain. He gathered up his pages. He'd have to slog at this thing till he got it right. He swallowed down the last of his coffee. Back to work.

The fire at any rate was going well. It was roaring up the chimney. The sun too was pouring into the room. Away across the river in a far field cattle were lying down: a sign of good weather it was said.

Hastily, James stepped back from the window and sat down at

his desk. It augured badly for his work when he was aware of the weather. Normally he couldn't have told if the day was wet or fine.

That was the odd thing about Dublin. There, the weather did matter. There he was aware of every fickle change in the sky, especially on a day like today that began with rain and later gave way to sunshine. The changes came so quick in the city. They took one by surprise, although one was alerted by a thousand small signs, whereas the sodden fields were slow to recover after the smallest shower. In Dublin the instant there was a break in the clouds, the pavements gave back an answering glint. And after that came a strange white light mingling water and sun, a light that could be perceived in the reflections under foot without raising one's eyes to the sky at all. And how fast then the paving stones dried out into pale patches. Like stepping stones, these patches acted strangely on him, putting a skip into his otherwise sober step!

Talk of the poetry of Spring. The earth's rebirth! Where was it more intoxicating than in the city, the cheeky city birds filling the air with song, and green buds breaking out on branches so black with grime it was as if iron bars had sprouted. Thinking of the city streets his feet ached to be pacing them. James glanced out again at the fields with hatred.

Damn, damn, damn. The damage was done. He'd let himself get unsettled. It would be Dublin for him today. He looked at the clock. He might even go on the early bus. Only what would he do up there all day? His interest in Dublin had dwindled to its core, and the core was Myra.

All the same, he decided to go on the early bus. 'Come on, James! Be a gay dog for once. Get the early bus. You'll find plenty to do. The bookshops! The National Library! Maybe a film? Come on. You're going whether you like it or not, old fellow.'

Catching up the poker James turned the blazing logs over to smother their flames. A pity he'd lit the fire, or rather it was a pity it couldn't be kept in till he got back. It would be nice to return to a warm house. But old Mrs Nully had a mortal dread of the cottage taking fire in his absence. James smiled thinking how she had recently asked why he didn't install central heating. In a three-roomed cottage! Now where on earth had she got that notion, he wondered, as he closed the door and put the key under the mat for her. Then, as he strode off down to the road, he remembered that a son of hers had been taken on as houseman in Asigh House, and the son's wife gave a hand there at weekends. The old woman had probably been shown over the house by them before the Balfes moved into it.

The Balfes! James was nearly at the road, and involuntarily he glanced back across the river to where a fringe of fir trees in the distance marked out the small estate of Asigh. Strange to think – laughable really – that Emmy, who once had filled every cranny of his mind, should only come to mind now in a train of thought that had its starting point in a plumbing appliance!

Here James called himself to order. It was a gross exaggeration to have said – even to himself – that Emmy had ever entirely filled his mind. He'd only known her for a year, and that was the year he finished his Ph.D. He submitted the thesis at the end of the year, and his marks, plus the winning of the travelling scholarship, surely spoke for a certain detachment of mind even when he was most obsessed by her?

He glanced back again at the fir trees. Emmy only stood out in his life because of the violence of his feeling for her. It was something he had never permitted himself before; and never would again. When the affair ended, it ended as completely as if she had been a little skiff upon a swiftly flowing river, which, when he'd cut the painter, was carried instantly away. For a time he'd no way of knowing whether it had capsized or foundered. As it happened, Emmy had righted herself and come to no harm.

Again, James had to call himself to order. How cruel he made himself seem by that metaphor. Yet for years that was how he'd felt obliged to put it to himself. That was how he'd put it to Myra when he first told her about Emmy. But Myra was quick to defend him, quick to see, and quick to show him how he had acted in self-defence. His career would have been wrecked, because of course with a girl like Emmy marriage would have become inescapable. And, of course, then as now, marriage for him was out. It was never really in the picture.

Later, after Myra appeared on the scene, he came to believe that a man and woman could enter into a marriage of minds.

'But when one is young, James,' Myra said, 'one can't be expected to be both wise and foolish at the same time.'

A good saying. He'd noticed, and appreciated, the little sigh with which she accompanied her words, as if she didn't just feel *for* him but *with* him. Then she asked the question that a man might have asked.

'She married eventually I take it, this Emmy?'

'Oh good lord, yes.' How happy he was to be able to answer in the affirmative. If Emmy had not married it would have worried him all his life. But she did. And, all things considered, surprisingly soon.

'Young enough to have a family?' Myra probed, but kindly, kindly. He nodded. 'I take it,' she said then, more easily, 'I take it she married that student who –'

James interrupted ' – the one she was knocking around with when I first noticed her?'

'Yes, the one that was wrestling with that window when you had to step down from the rostrum and yank it open yourself?'

Really Myra was unique. Her grasp of the smallest details of that incident, even then so far back in time, was very gratifying.

He had been conducting a tutorial and the lecture room got so stuffy he'd asked if someone would open a window? But when a big burly fellow – the footballer type – tried with no success, James strode down the classroom himself, irritably, because he half thought the fellow might be having him on to create a diversion. And when he had to lean in across a student whose chair was right under the window, he was hardly aware it was a girl, as he exerted all his strength to bring down the heavy sash. Only when the sash came down and the fresh air rushed in overhead did he find he was looking straight into the eyes of a girl – Emmy.

That was all. But during the rest of the class their eyes kept meeting. And the next day it was the same. Then he began to notice her everywhere, in the corridors, in the Main Hall, and once across the Aula Maxima at an inaugural ceremony. And she'd seen him too. He knew it. But for a long time, several weeks, there was nothing between them except this game of catch-catch with their eyes. And always, no matter how far apart they were, it was as if they had touched.

James soon found himself trembling all over when her eyes touched him. Then one day in the library she passed by his desk and he saw that a paper in her hand was shaking as if there was a breeze in the air. But there was no breeze. Still, deliberately, he delayed the moment of speaking to her because there was a kind of joy in waiting. And funnily enough when they did finally speak neither of them could afterwards remember what their first spoken words had been. They had already said so much with their eyes.

Myra's comment on this, though, was very shrewd. 'You had probably said all there was to say, James.' Again she gave that small sigh of hers that seemed to put things in proportion: to place him, and Emmy too, on the map of disenchantment where all mankind, it seems, must sojourn for a time. And indeed it was sad to think that out of the hundreds of hours that he and Emmy had spent together, wandering along the damp paths of Stephen's Green, sitting in little cafés, and standing under the lamps of Leeson Street where he was in lodgings, he could recall nothing of what was said. 'You probably spent most evenings trying out ideas for your thesis on her, poor girl.' Myra had a dry humour at times, but he had to acknowledge it was likely enough, although if so, Emmy used to listen as if she were drinking in every word.

When he'd got down at last to the actual writing of the thesis they did not meet so often. In fact he could never quite remember their last meeting either. Not even what they had said to each other at parting. Of course long before that they must have faced up to his situation. He'd been pretty sure of getting the travelling scholarship, so it must have been an understood thing that he'd be going away for at least two years. And in the end, he left a month sooner than he'd intended. They never actually did say good-bye. He'd gone without seeing her – just left a note at her digs. And for a while he wasn't even sure if she'd got it. She'd got it all right. She wrote and thanked him. How that smarted! *Thanked* him for breaking it off with her. Years later, telling Myra, he still felt the sting of that.

Myra was marvellous though.

'Hurt pride, my dear James. Nothing more, don't let it spoil what is probably the sweetest thing in life – for all of us, men or women – our first shy, timid love.' There was a tenderness in her voice. Was she remembering some girlish experience of her own?

The pang of jealousy that went through him showed how little Emmy had come to mean to him.

Myra put him at ease.

'We all go through it, James, it's only puppy love.'

'Puppy love! I was twenty-six, Myra!'

'Dear, dear James.' She smiled. 'Don't get huffy. I know quite well what age you were. You were completing your Ph.D., and you were old enough to conduct tutorials. You were not at the top of the tree, but you had begun the ascent!'

It was so exactly how he'd seen himself in those days, that he laughed. And with that laugh the pain went out of the past.

'Dear James,' she said again, 'anyone who knows you – and loves you,' she added quickly, because they tried never to skirt away from that word love, although they gave it a connotation all their own, 'anyone who loves you, James, would know that even then, where women were concerned, you'd be nothing but a lanky, bashful boy. Wait a minute!' She sprang up from the sofa. 'I'll show you what I mean.' She took down the studio photograph she'd made him get taken the day of his honorary doctorate. 'Here!' She shoved the silver frame into his hands, and going into the room where she slept, she came back with another photograph. 'You didn't know I had this one?' He saw with some chagrin that it was a blow-up from a group photograph taken on the steps of his old school at the end of his last year. 'See!' she said. 'It's the same face in both, the same ascetical features, the same look of dedication.' Then she pressed the frame end face inward, against her breast. 'Oh James, I bet Emmy was the first girl you ever looked at! My dear, it was not so much the girl as the experience itself that bowled you over.'

Emmy was not the first girl he'd looked at. In those days he was always looking at girls, but looking at them from an unbridgeable distance. When he looked at Emmy the space between them seemed to be instantly obliterated. Emmy had felt the same. That day in class her mind had been a million miles away. She was trying to make up her mind about getting engaged to the big burly fellow, the one who couldn't open the window; James could not remember his name, but he was a type that could be attractive to women. The fellow was pestering her to marry him, and the attentions of a fellow like that could have been very flattering to a girl like Emmy. She was so young. Yet, after she met *him* it was as if a fiery circle had been blazed around them, allowing no way out for either until he, James, in the end had to close his eyes and break through, not caring about the pain as long as he got outside again.

Because Myra was right. Marriage would have put an end to his academic career. For a man like him it would have been suffocating.

'Even now!' Myra said, and there was a humorous expression on her face, because of course, in their own way, he and Myra *were* married. Then, in a business-like way, as if she were filling up a form for filing away, she asked him another question. 'What family did they have?'

'She had five or six children, I think, although she must have been about thirty by the time she married.' James couldn't help throwing his eyes up to heaven at the thought of such a household. Myra too raised her eyebrows.

'You're joking?' she said. 'Good old Balfe!' But James was staring at her, hardly able to credit she had picked up Emmy's married name. He himself had hardly registered it, the first time *he'd* heard it, so that when last summer Asigh House had been bought by people named Balfe, it simply hadn't occurred to him that it could have been Emmy and her husband until one day on the road a car passed him and the woman beside the driver reminded him oddly of her. The woman in the car was softer and plumper and her hair was looser and more untidy – well fluffier anyway – than Emmy's used to be, or so he thought, until suddenly he realized it *was* her. Emmy! She didn't recognize him though. But then she wasn't looking his way. She was looking out over the countryside through which she was passing. It was only when the car turned left at the crossroad the thought hit him, that she had married a man named Balfe, and that Balfe was the name of the people who'd bought Asigh. It was a shock. Not only because of past associations, but more because he had never expected any invasion of his privacy down here. It was his retreat, from everything and everyone. Myra – even Myra – had never been down there. She was too sensible to suggest such a thing. And he wouldn't want her to come either.

Once when he'd fallen ill he'd lost his head and sent her a telegram, but even then she'd exercised extreme discrimination. She despatched a nurse to take care of him, arranging with the woman to phone her each evening from the village. Without once coming down, she had overseen his illness – which fortunately was not of long duration. She had of course ascertained to her satisfaction that his condition was not serious. The main thing was that she set a firm precedent for them both. It was different when he was convalescing. Then she insisted that he come up to town and stay in a small hotel near the flat, taking his evening meal with her, as on ordinary visits except – James smiled – except that she sent a taxi to fetch him, and carry him back, although the distance involved was negligible, only a block or two.

Remembering her concern for him on that occasion, James told himself that he could never thank her enough. He resolved to let her see he did not take her goodness for granted. Few women could be as self-effacing.

Yet, in all fairness to Emmy, she had certainly effaced herself fast. One might say drastically. After that one note of thanks – it jarred again that she had put it like that – he had never once heard or seen her until that day she passed him here on the road in her car. So much for his fears for his privacy. Unfounded! For days he'd half expected a courtesy call from them, but after a time he began to wonder if they were aware at all that he lived in the neighbourhood? After all, their property was three or four miles away, and the river ran between. It was just possible Emmy knew nothing of his existence. Yet somehow, he doubted it. As the crow flies he was less than two miles away. He could see their wood. And was it likely the local people would have made no mention of him? No, it was hard to escape the conclusion that Emmy might be avoiding him. Although Myra – who was never afraid of the truth – had not hesitated to say that Emmy might have forgotten him altogether!

'Somehow I find that hard to believe, Myra,' he'd said, although after he'd made the break, there had been nothing. Nothing, nothing, nothing.

But Myra was relentless.

'You may not like to believe it, James, but it could be true all the same,' she said. Then she tried to take the hurt out of her words by confessing that she herself found it dispiriting to think a relationship that had gone so deep, could be erased completely. 'I myself can't bear to think she did not recognize you that day she passed you on the road. *She* may have changed – you said she'd got stouter –' That wasn't the word he'd used, but he'd let it pass – 'whereas you, James, can hardly have changed at all, in essentials, I mean. Your figure must be the same as when you were a young man. I can't bear to think she didn't even *know* you.'

'She wasn't looking straight at me, Myra.'

'No matter! You'd think there'd have been some telepathy between you; some force that would *make* her turn. Oh, I can't bear it!'

She was so earnest he had to laugh.

'It is a good job she didn't see me,' he said. Emmy being nothing to him then, it was just as well there should be no threat to his peace and quiet.

Such peace; such quiet. James looked around at the sleepy countryside. The bus was very late though! What was keeping it?

Ah, here it came. Signalling to the driver, James stepped up quickly on to the running board so the man had hardly to do more than go down into first gear before starting off again. In spite of how few passengers there were, the windows were fogged up and James had to clear a space on the glass with his hand to see out. It was always a pleasant run through the rich Meath fields, but soon the unruly countryside gave way to neatly squared-off fields with pens and wooden palings, where cattle were put in for the night before being driven to the slaughter-house.

James shuddered. He was no country-man. Not by nature anyway. He valued the country solely for the protection it gave him from people. When he lived in Dublin he used to work in the National Library, but as he got older he began to feel that in the eyes of the students and the desk-messengers, he could have appeared eccentric. Not objectionably so, just rustling his papers too much, and clearing his throat too loudly; that kind of thing. He'd have been the first to find that annoying in others when he was young. The cottage was much better. It also served to put that little bit of distance between him and Myra which they both agreed was essential.

'If I lived in Dublin I'd be here at the flat every night of the week,' he'd once said to her. 'I'm better off down there – I suppose – stuck in the mud!'

That was an inaccurate – an unfair – description of his little retreat, but the words had come involuntarily to his lips which showed how he felt about the country in general. The city streets of Dublin were so full of life, and the people were so dapper and alert compared with the slow-moving country people. Every time he went up there he felt like an old fogy – that was until he got to Myra's – because Myra immediately gave him back a sense of being alive. Mentally at least Myra made him feel more alive than twenty men.

The bus had now reached O'Connell Bridge, where James usually descended, so he got out. He ought to have got out sooner and walked along the Quays. One could kill a whole morning looking over the book barrows. Now he would have to walk back to them.

Perhaps he ought not to have come on the early bus? It might not be so easy to pass the time. And after browsing to his heart's content and leaning for a while looking over the parapet on to the Liffey, it was still only a little after 1 o'clock when he strolled back to the centre of the city. He'd have to eat something and that would use up another hour or more. He'd buy a paper and sit on over his coffee.

James hadn't bargained on the lunchtime crowds though. All the popular places were crowded, and in a few of the better places, one look inside was enough to send him off! These places too were invaded by the lunchtime hordes, and the menu would cater for these barbarians. If there should by chance happen to be a continental dish on the menu – a goulash or pasta – it would nauseate him to see the little clerks attacking it with knife and fork as if it was a mutton chop.

At this late hour how about missing out on lunch altogether? It never hurt to skip a meal, although, mind you, he was peckish. How about a film? He hadn't been in a cinema for years. And just then, as if to settle the matter – James saw he was passing a cinema. It was exceptionally small for a city cinema, but without another thought he bolted inside.

Once inside, he regretted that he hadn't checked the time of the showings. He didn't fancy sitting through a newsreel, to say nothing of a cartoon. He had come in just in the middle of a particularly silly cartoon. He sat in the dark fuming. To think he'd let himself in for this stuff. It was at least a quarter of an hour before he realized with rage that he must have strayed into one of the new-fangled newsreel cinemas about which Myra had told him. For another minute he sat staring at the screen, trying to credit the mentality of people who voluntarily subjected themselves to this kind of stuff. He was about to leave and make for the street, when without warning his eyes closed. He didn't know for how long he had dozed off, but on waking he was really ravenous. But wouldn't it be crazy to eat at this hour and spoil his appetite for the meal with Myra? He could, he supposed, go around to the flat earlier – now – immediately? Why wait any longer? But he didn't know at what hour Myra herself got there. All he knew was that she was always there after seven, the time he normally arrived.

But wasn't it remarkable now he came to think of it, that she *was* always there when he called. Very occasionally at the start she had let drop dates on which she had to go to some meeting or other, and he'd made a mental note of them, but as time went on she gave up these time-wasting occupations. There had been one or two occasions she had been going out, but had cancelled her arrangements immediately he came on the scene. He had protested of course, but lamely, because quite frankly it would have been frightfully disappointing to have come so far and found she really had to go out.

Good God – supposing that were to happen now? James was so scared at the possibility of such a catastrophe he determined to lose no more time but get around there quick. Just in case. He stepped out briskly.

The lane at the back of Fitzwilliam Square, where Myra had her mews, was by day a hive of small enterprises. A smell of cellulosing and sounds of welding filled the air. In one courtyard there was a little fellow who dealt in scrap-iron and he made a great din. But by early evening, the big gates closed on these businesses, the high walls made the lane a very private place, and the mews-dwellers were disturbed by no sound harsher than the late song of the birds nesting in the trees of the doctors' gardens.

Walking down the lane and listening to those sleepy bird-notes gave James greater pleasure than walking on any country road. His feet echoed so loudly in the stillness that sometimes before he rapped on her gate at all, Myra would come running out across the courtyard to admit him. A good thing that! Because otherwise he'd have had to rap with his bare knuckles; Myra had no knocker.

'You know I don't encourage callers, James,' she'd said once smiling. 'Few people ferret me out here – except you; and, of course, the tradesmen. And I know their step too! It's nearly as quiet here as in your cottage.'

'Quiet?' He'd raised his eyebrows. 'Listen to those birds; I never heard such a din!'

Liking a compliment to be oblique, she'd squeezed his arm as she drew him inside.

This evening however James was less than halfway down the lane when at the other end he saw Myra appear at the wicket gate. If she hadn't been bareheaded he'd have thought she was going out!

'Myra?' he called in some dismay.

She laughed as she came to meet him. 'I heard your footsteps,' she said. 'I told you! I always do.'

'From this distance?'

She took his arm and smiled up at him. 'That's nothing! It's a wonder I don't hear you walking down the country road to get the bus.' She matched her step with his. Normally he hated to be linked, but with Myra it seemed to denote equality, not dependence. Suddenly she unlinked her arm. 'Well, I may as well confess something,' she said more seriously. 'This evening I was listening for you. I was expecting you.'

They had reached the big wooden gate of the mews and James, glancing in through the open wicket across the courtyard, was startled to see, through the enormous window by which she had replaced the doors of the coach-house, that the little table at which they ate was indeed set up, and with places laid for two! She wasn't joking then? An unpleasant thought crossed his mind – was she expecting someone else? But reading his mind, Myra shook her head.

'Only you, James.'

'I don't understand –'

'Neither do I!' she said quickly. 'I *was* expecting you though. And I ordered our trays!' Here she wrinkled her nose in a funny way she had. 'I made the order a bit more conservative than usual. No prawns!' He understood at once. He loved prawns. 'So you see,' she continued, 'if my oracle failed, and you didn't come, the food would do for sandwiches tomorrow. As you know, I'm no use at hotting up left-overs. It smacks too much of –'

He knew. He knew.

'Too wifey,' he smiled. And she smiled. This was the word they'd ear-marked to describe a certain type of woman they both abhorred.

'You could always have fed the prawns to the cat next door,' James said. 'Whenever I'm coming he's sitting on the wall smacking his lips.'

'But James,' she said, and suddenly she stopped smiling, 'he doesn't know when you're coming – any more than me!'

'Touché,' James admitted to being caught out there. He wasn't really good at smart remarks. 'Ah well, it's a lucky cat who knows there's an even chance of a few prawns once or twice a month. That's more than most cats can count on.' Bending his head he followed her in through the wicket. 'Some cats have to put up with a steady diet of shepherd's pie and meat loaf.'

They were inside now, and he sank down on the sofa. Myra, who was still standing, shuddered.

'What would I do if you were the kind of man who *did* like shepherd's pie?' she said. 'I'm sure there are such men.' But she couldn't keep up the silly chaff. 'I think maybe I'd love you enough to try and make it –' she laughed, '– if I could. I don't honestly think I'd be able. The main thing is that you are *not* that type. Let's stop fooling. Here, allow me to give you a kiss of gratitude – for being you.'

Lightly she laid her cheek against his, while he for his part took her hand and stroked it.

It was one of the more exquisite pleasures she gave him, the touch of her cool skin. His own hands had a tendency to get hot although he constantly wiped them with his handkerchief. He had always preferred being too cold to being too hot. Once or twice when he had a headache – which was not often – Myra had only to place her hand on his forehead for an instant and the throbbing ceased. This evening he didn't have a headache but all the same he liked the feel of her hand on his face.

'Do that again,' he said.

'How about fixing the drinks first?' she said.

That was his job. But he did not want to release her hand, and he made no attempt to stand up. Unfortunately just then there was a rap on the gate.

'Oh bother,' he said.

'It's only the Catering Service,' Myra said, and for a minute he didn't get the joke. She laughed then and he noticed she meant the grubby little pot-boy who brought the trays around from the café.

'Let me get them,' he said, but she had jumped up and in a minute she was back with them.

'I must tell you,' she said. 'You know the man who owns the café? Well, he gave me such a dressing-down this morning when I was ordering these.' James raised his eyebrows as he held open the door of the kitchenette to let her through. 'Just bring me the warming plate, will you please, James,' she said interrupting herself. 'I'll pop the food on it for a second while we have our little drink.' She glanced at her watch. 'Oh, it's quite early still.' She looked back at him. 'But you were a little later than usual, I think, weren't you?'

'I don't think so,' he said vaguely, as he fitted the plug of the food-warmer into the socket. 'If anything, I think I was a bit earlier. But I could be wrong. When one has time to kill it's odd how often one ends up being late in the end!'

'Time to kill?'

She looked puzzled. Then she seemed to understand. 'Oh James. You make me tired. You're so punctilious. Haven't I told you a thousand times that you don't have to be polite with me? If your bus got in early you should have come straight to the flat. Killing time indeed. Standing on ceremony, eh?'

He handed her her drink.

'You were telling me something about the proprietor of the café – that he was unpleasant about something? You weren't serious?'

'Oh that ! Of course not.'

Yet for some reason he was uneasy. 'Tell me,' he said authoritatively.

Naturally, she complied. 'He was really very nice,' she said. 'He intended phoning me. He just wanted to say there was no need to wash the plates before sending them back. I'm to hand them to the messenger in the morning just as they are – and not *attempt* to wash them.' Knowing how fastidious she was, James was about to pooh-pooh the suggestion, but she forestalled him. 'I can wrap them up in the napkins, and then I won't be affronted by the sight. And I need feel under no compliment to the café – it's in their own interests as much as in mine. They have a big washing machine – I've seen it – with a special compartment like a dentist's steriliz-ation cabinet, and of course they couldn't be sure that a customer would wash them properly. You can imagine the cat's lick some women would give them!'

James could well imagine it. He shuddered. Myra might hate housework, but anything she undertook she did to perfection. Unexpectedly she held out her glass.

'Let's have another drink,' she said. They seldom took more than one. 'Sit down,' she commanded. 'Let's be devils for once.' This time though she sat on the sofa and swung her feet up on it so he had to sit in the chair opposite. 'There's nothing that makes the ankles ache like thinking too hard,' she said.

James didn't really understand what she meant but he laughed happily.

'Seriously!' she said. 'I am feeling tired this evening. I'm so glad you came. I think maybe I worked extra hard this morning because I was looking forward to seeing you later. Oh, I'm so glad you came, James. I would have been bitterly disappointed if you hadn't showed up.'

James felt a return of his earlier uneasiness.

'I'm afraid that premonition of yours is more than I can under-stand,' he said, but he spoke patiently, because she was not a woman who had to be humoured. 'As a matter of fact I never had less intention of coming to town. I'd already lit the fire in my study when I suddenly took the notion. I had to put the fire out!'

At that, Myra left down her glass and swung her feet back on to the floor.

'What time did you leave?' she asked, and an unusually crisp note in her voice took him unawares.

'I thought I told you,' he said apologetically, although there was nothing for which to apologize. 'I came on the morning bus.'

'Oh!' It was only one word, but it fell oddly on his ears. She reached for her drink again then, and swallowed it down. Somehow that too bothered him. 'Is that what you meant by having to kill time?' she asked.

'Well –' he began, not quite knowing what to say. He took up his own drink and let it down fairly fast for him.

'Oh, don't bother to explain,' she said. 'I think you will agree though it would have been a nice gesture to have lifted a phone and let me know you were in town and coming here tonight.'

'But –'

'No buts about it. You knew I'd be here waiting whether you came or not. Isn't that it?'

'Myra!'

He hardly recognized her in this new mood. Fortunately the next moment she was her old self again.

'Oh James, forgive me. It's just that you've *no* idea – simply *no* idea how much it meant to me tonight to know in advance –' She stopped and carefully corrected herself '– to have had that curious feeling – call it instinct if you like – that you were coming. It made such a difference to my whole day. But now –' Her face clouded over, '– to think that instead of just having had a hunch about it, I could have known for certain. Oh, if only you'd been more thoughtful, James.' Sitting up straighter she looked him squarely in the eye. 'Or were you going somewhere else and changed your mind?'

What a foolish question.

'As if I ever go anywhere else!'

Her face brightened a bit at that, but not much.

'You'll hardly believe it,' she said after a minute, 'but I could have forgiven you more easily if you had been going somewhere else, and coming here *was* an afterthought. It would have excused you more.'

Excused? What was all this about? He must have looked absolutely bewildered, because she pulled herself up.

'Oh James, please don't mind me.' She leant forward and laid a hand on his knee. 'Your visits give me such joy – I don't need to tell you that – I ought to be content with what I have. Not knowing in advance is one of the little deprivations that I just have to put up with, I suppose.'

But now James was beginning to object strongly to the way she was putting everything. He stood up. As if his doing so unnerved her, she stood up too.

'It may seem a small thing to ask from you, James, but I repeat what I said – you could have phoned me.' Then, as if that wasn't bad enough, she put it into the future tense. 'If you would only try, once in a while, to give me a ring, even from the bus depot, so I could –'

'– could what?' James couldn't help the coldness in his voice, although considering the food that was ready on the food-warmer, his question, he knew, was ungenerous. On the other hand he felt it was absolutely necessary to keep himself detached, if the evening was not to be spoiled. He forced himself to speak sternly. 'Much as I enjoy our little meals together, it's not for the food I come here, Myra. You must know that.' He very, very nearly added that in any case he paid for his own tray, but when he looked at her he saw she had read these unsaid words from his eyes. He reddened. There was an awkward silence. Yet when she spoke she ignored everything he had said and harked back to what she herself had said.

'Wouldn't it be a very small sacrifice to make, James, when one thinks of all the sacrifices I've made for you? And over so many years?' Her words, which to him were exasperating beyond belief, seemed to drown her in a torrent of self-pity. 'So many, many years,' she whispered.

It was only ten.

'You'd think it was a lifetime,' he said irritably. Her face flushed.

'What is a lifetime, James?' she asked, and when he made no reply she helped him out. 'Remember it is not the same for a woman as for a man. *You* may think of yourself as a young blade, but I . . .'

She faltered again, as well she might, and bit her lip. She wasn't going to cry, was she? James was appalled. Nothing had ever before happened that could conceivably have given rise to tears, but it was an unspoken law with them that a woman should never shed tears in public. Not just unspoken either. On one occasion years ago she herself had been quite explicit about it.

'We do cry sometimes, we women, poor weaklings that we are. But I hope I would never be foolish enough to cry in the presence of a man. And to do it to you of all people, James, would be despicable.' At the time he'd wondered why she singled him out. Did she think him more sensitive than most? He'd been about to ask when she'd given one of her witty twists to things. 'If I did, I'd have you snivelling too in no time,' she said.

Yet here she was now, for no reason at all, on the brink of tears, and apparently making no effort to fight them back.

Myra was making no effort to stem her tears because she did not know she was crying. She really did despise tears. But now it seemed to her that perhaps she'd been wrong in always hiding her feelings. Other women had the courage to cry. Even in public too. She'd seen them at parties. And recently she'd seen a woman walking along the street in broad daylight with tears running down her cheeks, not bothering to wipe them away. Thinking of such women, she wondered if she perhaps had sort of – she paused to find the right word – sort of denatured herself for James?

Denatured: it was an excellent word. She'd have liked to use it then and there but she had just enough sense left to keep it to herself for the moment. Some other time when they were talking about someone else, she would bring it out and impress him. She must not forget the word.

When Myra's thoughts returned to James she felt calmer about him. He was not unkind. He was not cruel – the opposite in fact. What had gone wrong this evening was more her fault than his. When they'd first met she had sensed deep down in him a capacity for the normal feelings of friendship and love. Yet throughout the years she had consistently deflected his feelings away from herself and consistently encouraged him to seal them off. Tonight it seemed that his emotional capacity was completely dried up. Despair overcame her. She'd never change him now. He was fixed in his faults, cemented into his barren way of life. Tears gushed into her eyes again but this time she leant her head back quickly to try and prevent them rolling down, but they brimmed over and splashed down on her hands.

'Oh James, I'm sorry,' she whispered, but she saw her apology was useless; the damage was done. Then her heart hardened. What harm? She wasn't really sorry. Not for him anyway. Oh, not for him. It was for herself she was sorry.

Grasping at a straw, then, she tried to tell herself, nothing was ever too late. Perhaps tonight some lucky star had stood still in the sky over her head and forced her to be true to herself for once. James would see the real woman for a change. Oh, surely he would? And surely he would come over and put his arm around her. He would: he would. She waited.

When he did not move, and did not utter a single word, she had to look up.

'Oh no!' she cried. For what she saw in his eyes was ice. 'Oh James, have you no heart? What you have done to me is unspeakable! Yet you can't even pity me!'

James spoke at last. 'And what, Myra, what, may I ask, have I done to you?'

'You have –' She stopped, and for one second she thought she'd have control enough to bite back the word, but she hadn't. 'You have denatured me,' she said.

Oh God, what had she done *now*? Clapping her hands over her mouth too late, she wondered if she could pretend to some other meaning in the words. Instead, other words gushed out, words worse and more hideous. Hearing them she herself could not understand where they came from. It was as if, out of the corners of the room, she was being prompted by the voices of all the women in the world who'd ever been let down, or fancied themselves badly treated. The room vibrated with their whispers. Go on, they prompted. Tell him what you think of him. Don't let him get away with it. He has got off long enough. To stop the voices she stuck her fingers into her ears, but the voices only got louder. She had to shout them down. She saw James's lips were moving, trying to say something, but she could not hear him with all the shouting. When she finally caught a word or two of what he said she herself stopped trying to penetrate the noise. Silence fell. She saw James go limp with relief.

'What did you say? I – I didn't hear you,' she gulped.

'I said that if that's the way you feel, Myra, there's nothing for me to do but to leave.'

She stared at him. He was going over to the clothes' rack and was taking down his coat. What had got into them? How had they become involved in this vulgar scene? She had to stop him. If he went away like this would he ever come back? A man of his disposition? Could she take him back? Neither of them was of a kind to gloss over things and leave them unexplained knowing that unexplained they could erupt again – and again. Something had been brought to light that could never be forced back underground. Better all the same to let their happiness dry up if it must, than be blasted out of existence like this in one evening. Throwing out her arms she ran blindly towards him.

'James, I implore you. James! James! Don't let this happen to us.' She tried to enclose him with her arms, but somehow he evaded her and reached to take his gloves from the lid of the gramophone. Next thing she knew he'd be at the door.

'Do you realize what you're doing?' She pushed past him and ran to the door pressing her back against it, and throwing out her arms to either side. It was an outrageous gesture of crucifixion, and she knew she was acting out of character. She was making another and more frightful mistake. 'If you walk out this door, you'll never come through it again, James.'

All he did was try to push her to one side, not roughly, but gently.

'James! Look at me!'

But what he said then was so humiliating she wanted to die.

'I am looking, Myra,' he said.

There seemed nothing left to do but hit him. She thumped at his chest with her closed fists. That made him stand back all right. She had achieved that at least! If she was not going to get a chance to undo the harm she'd done, then she'd go the whole hog and let him think the worst of her. She was ashamed to think she had been about to renege on herself. She flung out her arms again, not hysterically this time, but with passion, real, real passion. Let him see what he was up against. But whatever he thought, James said nothing. And he'd have to be the one to speak first. Myra couldn't trust herself any more.

In the end, she did have to speak. 'Say something, James,' she pleaded.

'All right,' he said then. 'Be so kind, Myra, as to tell me what you think you're gaining by this performance?' he nodded at her outstretched arms. 'This nailing of yourself to the door like a stoat!'

The look in his eyes was ugly. She let her arms fall at once and running back to the sofa flung herself face down upon it screaming and kicking her feet.

She didn't even hear the door bang after him, or the gate slam.

Outside in the air James regretted that he had not shut the door more gently, but after the coarse and brutal words he had just used it was inconsistent to worry about the small niceties of the miserable business. His ugly words echoed in his mind, and he felt defiled by them. He had an impulse to go back and apologize, if only for his language. Nothing justified that kind of thing from a man. He actually raised his hand to rap on the gate, but he let it fall, overcome by a stronger impulse – to make good his escape. But as he hurried up the lane his unuttered words too seemed base and unworthy – a mean-minded figure of speech – that could only be condoned by the fact that he had been so grievously provoked, and by the overwhelming desire that had been engendered in him to get out in the air. If Myra had not stood aside and let him pass, he'd have used brute force. All the same nothing justified the inference that he was imprisoned. Never, never had she done anything to hold him. Never had he been made captive except perhaps by the pull of her mind upon his mind. He'd always been free to come or go as he chose. If in the flat they had become somewhat closed in of late it was from expediency – from not wanting to run into stupid people. If they had gone out to restaurants or cafés nowadays some fool would be sure to blunder over and join them, reducing their

evening to the series of banalities that passed for conversation with
most people. No, no, the flat was never a prison. Never. It was their
nest. And now he'd fallen out of the nest. Or worse still been
pushed out. All of a sudden James felt frightened. Was it possible
she had meant what she said? Could it be that he would never again
be able to go back there? Nonsense. She was hysterical.

He stood for a minute considering again whether he should not
perhaps go back? Not that he'd relish it. But perhaps he ought to do
so – in the interests of the future. No, he decided. Better give her
time to calm down. Another evening would be preferable. If
necessary he'd be prepared to come up again tomorrow evening. Or
later this same evening? That would be more sensible. He looked
back. She must be in a bad state when she hadn't run out after him.
Normally she'd come to the gate and stay standing in the lane until
he was out of sight. Even in the rain.

James shook his head. What a pity. If she'd come to the gate he
could have raised his hands or something, given some sign – there
merest indication would be enough – of his forgiveness. He could
have let her see he bore no rancour. But the gesture would not want
to be ambiguous. Not a wave; that would be over-cordial, and he
didn't want her stumbling up the lane after him. No more fire-
works thank you! But it would not want to appear final either. A
raised hand would have been the best he could do at that time. He
was going to walk on again when it occurred to him that if he'd gone
back he need not have gone inside. Just a few words at the gate, but
on the whole it was probably better to wait till she'd calmed down.
Then he could safely take some of the blame, and help her to save
face. Fortunately he did not have the vanity that, in another man,
might make such a course impossible. It was good for the soul
sometimes to assume blame – even wrongly. James immediately
felt better, less bottled up. He walked on. But he could not rid his
thoughts of the ugly business. He ought to have known that no
woman on earth but was capable, at some time or another, of a lapse
like Myra's. And Myra, of course, was a woman. How lacking he'd
been in foresight. He'd have to go more carefully with her in
future. Next time they met, although he would not try to exonerate
himself from the part he'd played in the regrettable scene, at the
same time it would not be right to rob her of the therapeutic effects

of taking her share of the blame. He felt sure that, being fair-minded people, both of them, they would properly apportion the blame.

Anyway he resolved to put the whole thing out of his mind until after he'd eaten. To think he'd eaten nothing since morning! After he'd had some food he'd be better able to handle the situation.

James had reached the other end of the lane now and gone out under the arch into Baggot Street again. Where would he eat? He'd better head towards the centre of the city. It ought not to be as difficult as it had been at midday, although an evening meal in town could be quite expensive. He didn't want a gala-type dinner, but not some awful slop either that would sicken him. He was feeling bad. The tension had upset his stomach and he was not sure whether he was experiencing hunger pangs or physical pain. Damn Myra. If she'd been spoiling for a fight, why the devil hadn't she waited till after their meal? She'd say this was more of his male selfishness, but if they had eaten they'd have been better balanced and might not have had a row at all. What a distasteful word – the word row! Yet, that's what it was – a common row. James came to a stand again. He wouldn't think twice of marching back and banging on the gate and telling her to stop her nonsense and put the food on the table. She was probably heartbroken. But if that was the case she'd have to come to the door with her face flushed and her hair in disorder. Sobered by such a distasteful picture he walked on. He could not possibly subject her to humiliation like that. It would be his duty to protect her from exposing herself further. Perhaps he'd write her a note and post it in the late-fee box at the G.P.O. before he got the bus for home. She'd have it first thing in the morning, and after a good night's sleep she might be better able to take what he had to say. He began to compose the letter.

'*Dear Myra* –' But he'd skip the beginning: that might be sticky. He'd have to give that careful thought. The rest was easy. Bits and pieces of sentences came readily to his mind – '*We must see to it that, like the accord that has always existed between us, discord too, if it should arise, must be –*'

That was the note to sound. He was beginning to feel his old self again. He probably ought to make reference to their next meeting?

Not too soon – this to strike a cautionary note – but it might not be wise to let too much time pass either –

'*because, Myra, the most precious element of our friendship* –'

No, that didn't sound right. After tonight's scene, friendship didn't appear quite the right word. A new colouring had been given to their relationship by their tiff. But here James cursed under his breath. Tiff. Such a word! What next? Where were these trite words coming from? She'd rattled him all right. Damn it. Oh damn it.

James abandoned the letter for a moment when he realized he had been plunging along without regard to where he was headed. Where would he eat? There used to be a nice quiet little place in Molesworth Street, nearly opposite the National Library. It was always very crowded but with quite acceptable sorts from the library or the Arts School. He made off down Kildare Street.

When James reached the café in Molesworth Street however and saw the padlock on the area railings, he belatedly remembered it was just a coffee-shop, run by voluntary aid for some charitable organization, and only open mornings. He stood, stupidly staring at the padlock. Where would he go now? He didn't feel like traipsing all over the city. Hadn't there been talk some time ago about starting a canteen in the National Library! Had that got under way? He looked across the street. An old gentleman was waddling in the Library gate with his brief case under his arm. James strode after him.

But just as he'd got to the entrance, the blasted porter slammed the big iron gate – almost in his face. He might have had his nose broken.

'Sorry, sir. The Library is closed. Summer holidays, sir.'

'But you just let in someone! I saw that man –'

James glared after the old man who was now ambling up the steps to the reading room.

'The gentleman had a pass, sir,' the porter said. 'There's a skeleton staff on duty in the stacks and the Director always gives out a few permits to people doing important research.' The fellow was more civil now. 'It's only fair, sir. It wouldn't do, sir, would it, to refuse people whose work is –' But here he looked closer at James and, recognizing him, his civility changed into servility. 'I beg your pardon, Professor,' he said. 'I didn't recognize you, sir. I would have thought you'd have applied for a permit. Oh dear, oh dear!' The man actually wrung his hands – 'if it was even yesterday, I could have got hold of the Director on the phone, but he's gone away – out of the country too I understand.'

'Oh, that's all right,' James said, somewhat mollified by being recognized and remembered. He was sorry that he, in turn, could not recall the porter's name. 'That's all right,' he repeated. 'I wasn't going to use the library anyway. I thought they might have opened that canteen they were talking about some time back – ?'

'Canteen, sir? When was that?' The fellow had clearly never heard of the project. He was looking at James as if he was Lazarus come out of the tomb.

'No matter. Good evening!' James said curtly, and he walked away. Then, although he had never before in his life succumbed to the temptation of talking to himself, now, because it was so important, he put himself a question out loud.

'Have I lost touch with Dublin?' he asked. And he had to answer simply and honestly. 'I have.' He should have known the library was always closed this month. If only there was a friend on whom he could call. But he'd lost touch with his friends too.

He looked around. There used to be a few eating places in this vicinity, or rather he could have sworn there were. It hardly seemed possible they were *all* closed down. Where on earth did people eat in Dublin nowadays? They surely didn't go to the hotels? In his day the small hotels were always given over at night to political rallies or football clubs. And the big hotels were out of the question. Not that he'd look into the cost at this stage. He stopped. If it was anywhere near time for his bus he wouldn't think twice of going straight back without eating at all.

It was all very well for Myra. She ate hardly anything anyway. He often felt that as far as food went, their meal together meant nothing to her. Setting up that damned unsteady card-table, and laying out those silly plates of hers shaped like vine leaves and too small to hold enough for a bird. They reminded him of when his sisters used to make him play babby-house.

Passing Trinity College, James saw there was still two hours to go before his bus, but it was just on the hour. There might be a bus going to Cavan? The Cavan bus passed through Garlow Cross, only a few miles from the cottage. How about taking that? He'd taken it once years ago, and although he was younger and fitter in those days, he was tempted to do it. His stomach was so empty it was almost caving in, but he doubted if he could eat anything now. He felt sickish. He might feel better after sitting in the bus. And better anything than hanging about the city.

At that moment on Aston Quay James saw the Cavan bus. It was filling up with passengers, and the conductor and driver, leaning on the parapet of the Liffey, were taking a last smoke. James was about to dash across the street, but first he dashed into a sweet shop to buy a bar of chocolate, or an apple. The sensation in his insides was like something gnawing at his guts. He got an apple and a bar of chocolate as well, but he nearly missed the bus. Very nearly. The driver was at the wheel and the engine was running. James had to put on a sprint to get across the street, and even then the driver was pulling on the big steering wheel and swivelling the huge wheels outward into the traffic before putting the bus in motion. James jumped on the step.

'Dangerous that, sir,' said the young conductor.

'You hadn't begun to move!' James replied testily, while he stood on the platform getting his breath back.

'Could have jerked forward, sir. Just as you were stepping up!'

'You think a toss would finish me off, eh?' James said. He meant the words to be ironical, but his voice hadn't been lighthearted enough to carry off the joke.

The conductor didn't smile. 'Never does any of us any good, sir, at any age.'

James looked at him with hatred. The fellow was thin and spectacled. Probably the over-conscientious sort. Feeling no inclination to make small talk he lurched into the body of the bus, and sat down on the nearest seat. He was certainly glad to be off his feet. He hadn't noticed until now how they ached. Such a day. Little did he think setting off that it would be a case of About Turn and Quick March.

James slumped down in his seat, but when he felt the bulge of the apple in his pocket he brightened up, and was about to take it out when he was overcome by a curious awkwardness with regard to the conductor. Instead, keeping his hand buried in his pocket he broke off a piece of the chocolate and surreptitiously put it into his mouth. He would nearly have been too tired to chew the apple. He settled back on the seat and tried to doze. But now Myra's words kept coming back. They were repeating on him, like indigestion.

To think she should taunt him with how long they'd known each other? Wasn't it a good thing they'd been able to put up with each other for so long? What else but time had cemented their relationship? As she herself had once put it, very aptly, they'd invested a lot in each other. Well, as far as he was concerned she could have counted on *her* investment to the end. Wasn't it their credo that it didn't take marriage lines to bind together people of their integrity. He had not told her, not in so many words – from delicacy – but he had made provision for her in his will. He'd been rather proud of the way he'd worded the bequest too, putting in a few lines of appreciation that were, he thought, gracefully, but more important, tactfully expressed.

Oh, why had she doubted him? Few wives could be as sure of their husbands as she of him – but he had to amend this – as she *ought* to be, because clearly she had set no value on his loyalty. What was that she'd said about the deprivations she'd suffered? *'One of the many deprivations'*! Those might not have been her exact words, but that was more or less what she'd implied. What had come over her? He shook his head. Had they not agreed that theirs was the perfect solution for facing into the drearier years of ageing and decay? That dreary time was not imminent, of course, but alas it would inevitably come. The process of ageing was not attractive, and they both agreed that if they were continually together – well, really married for instance – the afflictions of age would be doubled for them. On the other hand, with the system they'd worked out, neither saw anything but what was best, and best preserved, in the other. As the grosser aspects of age became discernible, if they could not conceal them from themselves, at least they could conceal them from each other. To put it flatly, if they had been married a dozen times over, that would still be the way he'd want things to be at the end. It was disillusioning now to find she had not seen eye to eye with him on this. Worse still, she'd gone along with him and paid lip-service to his ideals while underneath she must all the time have dissented.

Suddenly James sat bolt upright. That word she used: deprivation. She couldn't have meant that he'd done her out of children? What a thought! Surely it was unlikely that she could have had a child even when they first met? What age was she then? Well, perhaps not too old but surely to God she was at an age when she couldn't have fancied putting herself in *that* condition? And what about all the cautions that were given now on the danger of late conception? How would *she* like to be saddled with a retarded child? Why, it was her who first told him about recent medical findings! And – wait a minute – that was early in their acquaintance too, if he remembered rightly. He could recall certain particulars of the conversation. They had been discussing her work, and the demands it made on her. She was, of course, aware from the first that *he* never wanted children, that he abhorred the thought of a houseful of brats, crawling everywhere, and dribbling and spitting out food. They overran a place. As for the smell of wet diapers about a house, it nauseated him. She'd pulled him up on that though.

'Not soiled diapers, James. The most slovenly woman in the world has more self-respect than to leave dirty diapers lying about. But I grant you there often is a certain odour – I've found it myself at times in the homes of my friends, and it has surprised me, I must say – but it comes from *clean* diapers hanging about to air. At worst it's the smell of steam. They have to be boiled you know.' She made a face. 'I agree with you, though. It's not my favourite brand of perfume.'

Those were her very words. If he were to be put in the dock at this moment he could swear to it. Did that sound like a woman who wanted a family? Yet tonight she had insinuated – James was so furious he clenched his hands and dug his feet into the floorboards as if the bus were about to hurtle over the edge of an abyss and he could put a brake on it.

Then he thought of something else: something his sister Kay had said.

It was the time Myra had had to go into hospital for a few weeks. Nothing serious, she'd said. Nothing to worry about, or so she'd told him. Just a routine tidying up job that most people – presumably she meant women – thought advisable. Naturally he'd encouraged her to get it over and done with: not to put it on the long finger. The shocking thing was how badly it had shaken her. He was appalled at how frightful she'd looked for months afterwards. Finally the doctors ordered her to take a good holiday, although it hadn't been long since her summer holidays. She hadn't gone away that summer, except for one long week-end in London, but she'd packed up her work and he'd gone up more often. But the doctor was insistent that this time she was to go away. Oddly enough, her going away had hit him harder than her going into hospital. If they could have gone away together it would have been different. That, of course, was impossible. There was no longer a spot on the globe where one mightn't run the risk of bumping into some busybody from Dublin.

'What will I do while you're away?' he'd asked.

'Why don't you come up here as usual,' she suggested, 'except you need order only one tray.'

But she over-estimated the charm of the flat for its own sake. And he told her so.

'Nonsense,' she said. 'Men are like cats and dogs; it's their habitat they value, not the occupants.'

'I'll tell you what I'll do,' he said finally. 'I'll come up the day you're coming back and I'll have a fire lit – how about that?'

'Oh James, you are a dear. It would make me so glad to be coming back.'

'I should hope you'd be glad to be coming back anyway?'

'Oh yes, but you must admit it would be extra special to be coming back to find you here – in our little nest.'

There! James slapped his knee. *That* was where he'd got the word nest. He had to hand it to her; she was very ingenious in avoiding the word 'home'. She was at her best when it came to these small subtleties other people overlooked. And the day she was due back he had fully intended to be in the flat before her, were it not for a chance encounter with his sister Kay and a remark of hers that upset him.

Kay knew all about Myra. Whether she approved of her or not James did not know: Kay and himself were too much alike to embarrass each other by confidences. That was why he found what she said that day so extraordinary.

'Very sensible of her to go away,' Kay had said, 'otherwise it takes a long time, I believe, to recover from that beastly business.' Beastly business? What did she mean? Unlike herself, Kay had gone on and on. 'Much messier than childbirth I understand. Also, I've heard, James, that it's worse for an unmarried woman –' she paused – 'I mean a childless woman.' Then feeling – as well she might – that she'd overstepped herself, she looked at her watch. 'I'll have to fly,' she said. And perhaps to try and excuse her indiscretion she resorted to something else that was rare for Kay – banality. 'It's sort of the end of the road for them, I suppose,' she said, before she hurried away leaving him confused and dismayed.

He had never bothered to ask Myra what her operation had been. He didn't see that it concerned him. At any age there were certain danger zones for a woman that had to be kept under observation. But what if it had been a hysterectomy! Was that any business of his? Medically speaking, it wasn't all that different from any other ectomy – tonsillectomy, appendectomy. What was so beastly about it? If it came to that, the most frightful mess of all was getting one's antrums cleaned out. He knew all about *that*. Anyway the whole business was outside his province. Or at least he had thought so then.

Then, then, then. But now, now it was as if he'd been asked to stand up and testify to something. It was most unfair. Myra herself had never arraigned him. Neither before nor after. Admittedly he had not given her much encouragement. But he could have sworn that she herself hadn't given a damn at the time. Ah, but – and this was the rub, the whole business could have bred resentment, could have rankled within her and gone foetid. Considered in this new light the taunts she had flung at him tonight could no longer be put down to hysteria and written off – something long festering had suppurated. He put his hand to his head. Dear God, to think she had allowed him to bask all those years in a fool's paradise!

He closed his eyes. Thank heavens he hadn't demeaned himself by going back to try and patch things up. He'd left the way open should he decide to sever the bond completely. Perhaps he ought to sever it, if only on the principle that if a person once tells you a lie, that puts an end to truth between you forever. A lie always made him feel positively sick. And God knows he felt sick enough as it was. There was a definite burning sensation now in his chest as well as his stomach. He looked around the steamy bus. Could it be the fumes of the engine that were affecting him? He'd have liked to go and stand on the platform to get some fresh air, but he hated to make himself noticeable, although the bus was now nearly empty. He stole a look at the other passengers to see if anyone was watching him. He might have been muttering to himself, or making peculiar faces. Just to see if anyone would notice he stealthily, but deliberately, made a face into the window, on which the steam acted like a backing of mercury. And sure enough the damn conductor was looking straight at him. James felt he had to give the fellow a propitiating grin, which the impudent fellow took advantage of immediately.

'Not yet, sir,' he said. 'I'll tell you when you're there!'

Officious again. Well, smart as he was, he didn't know his countryside. Clearing a space on the foggy glass, James looked out. It was getting dark outside now but the shape of the trees could still be seen against the last light in the west. The conductor was wrong! They *were* there! He jumped to his feet.

'Not yet, sir,' the blasted fellow called out again, and loudly this time for all to hear.

Ignoring him, James staggered down the bus to the boarding-platform, where, without waiting for the conductor to do it, he defiantly hit the bell to bring the bus to a stop. The fellow merely shrugged his shoulders. James threw an angry glance at him, and then, although the bus had not quite stopped, deliberately and only taking care to face the way the bus was travelling so that if he did fall it would be less dangerous, he jumped off.

Luckily he did not fall. He felt a bit shaken, as he regained his balance precariously on the dark road. He was glad to think he had spiked that conductor. He could tell he had by the smart way the fellow hit the bell again and set the bus once more in motion, that for all his solicitude on the Quays, he'd hardly have noticed if one had fallen on one's face on the road: or cared.

And Myra? If Myra were to read a report of the accident in the newspaper tomorrow, how would *she* feel? More interesting still –

what would she tell her friends? Secretive as their relationship was supposed to be, James couldn't help wondering if she might not have let the truth leak out to some people. Indeed, this suspicion had lurked in his mind for some time, but he only fully faced it now.

What about those phone calls she sometimes got? Those times when she felt it necessary to plug out the phone and carry it into her bedroom? Or else talk in a lowered voice, very different from the normal way in which she'd call out 'wrong number' and bang down the receiver? Now that he thought about it, the worst give-away was when she'd let the phone ring and ring without answering it at all. It nearly drove him mad listening to that ringing.

'What will they think, Myra?' he'd cry. When she used to say the caller would think she was out, he nearly went demented altogether at her lack of logic.

'They wouldn't keep on ringing if they didn't suspect you were here,' he exploded once.

Ah! The insidiousness of her answer hadn't fully registered at the time. *Now* it did though.

'Oh, they'll understand.' That was what she'd said.

Understand what? He could only suppose she had given her friends some garbled explanation of things.

'Oh damn her! Damn her!' he said out loud again. There was no reason now why he shouldn't talk out loud or shout if he liked here on the lonely country road. 'Damn, damn,' he shouted. 'Damn, damn, damn!'

Immediately James felt uncomfortable. What if there was someone listening? A few yards ahead, to the left, there was a lighted window. But suddenly he was alerted to something odd. There should not be a light on the left. The shop at the crossroads should be on the other side. He looked around. Could that rotten little conductor have been right? Had he got off too soon? Perhaps that was why the fellow had hit that bell so smartly? To give him no time to discover his mistake?

For clearly he *had* made a mistake, and a bloody great one. He peered into the darkness. But the night was too black, he could see nothing. He had no choice but to walk on.

By the time James had passed the cottage with the lighted

window, his eyes were getting more used to the dark. All the same when a rick of hay reared up to one side of the road it might have been a mountain! Where was he at all? And a few seconds later when unexpectedly the moon slipped out from behind the clouds and glinted on the tin roof of a shed in the distance it might have been the sheen of a lake for all he recognized of his whereabouts. Just then, however, he caught sight of the red tail light of the bus again. It had only disappeared because the bus had dipped into a valley. It was now climbing out of the dip again, and going up a steep hill. Ah! he knew that hill. He wasn't as far off his track as he thought. Only a quarter of a mile or so, but he shook his head. In his present state that was about enough to finish him. Still, things could have been worse.

Meanwhile a wisp of vapoury cloud had come between the moon and the earth and in a few minutes it was followed by a great black bank of cloud. Only for a thin green streak in the west it would have been pitch dark again. This streak shed no light on his way but it acted on James like a sign, an omen.

He passed the hayrick. He passed the tin shed. But now another mass of blackness rose up to the left and came between him and the sky. It even hid the green streak this time though he was able to tell by a sudden resinous scent in the air and a curious warmth that the road was passing through a small wood. His spirits rose at once. These were the trees he could see from his cottage. Immediately, his mistake less disastrous, the distance lessened. If only that conductor could know how quickly he had got his bearings! The impudent fellow probably thought he'd left him properly stranded. And perhaps as much to spite the impudent fellow as anything else, when at that instant a daring thought entered his mind and he gave it heed. What if he were to cut diagonally across this wood? It could save him half a mile. It would actually be putting his mistake to work for him.

'What about it, James? Come on. Be a sport,' he jovially exhorted himself.

And seeing that his green banner was again faintly discernible through the dark trees, he called on it to be his lodestar, and scrambled up on the grass bank that separated the road from the wood.

James was in the wood before it came home to him that of course this must be Asigh wood – it must belong to the Balfes! No matter. Why should he let that bother him? The wood was nowhere near their house as far as he remembered its position by daylight. It was composed mostly of neglected, self-seeded trees, more scrub than timber – almost waste ground – ground that had probably deteriorated into commonage.

As he advanced into the little copse – wood was too grand a designation for it – James saw it was not as dense as it seemed from the road, or else at this point there was a pathway through it. Probably it was a short cut well known to the locals, because even in the dark he thought he saw sodden cigarette packets on the ground, and there were toffee wrappers and orange peels lodged in the bushes. Good signs.

Further in, however, his path was unexpectedly blocked by a fallen tree. It must have been a long time lying on the ground because when he put his hand on it to climb over, it was wet and slimy. He quickly withdrew his hand in disgust. He'd have to make his way round it.

The path was not very well defined on the other side of the log. It looked as if people did not after all penetrate this far. The litter at the edge of the wood had probably been left by children. Or by lovers who only wanted to get out of sight of the road? Deeper in, the scrub was thicker, and in one place he mistook a strand of briar for barbed wire it was so tough and hard to cut through. You'd need wire clippers!

James stopped. Was it foolhardy to go on? He'd already ripped the sleeve of his suit. However, the pain in his stomach gave him his answer. Nothing that would get him home quicker was foolish.

'Onward, James,' he said wearily.

And then, damn it, he came to another fallen tree. Again he had to work his way around it. Mind you, he hadn't counted on this kind of thing. The upper branches of this tree spread out over an incredibly wide area. From having to look down, instead of up, he found that – momentarily of course – he'd lost his sense of direction. Fortunately, through the trees, he could take direction from his green banner. Fixing on it, he forged ahead.

But now there were new hazards. At least twice, tree stumps

nearly tripped him, and there were now dried ruts that must have been made by timber lorries at some distant date. Lucky he didn't sprain his ankle. He took out his handkerchief and wiped his forehead. At this rate he wouldn't make very quick progress. He was beginning to ache in every limb, and when he drew a breath, a sharp pain ran through him. The pains in his stomach were indistinguishable now from all the other pains in his body. It was like the way a toothache could turn the whole of one's face into one great ache. The thought of turning back plagued him too at every step. Stubbornly, though, he resisted the thought of turning. To go on could hardly be much worse than to go back through those briars?

A second later James got a fall, a nasty fall. Without warning, a crater opened up in front of him and he went head-first into it. Another fallen tree, blown over in a storm evidently, because the great root that had been ripped out of the ground had taken clay and all with it, leaving this gaping black hole. Oh God! He picked himself up and mopped his forehead with his sleeves.

This time he had to make a wide detour. Luckily after that the wood seemed to be thinning out. He was able to walk a bit faster, and so it seemed reasonable to deduce that he might be getting near to the road at the other end. His relief was so great that perhaps that was why he did not pause to take his bearings again, and when he did look up he was shocked to see the green streak in the sky was gone. Or was it? He swung around. No, it was there, but it seemed to have veered around and was now behind him. Did that mean he was going in the wrong direction? Appalled, he leant back against a tree. His legs were giving way under him. He would not be able to go another step without a rest. And now a new pain had struck him between the shoulders. He felt around with his foot in the darkness looking for somewhere to sit, but all he could feel were wads of soggy leaves from summers dead and gone.

Perhaps it was just as well – if he sat down he might not be able to get up again. Then the matter was taken out of his hands. He was attacked by a fit of dizziness, and his head began to reel. To save himself from falling he dropped down on one knee and braced himself with the palms of his hands against the ground. Bad as he was, the irony of his posture struck him – the sprinter, tensed for the starter's pistol! Afraid of cramp he cautiously got to his feet. And he thought of the times when, as a youngster playing hide and seek, a rag would be tied over his eyes and he would be spun around like a top, so that when the blindfold was removed, he wouldn't know which way to run.

Ah, there was the green light! But how it had narrowed! It was only a thin line now. Still, James lurched towards it. The bushes had got dense again and he was throwing himself against them, as against a crashing wave, while they for their part seemed to thrust him back. Coming to a really thick clump he gathered up enough strength to hurl himself against it, only to find that he went through it as if it was a bank of fog, and sprawled out into another clearing.

Was it the road at last? No. It would have been lighter overhead. Instead a solid mass of blackness towered over him, high as the sky. Were it not for his lifeline of light he would have despaired. As if it too might quench he feverishly fastened his eyes on it. It was not a single line any more. There were three or four lines. Oh God, no? It was a window, a window with a green blind drawn down, that let out only the outline of its light. A house? Oh God, not Balfe's? In absolute panic James turned and with the vigour of frenzy crashed back through the undergrowth in the way he had come. This time the bushes gave way freely before him, but the silence that had pressed so dank upon him was shattered at every step and he was betrayed by the snapping and breaking of twigs. When a briar caught on his sleeve it gave out a deafening rasp. Pricks from a gorse bush bit into his flesh like sparks of fire, but worse still was the prickly heat of shame that ran over his whole body.

'Damn, damn, damn,' he cried, not caring suddenly what noise he made. Why had he run like that? – Like a madman? – Using up his last store of strength? What did he care about anyone or anything if only he could get out of this place? What if it was Balfe's? It was hardly the house? Probably an outbuilding? Or the quarters of a hired hand? Why hadn't he called out?

Sweat was breaking out all over him now and he had to exert a superhuman strength not to let himself fall spent, on the ground, because if he did he'd stay there. He wouldn't be able to get up. To rest for a minute he dropped on one knee again. The pose of the athlete again! Oh, it was a pity Myra couldn't see him, he thought bitterly, but then for a moment he had a crazy feeling that the pose was for real. He found himself tensing the muscles of his face, as if at any minute a real shot would blast-off and he would spring up and dash madly down a grassy sprint-track.

It was then that a new, a terrible, an utterly unendurable pain exploded in his chest.

'God, God!' he cried. His hands under him were riveted to the ground. Had he been standing he would have been thrown. 'What is the matter with me?' he cried. And the question rang out over all the wood. Then, as another spasm went through him other questions were torn from him. Was it a heart attack? A stroke? – In abject terror, not daring to stir, he stayed crouched. 'Ah, Ah, Ahh . . .' The pain again. The pain, the pain, the pain.

'Am I dying?' he gasped, but this time it was the pain that answered, and answered so strangely James didn't understand because it did what he did not think possible: it catapulted him to his feet, and filled him with a strength that never, never in his life had he possessed. It ran through him like a bar of iron – a stanchion that held his ribs together. He was turned into a man of iron! If he raised his arms now and thrashed about, whole trees would give way before him, and their branches, brittle as glass, would clatter to the ground. 'See Myra! See!' he cried out. So he had lost his vigour? He'd show her! But he had taken his eyes off the light. Where was it? Had it gone out? 'I told you not to go out,' he yelled at it, and lifting his iron feet he went crashing towards where he had seen it last.

But the next minute he knew there was something wrong. Against his face he felt something wet and cold, and he was almost overpowered by the smell of rank earth and rotting leaves. If he'd fallen he hadn't felt the fall. Was he numbed? He raised his head. He'd have to get help. But when he tried to cry out no sound came.

The light? Where was it. 'Oh, don't go out,' he pleaded to it, as if it was the light of life itself, and to propitiate it, he gave it a name. 'Don't go out, Emmy,' he prayed. Then came the last and most anguished question of all. Was he raving? No, no. It was only a window. But in his head there seemed to be a dialogue of two voices, his own and another that answered derisively. 'What window?' James tried to explain that it was the window in the classroom. Hadn't he opened it when the big footballer wasn't able to pull down the sash? He, James, had leant across the desk and brought it down with one strong pull. But where was the rush of sweet summer air? There was only a deathly chill. And where was Emmy?

With a last desperate effort James tried to stop his mind from stumbling and tried to fasten it on Myra. Where was *she*? She wouldn't have failed him. But she *had* failed him. Both of them had failed him. Under a weight of bitterness too great to be borne his face was pressed into the wet leaves, and when he gulped for breath, the rotted leaves were sucked into his mouth.

from *A Memory & Other Stories*, 1972

A Ball of Malt and Madame Butterfly

BENEDICT KIELY

On a warm but not sunny June afternoon on a crowded Dublin street, by no means one of the city's most elegant streets, a small hotel, a sort of bed-and-breakfast place, went on fire. There was pandemonium at first, more panic than curiosity in the crowd. It was a street of decayed Georgian houses, high and narrow, with steep wooden staircases, and cluttered small shops on the ground floors: all great nourishment for flames. The fire, though, didn't turn out to be serious. The brigade easily contained and controlled it. The panic passed, gave way to curiosity, then to indignation and finally, alas, to laughter about the odd thing that happened when the alarm was at its worst.

This was it.

From a window on the topmost floor a woman, scantily clad, puts her head out and waves a patchwork bed coverlet, and screams for help. The stairway, she cries, is thick with smoke, herself and her husband are afraid to face it. On what would seem to be prompting from inside the room, she calls down that they are a honeymoon couple up from the country. That would account fairly enough for their still being abed on a warm June afternoon.

The customary ullagone and ullalu goes up from the crowd. The fire-engine ladder is aimed up to the window. A fireman begins to run up the ladder. Then suddenly the groom appears in shirt and trousers, and barefooted. For, to the horror of the beholders, he makes his bare feet visible by pushing the bride back into the room, clambering first out of the window, down the ladder like a monkey although he is a fairly corpulent man; with monkey-like agility dodging round the ascending fireman, then disappearing through the crowd. The people, indignant enough to trounce him, are still too concerned with the plight of the bride, and too astounded to seize him. The fireman ascends to the nuptial casement, helps the lady through the window and down the ladder, gallantly offering his jacket which covers some of her. Then when they are halfways down, the fireman, to the amazement of all, is seen to be laughing right merrily, the bride vituperating. But before they reach the ground she is also laughing. She is brunette, tall, but almost Japanese in appearance, and very handsome. A voice says: If she's a bride I can see no confetti in her hair.

She has fine legs which the fireman's jacket does nothing to conceal and which she takes pride, clearly, in displaying. She is a young woman of questionable virginity and well known to the firemen. She is the toast of a certain section of the town to whom she is affectionately known as Madame Butterfly, although unlike her most famous namesake she has never been married, nor cursed by an uncle bonze for violating the laws of the gods of her ancestors. She has another, registered, name: her mother's name. What she is her mother was before her, and proud of it.

The barefooted fugitive was not, of course, a bridegroom, but a long-established married man with his wife and family and a prosperous business in Longford, the meanest town in Ireland. For the fun of it the firemen made certain that the news of his escapade in the June afternoon got back to Longford. They were fond of, even proud of, Butterfly as were many other men who had nothing at all to do with the quenching of fire.

But one man loved the pilgrim soul in her and his name was Pike Hunter.

Like Borgnefesse, the buccaneer of Saint Malo on the Rance, who had a buttock shot or sliced off in action on the Spanish Main, Pike Hunter had a lopsided appearance when sitting down. Standing up he was as straight and well-balanced as a man could be: a higher civil servant approaching the age of forty, a shy bachelor, reared, nourished and guarded all his life by a trinity of upper-middle-class aunts. He was pink-faced, with a little fair hair left to emphasize early baldness, mild in his ways, with a slight stutter, somewhat afraid of women. He wore always dark-brown suits with a faint red stripe, dark-brown hats, rimless spectacles, shiny square-toed brown hand-made shoes with a wide welt. In summer, even on the hottest day, he carried a raincoat folded over his arm, and a rolled umbrella. When it rained he unfolded and wore the raincoat and opened and raised the umbrella. He suffered mildly from hay fever. In winter he belted himself into a heavy brown overcoat and wore galoshes. Nobody ever had such stiff white shirts. He favoured brown neckties distinguished with a pearl-headed pin. Why he sagged to one side, just a little to the left, when he sat down, I never knew. He had never been sliced or shot on the Spanish Main.

But the chance of a sunny still Sunday afternoon in Stephen's Green and Grafton Street, the select heart or soul of the city's south side, made a changed man out of him.

He had walked at his ease through the Green, taking the sun gratefully, blushing when he walked between the rows of young ladies lying back in deck chairs. He blushed for two reasons: they were reclining, he was walking; they were as gracefully at rest as the swans on the lake, he was awkwardly in motion, conscious that his knees rose too high, that his sparse hair – because of the warmth he had his hat in his hand – danced long and ludicrously in the little wind, that his shoes squeaked. He was fearful that his right toe might kick his left heel, or vice versa, and that he would fall down and be laughed at in laughter like the sound of silver bells. He was also alarmingly aware of the bronze knees, and more than knees, that the young ladies exposed as they leaned back and relaxed in their light summer frocks. He would honestly have liked to stop and enumerate those knees, make an inventory – he was in the Department of Statistics; perhaps pat a few here and there. But the fearful regimen of that trinity of aunts forbade him even to glance sideways, and he stumbled on like a winkered horse, demented by the flashing to right and to left of bursting globes of bronze light.

Then on the park pathway before him, walking towards the main gate and the top of Grafton Street, he saw the poet. He had seen him before, but only in the Abbey Theatre and never on the street. Indeed it seemed hardly credible to Pike Hunter that such a man would walk on the common street where all ordinary or lesser men were free to place their feet. In the Abbey Theatre the poet had all the strut and style of a man who could walk with the gods, the Greek gods that is, not the gods in the theatre's cheapest seats. His custom was to enter by a small stairway, at the front of the house and in full view of the audience, a few moments before the lights dimmed and the famous gong sounded and the curtain rose. He walked slowly, hands clasped behind his back, definitely balancing the prone brow oppressive with its mind, the eagle head aloft and crested with foaming white hair. He would stand, his back to the curtain and facing the house. The chatter would cease, the fiddlers in the orchestra would saw with diminished fury. Some of the city wits said that what the poet really did at those times was to count the empty seats in the house and make a rapid reckoning of the night's takings. But their gibe could not diminish the majesty of those entrances, the majesty of the stance of the man. And there he was now, hands behind back, noble head high, pacing slowly, beginning the course of Grafton Street. Pike Hunter walked behind him, suiting his pace to the poet's, to the easy deliberate rhythms of the early love poetry: I would that we were, my beloved, white birds on the foam of the sea. There is a queen in China or, maybe, it's in Spain.

They walked between the opulent windows of elegant glittering shops, doors closed for Sunday. The sunshine had drawn the people from the streets: to the park, to the lush green country, to the seaside. Of the few people they did meet, not all of them seemed to know who the poet was, but those who did know saluted quietly, with a modest and unaffected reverence, and one young man with a pretty girl on his arm stepped off the pavement, looked after the poet, and clearly whispered to the maiden who it was that had just passed by the way. Stepping behind him at a respectful distance Pike felt like an acolyte behind a celebrant and regretted that there was no cope or cloak of cloth of gold of which he could humbly carry the train.

So they sailed north towards the Liffey, leaving Trinity College, with Burke standing haughty-headed and Goldsmith sipping at his honeypot of a book, to the right, and the Bank and Grattan orating Esto Perpetua, to the left, and Thomas Moore of the Melodies, brown, stooped and shabby, to the right; and came into West-moreland Street where the wonder happened. For there approaching them came the woman Homer sung: old and grey and, perhaps, full of sleep, a face much and deeply lined and haggard, eyes sunken, yet still the face of the queen she had been when she and the poet were young and they had stood on the cliffs on Howth

Head, high above the promontory that bears the Bailey Lighthouse as a warning torch and looks like the end of the world; and they had watched the soaring of the gulls and he had wished that he and she were only white birds, my beloved, buoyed out on the foam of the sea. She was very tall. She was not white, but all black in widow's weeds for the man she had married when she wouldn't marry the poet. Her black hat had a wide brim and, from the brim, an old-fashioned veil hung down before her face. The pilgrim soul in you, and loved the sorrows of your changing face.

Pike stood still, fearing that in a dream he had intruded on some holy place. The poet and the woman moved dreamlike towards each other, then stood still, not speaking, not saluting, at opposite street corners where Fleet Street comes narrowly from the east to join Westmoreland Street. Then still not speaking, not saluting, they turned into Fleet Street. When Pike tiptoed to the corner and peered around he saw that they had walked on opposite sides of the street for, perhaps, thirty paces, then turned at right angles, moved towards each other, stopped to talk in the middle of the street where a shaft of sunlight had defied the tall overshadowing buildings. Apart from themselves and Pike that portion of the town seemed to be awesomely empty; and there Pike left them and walked in a daze by the side of the Liffey to a pub called the Dark Cow. Something odd had happened to him: poetry, a vision of love?

It so happened that on that day Butterfly was in the Dark Cow, as, indeed, she often was: just Butterfly and Pike, and Jody with the red carbuncled face who owned the place and was genuinely kind to the girls of the town, and a few honest dockers who didn't count because they had money only for their own porter and were moral men, loyal to wives or sweethearts. It wasn't the sort of place Pike frequented. He had never seen Butterfly before: those odd slanting eyes, the glistening high-piled black hair, the well-defined bud of a mouth, the crossed legs, the knees that outclassed to the point of mockery all the bronze globes in Stephen's Green. Coming on top of his vision of the poet and the woman, all this was too much for him, driving him to a reckless courage that would have flabbergasted the three aunts. He leaned on the counter. She sat in an alcove that was a sort of throne for her, where on busier days she sat surrounded by her sorority. So he says to Jody whom he did not yet know as Jody: May I have the favour of buying the lady in the corner a drink?

— That you may, and more besides.
— Please ask her permission. We must do these things properly.
— Oh there's a proper way of doing everything, even screwing a goose.

But Jody, messenger of love, walks to the alcove and formally asks the lady would she drink if the gentleman at the counter sends it over. She will. She will also allow him to join her. She whispers: Has he any money?

— Loaded, says Jody.
— Send him over so. Sunday's a dull day.

Pike sits down stiffly, leaning a little away from her, which seems to her quite right for him as she has already decided that he's a shy sort of man, upper class, but shy, not like some. He excuses himself from intruding. She says: You're not inthrudin'.

He says he hasn't the privilege of knowing her name.

Talks like a book, she decides, or a play in the Gaiety.

— Buttherfly, she says.
— Butterfly, he says, is a lovely name.
— Me mother's name was Trixie, she volunteers.
— Was she dark like you?
— Oh, a natural blonde and very busty, well developed, you know. She danced in the old Tivoli where the newspaper office is now. I'm neat, not busty.

To his confusion she indicates, with hands moving in small curves, the parts of her that she considers are neat. But he notices that she has shapely long-fingered hands and he remembers that the poet had admitted that the small hands of his beloved were not, in fact, beautiful. He is very perturbed.

— Neat, she says, and well made. Austin McDonnell, the fire-brigade chief, says that he read in a book that the best sizes and shapes would fit into champagne glasses.

He did wonder a little that a fire-brigade chief should be a quotable authority on female sizes and shapes, and on champagne glasses. But then and there he decided to buy her champagne, the only drink fit for such a queen who seemed as if she came, if not from China, at any rate from Japan.

– Champagne, he said.

– Bubbly, she said. I love bubbly.

Jody dusted the shoulders of the bottle that on his shelves had waited a long time for a customer. He unwired the cork. The cork and the fizz shot up to the ceiling.

– This, she said, is my lucky day.

– The divine Bernhardt, said Pike, had a bath in champagne presented to her by a group of gentlemen who admired her.

– Water, she said, is better for washing.

But she told him that her mother who knew everything about actresses had told her that story, and told her that when, afterwards, the gentlemen bottled the contents of the bath and drank it, they had one bottleful too many. He was too far gone in fizz and love's frenzy to feel embarrassed. She was his discovery, his oriental queen.

He said: You're very oriental in appearance. You could be from Japan.

She said: My father was, they say. A sailor. Sailors come and go.

She giggled. She said: That's a joke. Come and go. Do you see it?

Pike saw it. He giggled with her. He was a doomed man.

She said: Austin McDonnell says that if I was in Japan I could be a geisha girl if I wasn't so tall. That's why they call me Buttherfly. It's the saddest story. Poor Madame Buttherfly died that her child could be happy across the sea. She married a sailor, too, an American lieutenant. They come and go. The priest, her uncle, cursed her for marrying a Yank.

– The priests are good at that, said Pike who, because of his reading allowed himself, outside office hours, a soupçon of anticlericalism.

Touched by Puccini they were silent for a while, sipping champagne. With every sip Pike realized more clearly that he had found what the poet, another poet, an English one, had called the long-awaited long-expected Spring, he knew his heart had found a time to sing, the strength to soar was in his spirit's wing, that life was full of a triumphant sound and death could only be a little thing. She was good on the nose, too. She was wise in the ways of perfume. The skin of her neck had a pearly glow. The three guardian aunts were as far away as the moon. Then one of the pub's two doors – it was a corner house – opened with a crash and a big man came in, well drunk, very jovial. He wore a wide-brimmed grey hat. He walked to the counter. He said: Jody, old bootlegger, old friend of mine, old friend of Al Capone, serve me a drink to sober me up.

– Austin, said Jody, what will it be?

– A ball of malt, the big man said, and Madame Butterfly.

– That's my friend, Austin, she said, he always says that for a joke.

Pike whose face, with love or champagne or indignation, was taut and hot all over, said that he didn't think it was much of a joke.

– Oh, for Janey's sake, Pike, be your age.

She used his first name for the first time. His eyes were moist.

– For Janey's sake, it's a joke. He's a father to me. He knew my mother.

– He's not Japanese.

– Mind your manners. He's a fireman.

– Austin, she called. Champagne. Pike Hunter's buying champagne.

Pike bought another bottle, while Austin towered above them, swept the wide-brimmed hat from his head in a cavalier half-circle, dropped it on the head of Jody whose red carbuncled face was thus half-extinguished. Butterfly giggled. She said: Austin, you're a scream. He knew Trixie, Pike. He knew Trixie when she was the queen of the boards in the old Tivoli.

Sitting down, the big man sang in a ringing tenor: For I knew Trixie when Trixie was a child.

He sipped at his ball of malt. He sipped at a glass of Pike's champagne. He said: It's a great day for the Irish. It's a great day to break a fiver. Butterfly, dear girl, we fixed the Longford lout. He'll never leave Longford again. The wife has him tethered and spanceled in the haggard. We wrote poison-pen letters to half the town, including the parish priest.

– I never doubted ye, she said. Leave it to the firemen, I said.

– The Dublin Fire Brigade, Austin said, has as long an arm as the Irish Republican Army.

– Austin, she told Pike, died for Ireland.

He sipped champagne. He sipped whiskey. He said: Not once, but several times. When it was neither popular nor profitable. By the living God, we was there when we was wanted. Volunteer McDonnell, at your service.

His bald head shone and showed freckles. His startlingly blue eyes were brightened and dilated by booze. He said: Did I know Trixie, light on her feet as the foam on the fountain? Come in and see the horses. That's what we used to say to the girls when I was a young fireman. Genuine horsepower the fire engines ran on then, and the harness hung on hooks ready to drop on the horses as the firemen descended the greasy pole. And where the horses were, the hay and the straw were plentiful enough to make couches for Cleopatra. That was why we asked the girls in to see the horses. The sailors from the ships, homeless men all, had no such comforts and conveniences. They used to envy us. Butterfly, my geisha girl, you should have been alive then. We'd have shown you the jumps.

Pike was affronted. He was almost prepared to say so and take the consequences. But Butterfly stole his thunder. She stood up, kissed the jovial big man smack on the bald head, and then, as light on her feet as her mother ever could have been, danced up and down the floor, tight hips bouncing, fingers clicking, singing: I'm the smartest little geisha in Japan, in Japan. And the people call me Rolee Polee Nan, Polee Nan.

Drowning in desire, Pike forgot his indignation and found that he was liking the man who could provoke such an exhibition. Breathless, she sat down again, suddenly kissed Pike on the cheek, said: I love you too. I love champagne. Let's have another bottle.

They had.

– Rolee Polee Nan, she sang as the cork and the fizz ascended.

– A greater writer, a Russian, Pike said, wrote that his ideal was to be idle and to make love to a plump girl.

– The cheek of him. I'm not plump. Turkeys are plump. I love being tall, with long legs.

Displaying the agility of a trained high-kicker with hinges in her hips she, still sitting, raised her shapely right leg, up and up as if her toes would touch the ceiling, up and up until stocking top,

suspender, bare thigh, and a frill of pink panties showed. Something happened to Pike that had nothing at all to do with poetry or
Jody's champagne. He held Butterfly's hand. She made a cat's
cradle with their fingers and swung the locked hands pendulum-
wise. She sang: Janey Mac, the child's a black, what will we do on
Sunday? Put him to bed and cover his head and don't let him up
until Monday.

Austin had momentarily absented himself for gentlemanly
reasons. From the basement jakes his voice singing rose above the
soft inland murmur of falling water: Oh my boat can lightly float in
the heel of wind and weather, and outrace the smartest hooker
between Galway and Kinsale.

The dockers methodically drank their pints of black porter and
paid no attention. Jody said: Time's money. Why don't the two of
you slip upstairs. Your heads would make a lovely pair on a pillow.

Austin was singing: Oh she's neat, oh she's sweet, she's a beauty
every line, the Queen of Connemara is that bounding barque of
mine.

He was so shy, Butterfly said afterwards, that he might have been
a Christian Brother and a young one at that, although where or how
she ever got the experience to enable her to make the comparison,
or why she should think an old Christian Brother less cuthallacht
than a young one, she didn't say. He told her all about the aunts and
the odd way he had been reared and she, naturally, told Austin and
Jody and all her sorority. But they were a kind people and no
mockers, and Pike never knew, Austin told me, that Jody's
clientele listened with such absorbed interest to the story of his life,
and of his heart and his lovemaking. He was something new in their
experience, and Jody's stable of girls had experienced a lot, and
Austin a lot more, and Jody more than the whole shebang, and all
the fire brigade, put together.

For Jody, Austin told me, had made the price of the Dark Cow in
a basement in Chicago. During the prohibition, as they called it,
although what they prohibited it would be hard to say. He was one
of five brothers from the bogs of Manulla in the middle of nowhere
in the County of Mayo. The five of them emigrated to Chicago.
When Al Capone and his merry men discovered that Jody and his

brother had the real true secret about how to make booze, and to make it good, down they went into the cellar and didn't see daylight nor breathe fresh air, except to surface to go to Mass on Sundays, until they left the USA. They made a fair fortune. At least four of them did. The fifth was murdered.

Jody was a bachelor man and he was good to the girls. He took his pleasures with them as a gentleman might, with the natural result that he was poxed to the eyebrows. But he was worth more to them than the money he quite generously paid after every turn or trick on the rumpled, always unmade bed in the two-storied apartment above the pub. He was a kind uncle to them. He gave them a friendly welcome, a place to sit down, free drink and smokes and loans, or advances for services yet to be rendered, when they were down on their luck. He had the ear of the civic guards and could help a girl when she was in trouble. He paid fines when they were unavoidable, and bills when they could no longer be postponed, and had an aunt who was reverend mother in a home for unmarried mothers and who was, like her nephew, a kindly person. Now and again, like the Madame made immortal by Maupassant, he took a bevy or flock of the girls for a day at the seaside or in the country. A friend of mine and myself, travelling into the granite mountains south of the city, to the old stonecutters' villages of Lackan and Ballyknockan where there were aged people who had never seen Dublin, thirty miles away, and never wanted to, came upon a most delightful scene in the old country pub in Lackan. All around the bench around the walls sat the mountainy men, the stonecutters, drinking their pints. But the floor was in the possession of a score of wild girls, all dancing together, resting off and on for more drink, laughing, happy, their gaiety inspired and directed by one man in the middle of the floor: red-faced, carbuncled, oily black hair sleeked down and parted up the middle in the style of Dixie Dean, the famous soccer centre-forward, whom Jody so much admired. All the drinks were on generous Jody.

So in Jody's friendly house Pike had, as he came close to forty years, what he never had in the cold abode of the three aunts: a home with a father, Austin, and a brother, Jody, and any God's amount of sisters; and Butterfly who, to judge by the tales she told afterwards, was a motherly sort of lover to him and, for a while, a sympathetic listener. For a while, only: because nothing in her birth, background, rearing or education had equipped her to listen to so much poetry and talk about poetry.

– Poor Pike, she'd say, he'd puke you with poethry. Poethry's all very well, but.

She had never worked out what came after that qualifying: But.

– Give us a bar of a song, Austin. There's some sense to singing. But poethry. My heart leaps up when I behold a rainbow in the sky. On Linden when the sun was low. The lady of Shalott left the room to go to the pot. Janey preserve us from poethry.

He has eyes, Jody told Austin and myself, for no girl except Butterfly. Reckon, in one way, we can't blame him for that. She sure is the smartest filly showing in this paddock. But there must be moderation in all things. Big Anne, now, isn't bad, nor her sister, both well-built Sligo girls and very cooperative, nor Joany Maher from Waterford, nor Patty Daley from Castleisland in the County Kerry who married the Limey in Brum but left him when she found he was as queer as a three-dollar bill. And what about little Red Annie Byrne from Kilkenny City, very attractive if it just wasn't for the teeth she lost when the cattleman that claimed he caught gonorrhea from her gave her an unmerciful hammering in Cumberland Street. We got him before he left town. We cured more than his gonorrhea.

– But, Austin said, when following your advice, Jody, and against my own better judgement, I tried to explain all that to Pike, what does he do but quote to me what the playboy of the Abbey Theatre, John M. Synge, wrote in a love poem about counting queens in Glenmacnass in the Wicklow mountains.

– In the Wicklow mountains, said Jody. Queens? With the smell of the bog and the peat smoke off them.

Austin, a great man, ever, to sing at the top of his tenor voice about Dark Rosaleen and the Queen of Connemara and the County of Mayo, was a literary class of fireman. That was one reason why Pike and himself got on so well together, in spite of that initial momentary misunderstanding about the ball of malt and Madame Butterfly.

– Seven dog days, Austin said, the playboy said he let pass, he and his girl, counting queens in Glenmacnass. The queens he mentions, Jody, you never saw, even in Chicago.

– Never saw daylight in Chicago.

– The Queen of Sheba, Austin said, and Helen, and Maeve the warrior queen of Connacht, and Deirdre of the Sorrows and Gloriana that was the great Elizabeth of England and Judith out of the Bible that chopped the block of Holofernes.

– All, said Jody, in a wet glen in Wicklow. A likely bloody story.

– There was one queen in the poem that had an amber belly.

– Jaundice, said Jody. Or Butterfly herself that's as sallow as any Jap. Austin, you're a worse lunatic than Pike.

– But in the end, Jody, his own girl was the queen of all queens. They were dead and rotten. She was alive.

– Not much of a compliment to her, Jody said, to prefer her to a cartload of corpses.

– Love's love, Jody. Even the girls admit that. They've no grudge against him for seeing nobody but Butterfly.

– They give him a fool's pardon. But no doll in the hustling game, Austin, can afford to spend all her time listening to poetry. Besides, girls like a variety of pricks. Butterfly's no better or worse than the next. When Pike finds that out he'll go crazy. If he isn't crazy already.

That was the day, as I recall, that Butterfly came in wearing the fancy fur coat – just a little out of season. Jody had, for some reason or other, given her a five-pound note. Pike knew nothing about that. And Jody told her to venture the five pounds on a horse that was running at the Curragh of Kildare, that a man in Kilcullen on the edge of the Curragh had told him that the jockey's wife had already bought her ball dress for the victory celebration. The Kilcullen man knew his onions, and his jockeys, and shared his wisdom only with a select few so as to keep the odds at a good twenty to one.

– She's gone out to the bookie's, said Jody, to pick up her winnings. We'll have a party tonight.

Jody had a tenner on the beast.

– She could invest it, said Austin, if she was wise. The day will come when her looks will go.

– Pike might propose to her, said Jody. He's mad enough for anything.

– The aunts would devour him. And her.

– Here she comes, Jody said. She invested her winnings on her fancy back.

She had too, and well she carried them in the shape of pale or silver musquash, and three of her sorority walked behind her like ladies-in-waiting behind the Queen of England. There was a party in which even the dockers joined, but not Pike, for that evening and night one of his aunts was at death's door in a nursing home, and Pike and the other two aunts were by her side. He wasn't to see the musquash until he took Butterfly on an outing to the romantic hill of Howth where the poet and the woman had seen the white birds. That was the last day Pike ever took Butterfly anywhere. The aunt recovered. They were a thrawn hardy trio.

Pike had become a devotee. Every day except Sunday he lunched in Jody's, on a sandwich of stale bread and leathery ham and a glass of beer, just on the off-chance that Butterfly might be out of the doss and abroad, and in Jody's, at that, to her, unseasonable hour of the day. She seldom was, except when she was deplorably short of money. In the better eating places on Grafton Street and Stephen's Green, his colleagues absorbed the meals that enabled higher civil servants to face up to the afternoon and the responsibilities of State: statistics, land commission, local government, posts and tele-graphs, internal revenue. He had never, among his own kind, been much of a mixer: so that few of his peers even noticed the speed with which, when at five in the evening the official day was done, he took himself, and his hat and coat and umbrella, and legged it off to Jody's: in the hope that Butterfly might be there, bathed and perfumed and ready for wine and love. Sometimes she was. Sometimes she wasn't. She liked Pike. She didn't deny it. She was always an honest girl, as her mother, Trixie, had been before her – so Austin said when he remembered Trixie who had died in a hurry, of peritonitis. But, Janey Mac, Butterfly couldn't have Pike Hunter for breakfast, dinner, tea, and supper, and nibblers as well, all the livelong day and night. She still, as Jody said, had her first million to make, and Pike's inordinate attachment was coming between her and the real big business, as when, say, the country cattlemen were in town for the market. They were the men who knew how to get rid of the money.

– There is this big cattleman, she tells Austin once, big he is in every way, who never knows or cares what he's spending. He's a gift and a godsend to the girls. He gets so drunk that all you have to do to humour him is play with him a little in the taxi going from pub to pub and see that he gets safely to his hotel. The taximen are on to the game and get their divvy out of the loot.

One wet and windy night, it seems, Butterfly and this philan-thropist are flying high together, he on brandy, she on champagne, for which that first encounter with Pike has given her a ferocious drouth. In the back of the taxi touring from pub to pub, the five-pound notes are flowing out of your man like water out of a pressed sponge. Butterfly is picking them up and stuffing them into her handbag, but not all of them. For this is too good and too big for any taximan on a fair percentage basis. So for every one note she puts into her handbag she stuffs two or three down into the calf-length boots she is wearing against the wet weather. She knows, you see, that she is too far gone in bubbly to walk up the stairs to her own room, that the taximan, decent fellow, will help her up and then, fair enough, go through her bag and take his cut. Which, indeed, in due time he does. When she wakes up, fully clothed, in the morning on her own bed, and pulls off her boots, her ankles, what with the rain that had dribbled down into her boots, are poulticed and plastered with notes of the banks of Ireland and of England, and one moreover of the Bank of Bonnie Scotland.

– Rings on my fingers, she says, and bells on my toes.

That was the gallant life that Pike's constant attendance was cutting her off from. She also hated being owned. She hated other people thinking she was owned. She hated like hell when Pike would enter the Dark Cow and one of the other girls or, worse still, another man, a bit of variety, would move away from her side to let Pike take the throne. They weren't married, for Janey's sake. She could have hated Pike, except that she was as tenderhearted as Trixie had been, and she liked champagne. She certainly felt at liberty to hate the three aunts who made a mollycoddle out of him. She also hated, with a hatred that grew and grew, the way that Pike puked her with poethry. And all this time poor Pike walked in a dream that he never defined for us, perhaps not even for himself, but that certainly must have looked higher than the occasional trick on Jody's rumpled bed. So dreaming, sleepwalking, he persuaded Butterfly to go to Howth Head with him one dull hot day when the town was empty and she had nothing better to do. No place could have been more fatally poetic than Howth. She wore her musquash. Not even the heat could part her from it.

– He never let up, she said, not once from the moment we boarded the bus on the quays. Poethry. I had my bellyful.

– Sure thing, said Jody.

– Any man, she said, that won't pay every time he performs is a man to keep a cautious eye on. Not that he's not generous. But at the wrong times. Money down or no play's my motto.

– Well I know that, Jody said.

– But Pike Hunter says that would make our love mercenary, whatever that is.

– You're a great girl, said Austin, to be able to pronounce it.

– Your middle name, said Jody, is mercenary.

– My middle name, thank you, is Imelda. And the cheek of Pike Hunter suggesting to me to go to a doctor because he noticed something wrong with himself, a kidney disorder, he said. He must wet the bed.

– Butterfly, said Austin, he might have been giving you good advice.

– Nevertheless. It's not for him to say.

When they saw from the bus the Bull Wall holding the northern sand back from clogging up the harbour, and the Bull Island, three miles long, with dunes, bent grass, golfers, bathers and skylarks, Pike told her about some fellow called Joyce – there was a Joyce in the Civic Guards, a Galwayman who played county football, but no relation – who had gone walking on the island one fine day and laid eyes on a young one, wading in a pool, with her skirts well pulled up; and let a roar out of him. By all accounts this Joyce was no addition to the family for, as Pike told the story, Butterfly worked out that the young one was well under age.

Pike and Butterfly had lunch by the edge of the sea, in the Claremont Hotel, and that was all right. Then they walked in the

grounds of Howth Castle, Pike had a special pass, and the flowers
and shrubs were a sight to see if only Pike had kept his mouth shut
about some limey by the name of Spenser who landed there in the
year of God, and wrote a poem as long as from here to Killarney
about a fairy queen and a gentle knight who was pricking on the
plain like the members of the Harp Cycling Club, Junior Branch,
up above there in the Phoenix Park. He didn't get time to finish the
poem, the poet that is, not Pike, for the Cork people burned him
out of house and home and, as far as Butterfly was concerned, that
was the only good deed she ever heard attributed to the Cork
people.

The Phoenix Park and the Harp Club reminded her that one day
Jody had said, meaning no harm, about the way Pike moped
around the Dark Cow when Butterfly wasn't there, that Pike was
the victim of a semihorn and should go up to the Fifteen Acres in
the Park and put it in the grass for a while and run around it. But
when, for fun, she told this to Pike he got so huffed he didn't speak
for half an hour, and they walked Howth Head until her feet were
blistered and the heel of her right shoe broke, and the sweat, with
the weight of the musquash and the heat of the day, was running
between her shoulder blades like a cloudburst down the gutter.
Then the row and the ructions, as the song says, soon began. He
said she should have worn flat-heeled shoes. She said that if she had
known that he was conscripting her for a forced march over a
mountain she'd have borrowed a pair of boots from the last soldier
she gave it to at cut price, for the soldiers, God help them, didn't
have much money but they were more openhanded with what they
had than some people who had plenty, and soldiers didn't waste
time and breath on poetry: Be you fat or be you lean there is no soap
like Preservene.

So she sat on the summit of Howth and looked at the lighthouse
and the seagulls, while Pike walked back to the village to have the
broken heel mended, and the sweat dried cold on her, and she was
perished. Then when he came back, off he was again about how
that white-headed old character that you'd see across the river there
at the Abbey Theatre, and Madame Gone Mad McBride that was
the age of ninety and looked it, and known to all as a roaring rebel,
worse than Austin, had stood there on the very spot, and how the

poet wrote a poem wishing for himself and herself to be turned into seagulls, the big dirty brutes that you'd see along the docks robbing the pigeons of their food. Butterfly would have laughed at him, except that her teeth by this time were tap-dancing with the cold like the twinkling feet of Fred Astaire. So she pulled her coat around her and said: Pike, I'm no seagull. For Janey's sake take me back to civilization and Jody's where I know someone.

But, God sees, you never knew anybody, for at that moment the caveman came out in Pike Hunter, he that was always so backward on Jody's bed and, there and then, he tried to flatten her in the heather in full view of all Dublin and the coast of Ireland as far south as Wicklow Head and as far north as where the Mountains of Mourne sweep down to the sea.

– Oh none of that, Pike Hunter, she says, my good musquash will be crucified. There's a time and a place and a price for everything.

You and your musquash, he tells her.

They were wrestling like Man Mountain Dean and Jack Doyle, the Gorgeous Gael.

– You've neither sense nor taste, says he, to be wearing a fur coat on a day like this.

– Bloody well for you to talk, says she, with your rolled umbrella and your woollen combinations and your wobbly ass that won't keep you straight in the chair, and your three witches of maiden aunts never touched, tasted, or handled my mortal man, and plenty of money, and everything your own way. This is my only coat that's decent, in case you haven't noticed, and I earned it hard and honest with Jody, a generous man but a monster on the bed. I bled after him.

That put a stop to the wrestling. He brought her back to the Dark Cow and left her at the door and went his way.

He never came back to the Dark Cow but once, and Butterfly wasn't on her throne that night. It was the night before the cattle market. He was so lugubrious and woebegone that Jody and Austin and a few merry newspaper men, including myself, tried to jolly him up, take him out of himself, by making jokes at his expense that would force him to come alive and answer back. Our efforts failed. He looked at us sadly and said: Boys, Beethoven, when he was dying, said: Clap now, good friends, the comedy is done.

He was more than a little drunk and, for the first time, seemed lopsided when standing up; and untidy.

– Clap now indeed, said Jody.

Pike departed and never returned. He took to steady drinking in places like the Shelbourne Hotel or the Buttery in the Hibernian where it was most unlikely, even with Dublin being the democratic sort of town that it is, that he would ever encounter Madame Butterfly. He became a great problem for his colleagues and his superior officers in the civil service, and for his three aunts. After careful consultation they, all together, persuaded him to rest up in Saint Patrick's Hospital where, as you all may remember, Dean Swift died roaring. Which was, I feel sure, why Pike wasn't there to pay the last respects to the dead when Jody dropped from a heart attack and was waked in the bedroom above the Dark Cow. The girls were there in force to say an eternal farewell to a good friend. Since the drink was plentiful and the fun and the mourning intense, somebody, not even Austin knew who, suggested that the part of the corpse that the girls knew best should be tastefully decorated with black crepe ribbon. The honor of tying on the ribbon naturally went to Madame Butterfly but it was Big Anne who burst into tears and cried out: Jody's dead and gone forever.

Austin met her, Butterfly not Big Anne, a few days afterwards at the foot of the Nelson Pillar. Jody's successor had routed the girls from the Dark Cow. Austin told her about Pike and where he was. She brooded a bit. She said it was a pity, but nobody could do nothing for him, that those three aunts had spoiled him for ever and, anyway, didn't Austin think that he was a bit astray in the head.

– Who knows, Butterfly? Who's sound or who's silly? Consider yourself for a moment.

– What about me, Austin?

– A lovely girl like you, a vision from the romantic East, and think of the life you lead. It can have no good ending. Let me tell you a story, Butterfly. There was a girl once in London, a slavey, a poor domestic servant. I knew a redcoat here in the old British days who said he preferred slaveys to anything else because they were clean, free and flattering.

– Austin, I was never a slavey.

– No Butterfly, you have your proper pride. But listen: this slavey is out one morning scrubbing the stone steps in front of the big house she works in, bucket and brush, carbolic soap and all that, in one of the great squares in one of the more classy parts of London Town. There she is on her bended knees when a gentleman walks past, a British army major in the Coldstream Guards or the Black Watch or something.

– I've heard of them, Austin.

– So this British major looks at her, and he sees the naked backs of her legs, thighs you know, and taps her on the shoulder or somewhere and he says: Oh rise up, lovely maiden and come along with me, there's a better life in store for you somewhere else. She left the bucket and the brush, and the stone steps half-scrubbed, and walked off with him and became his girl. But there were even greater things in store for her. For, Butterfly, that slavey became Lady Emma Hamilton, the beloved of Lord Nelson, the greatest British sailor that ever sailed, and the victor of the renowned battle of Trafalgar. There he is up on the top of the Pillar.

– You wouldn't think to look at him, Austin, that he had much love in him.

– But, Butterfly, meditate on that story, and rise up and get yourself out of the gutter. You're handsome enough to be the second Lady Hamilton.

After that remark, Austin brought her into Lloyd's, a famous house of worship in North Earl Street under the shadow of Lord Nelson and his pillar. In Lloyd's he bought her a drink and out of the kindness of his great singing heart, gave her some money. She shook his hand and said: Austin, you're the nicest man I ever met.

Austin had, we may suppose, given her an image, an ideal. She may have been wearied by Pike and his sad attachment to poetry, but she rose to the glimmering vision of herself as a great lady beloved by a great and valiant lord. A year later she married a docker, a decent quiet hardworking fellow who had slowly sipped his pints of black porter and watched and waited all the time.

– Oddly enough, Austin told me when the dignity of old age had gathered around him like the glow of corn stubble in the afterwards of harvest.

He could still sing. His voice never grew old.

– Oddly enough, I never had anything to do with her. That way, I mean. Well you know me. Fine wife, splendid sons, nobody like them in the world. Fine daughters, too. But a cousin of mine, a ship's wireless operator who had been all round the world from Yokohama to the Belgian Congo and back again, and had had a ship burned under him in Bermuda and, for good value, another ship burned under him in Belfast, said she was the meanest whore he ever met. When he had paid her the stated price, there were some coppers left in his hand and she grabbed them and said: give us these for the gas meter.

But he said, also, that at the high moments she had a curious and diverting way of raising and bending and extending her left leg – not her right leg which she kept as flat as a plumb level. He had never encountered the like before, in any colour or in any country.

from *A Ball of Malt and Madame Butterfly & other Stories*, 1973

Not Quite The Same

JOHN JORDAN

'Aye,' said Thomas.

'And then,' said Mrs McMenamin, eyes French-polished with intense recollection, 'then, they gave the mouse to the dog, a poodle it was, very badly kept, but not, I would have thought, *given* to mice.'

'A decent beast,' said Thomas.

'O Thomas,' she cried, 'you put things so well.'

'So well you might say,' said Thomas. He was getting restive. Before Mrs McMenamin had time to draw in her bosom for another episode about the poodle and the mouse, he let out a ferocious blast compounded of yawn, snarl, growl, screech, threnody, ode, hallelujah, belch. Thomas was invoking Our Blessed Lord.

'No singing,' said Dr Dargan, a venerable person who had abandoned for the licensing trade a distinguished career as a general practitioner. He was hard of hearing.

'I'm not singing,' said Thomas humbly.

'Sounded very like it to me,' said Dr Dargan. Eyes like perished finger-tips dared Thomas to answer back. He didn't, but when Dr Dargan had wheeled about and in the pretence of washing glasses, was making frantic sweeps with an odious cloth, Thomas bent over to Mrs McMenamin and said, 'Rose, I'd be nervous of that fellow. I'm sure he's a sex maniac.'

'O no,' she said, and she put her hand on her heart.

'What I want to say is this,' said Thomas, and as he tongued his splendid moustaches he took on the look of a dead ringer for Dr Schweitzer.

'Well now, as I was saying. . . .' Mrs McMenamin opened her mouth and Thomas began to sing a hymn called, 'I'll sing a hymn to Mary'. Mrs McMenamin assumed a devotional expression and were it not that she had one hand about a glass of brandy, she would unquestionably have joined it with the other. Those Homeric blue eyes brimmed, those impossible lashes quivered, that masterpiece of a mouth champed a little. Five minutes or so and the sacrifice of Melchisedech would be consummated and little Rose, dear little sweet little so winning Rose, would be walking the streets of Paradise. 'I'll love and bless Thy name,' Thomas wound up with gusto. From around the corner, like an orchestrated ass's bray, came the blind fiddler's rendition of 'The Blue Danube'. Through the window Mrs McMenamin could see a stopped clock and a hideous brick building the colour of rose in an unnatural late sunlight. Dr Dargan was muttering to himself, and his apprentice was scurrying about doing nothing. He had an odd hairstyle and wore badly scuffed winkle-pickers. His name was Aubrey and he was a great admirer of Mrs McMenamin.

'It's not quite the same,' said Mrs McMenamin.

'What's that you say?' growled Thomas.

'That hymn,' she gulped. 'When I think of My Childhood, and Thomas, it meant so much to me, and you know I really am religious, and Roddy – you remember darling Roddy? – says he thinks I need the Church and he *really* loves me.'

'That fellow Roddy,' said Thomas benignly, 'talks too much about love.'

'How can you say such a thing,' said Mrs McMenamin. She was genuinely aghast.

'I mean to say, you can talk about horses or drink or women, but you never talk about love.' He cleared his throat genteely, and carefully de-irrigated his moustaches with a large scarlet handkerchief on which was picked out in yellow the word 'Miami'.

'Thomas,' she said, 'you disappoint me.'

'You disappoint me. Aubrey,' he exploded. He pronounced the first syllable to rhyme with 'cow'.

'Yes sir,' said Aubrey.

'Give us a large Jameson Ten and whatever that woman wants.'

'Brandy,' said Mrs McMenamin peevishly. She objected, on the soundest possible principles, to being called a woman, and especcially by Thomas who most of the time was a perfect gentleman. Aubrey brought the drinks and waited while Thomas dug deep into the caverns of his ducks. A couple of pious ejaculations assisted in the production of a ten-shilling note. Aubrey swooped and in full descent was clutched by a hand of gun-metal.

'Manners,' said Thomas paternally. 'A young fellow like you cannot get on without manners. Christ, where did you get those shoes?'

'They're winkle-pickers. Did you never hear of them?'

'I did indeed.' He swivelled and bayed, 'Is that yourself, Packy.' Packy came crab-wise in his decent professional suit and said, 'I'm very glad to see you Thomas, and you Mrs McMenamin.'

'Twelve-and-four,' said Aubrey.

'You'll be paid,' said Thomas. 'Now Packy, you're a highly sophisticated and knowledgeable fellow. You've been to three schools and the U.C.D. You'd know about winkle-pickers.'

'Yes indeed Thomas,' said Packy.

'Well now, there's a young fellow comes in here. A young fella,' he said disgustedly. 'He wears a kind of shoe, a bit like Aubrey's there.'

'Oh yes,' said Packy. 'He wears elephant-skin sawn-off winkle-pickers.'

'I remember particularly the lovely gnawing sensation coming back from Communion,' said Mrs McMenamin. She was not interested in winkle-pickers. She could not see their relevance to the human heart. 'I grew up, and you know, it wasn't quite the same.'

'You're perfectly right,' said Thomas. 'But I'd love to know how they got the elephant-skin.'

'You know I'm not an intellectual,' said Mrs McMenamin, 'but I love that bit in Colette about coming back from Communion.'

'Elephants are highly intelligent beasts,' said Thomas.

'I'll *never* forget the poodle and the mouse,' said Mrs McMenamin.

'There is no world outside Verona walls,' said Packy absently. On the side he had procured for himself a modest glass of cider. He could be forgiven because he had loved much. In his eyes was the cunning of lost love, the watchfulness of the betrayed.

High above the madness of cars, driving to hell down Grafton Street, the blind fiddler importuned late-shoppers and tourists with 'Peggy O'Neill'. Suddenly there was a purity in the air, a girl's voice true as a lark, testifying to the childhood of Mrs McMenamin, and to Packy's lost love and to Thomas's inordinate pain at the fate of elephants. 'Did the poodle eat the mouse?' said Thomas.

'All that sand and all that sun and the feeling like hot cocoa in the tummy,' said Mrs McMenamin. 'I didn't look to see if it ate the mouse.'

'It's a hard world,' said Packy. 'I once had an air-gun and I shot a thrush. I've never killed anything since.'

'Except my heart,' said Mrs McMenamin, with exemplary insincerity.

'I hate that word heart,' said Thomas. His voice was heavy with the doom of the humble. And the lark's voice sang out again and a girl with eyes that were an even truer blue than Mrs McMenamin's and hair that looked argent in the perverse sunlight stumbled in.

'The poor bitch,' said Packy judicially.

'You pipsqueak you,' said Mrs McMenamin. 'Poor Primrose – you've got to have heart.'

'I hate that word,' said Thomas. 'What are you having Prim?'

'No singing here,' said Dr Dargan, dragged out of private madness by a lark's voice.

'Thank you Thomas,' said Primrose, 'I'm very drunk.'

'Indeed you're not,' said Thomas. 'Now Rosie here and Packy and myself were discussing elephants. Do they have those beasts in Spain?'

'I once,' said Primrose, 'saw a drunken elephant.'

'God that must have been very interesting.'

'Aubrey,' said Primrose, 'please give me a drink. I won't sing.'

'You can sing if I'm here,' said Thomas.

'Indeed you may,' said Packy.

Dr Dargan said that there was to be no bad language. The lark's voice sang out again and intolerable peace descended, light as silk, like the small rains of early spring.

'Love,' said Thomas gloomily.

'Thomas,' said Mrs McMenamin, 'I hate that word.'

'Aye,' said Thomas. 'I once knew a fella who was in love. A fella a bit like myself. A terrible poor bastard. So I said to him, "Do you know what you can do?" And he said "What?" and I said "Go up to the Zoo".'

And they all thought about animals and themselves. Dr Dargan rinsed glasses and Aubrey whistled a pop-song and Roddy came in.

II

He had not changed in the two years since Mrs McMenamin fell in love with the Civic Guard on pointduty, and knew from the start it was impossible. The curve from stud to trouser-belt buckle had not increased, nor had it diminished. But lately he tended to carry his drink unsteadily and although he still worshipped Mrs McMenamin, yet that acolyte's patience of his was showing signs of wear and tear. When Rose was behaving outrageously he would rap his finger on the table and say, 'You can't go on like this' and she would spit back, 'What right have you to talk to me like this,' and he would say 'Because I love you.' Then on like corny stage-effect would come the tears, and the early more deplorable repertoire of striking gestures and husky vocalization would be played out until he took her home and sat with her until she'd drunk and cried herself to sleep. Sometimes he slept in the spare room and in the very late morning was permitted to assist at the reconstruction of that marvellous face. As he watched the profile being painted and shadowed back into mature girlhood, Roddy's tenderness would catch him by the throat and in that room smelling of *eau-de-cologne* and brandy and French cigarettes he would live over in stinging minutes the decades of his service.

'Roddy,' said Thomas, 'come over here.'

'Yes, Thomas?'

'Hold out your hand till I give you a smack'.

'Don't mind him,' said Mrs McMenamin. Warm, indulgent, with all her boys about her.

'Roddy,' said Primrose, 'my first and only love.' She had met him for the first time ten years ago, and had got it into her head that he had, as she put it, 'taken quite a fancy' to her.

'Great God,' said Thomas. He was about to let loose on Primrose when a new round came up in double-quick time. Dr Dargan considered that Roddy was a gentleman, and in his case service was uninterrogated and speedy.

'Rose,' said Roddy. 'I've bad news for you.'

'O no.' She got the hand to her heart too quickly.

'I called for you this morning,' he let this sink in, 'and Mr App bearded me in the hall.'

'That App,' said Thomas, 'is a scoundrel. What's worse he's a fraud.'

'He's coming in here to look for you, Rose.'

'I've paid my rent.' A great and gallant lady.

'He says you must stop offering insults to his wife when you are intoxicated.'

'App was in Africa,' said Thomas, 'or maybe in India. He must know a fair share about elephants.'

'I can't see why App should care,' said Mrs McMenamin. 'He treats that poor Leah like dirt.'

'He says your comments on her study of the Works of Shakespeare upset her very much. She's very sensitive.'

'*She calls me in,*' said Mrs McMenamin fiercely. 'I can't pass her bloody door but she pops out and insists I have a snifter from her gin-bottle. Yesterday,' she glowed, 'I was up early. Half-past nine. I *crept* past the door but out she came and it was half-past ten before I got away. She was reading *The Merchant of Venice* and so naturally I made a little joke about Leah and the wilderness of monkeys. I suppose she told Nugent App I compared him to Shylock.' She swigged and said happily, 'I wish I had.'

'Where did App get that Leah?' said Thomas.

'He says he met her on tour in the Provinces,' said Mrs McMenamin. 'I don't believe she's his wife at all.'

'You might be right there,' said Thomas. 'Many illicitous unions are contracted by mummers. I remember there was a fellow used to come down the country with a performing bear. One day he was there, and the next he was gone, and the cobbler's daughter with him. There were some people said she was eaten by the bear, but they were seen afterwards, the three of them, in Wigan, Lancs., by a fellow from the neighbourhood. Her face was destroyed with paint and you could see a fair amount of her bosom. Shockin' altogether.'

'Mind you,' said Packy, who had been whispering in the little pink ear of Primrose, 'I've heard that Nugent was once a very good actor and that he gave up a career in the West End to look after Leah, who isn't his wife, but his mother'.

'Don't be ridiculous,' said Mrs McMenamin. 'App's too old to be her son.'

'You'd never know,' said Packy, 'with that yellowy face of hers. He's about fifty-five. If she was seventy she could have had him when she was fifteen.' A little in drink, Packy's prose became less formal and his careful legal voice took on the shrewd lilt of his native parts.

Something had electrified Dr Dargan. He belted around the counter to the door, where half-way through, a hand almost entirely hidden by a great folly of white lilac, was trying to push in. Dr Dargan yanked back the door viciously and a very odd person plunged through. White lilac foamed about the torso and most of the face, and from the other hand dangled a string bag which appeared to contain jam-pots.

'Thank you, thank you,' said the person in a high silvery voice. 'God bless you, God bless.'

'App,' said Packy.

'Nugent App,' said Mrs McMenamin.

'The low bastard,' said Thomas.

'Ah my darlings,' said App, and the lilac and the jam-pots were dumped with a swish and a clatter on the counter.

'Rose my love, Thomas my dear fellow, Packy you naughty boy you, Roddy my old faithful and – do I know this little lady?' He leered at Primrose.

'I don't want to know a man who married his mother.'

'Oh boys oh boys,' chanted App. 'What a pretty wit you have. If only my Leah could hear you!'

'Take that bloody lilac out of my way,' said Thomas.

'It's for you Rose!' sang App. 'I picked it this morning on the way back from an early elocution class in the Convent of the Most Immaculate. All the way back to Fitzwilliam Square I carried it, and all the way here.'

'What are the jam-jars for?' asked Packy.

'Returns, dear, returns. Bloody empties. Tuppence each pot.

My Leah's such an economical housekeeper, which reminds me, Rose angel honey-bunch, what with her housework and her intensive study of the Works of Shakespeare, my Leah mustn't be upset by your naughty remarks. Why dear she said that you said I was like Shylock. Me dear! A wild spendthrift like me!'

This performance was given in a voice of campanile splendour, except when it cracked. De-lilaced, Mr App displayed a fine physique and a thinning mane of chemically black hair. He wore an orange shirt with a black tie, a royal blue suit and tan suede shoes. He had a gold wristlet watch and a gold wedding ring, and he used a gold lighter for a Turkish cigarette from a gold case which he did not offer.

'O Nugent,' said Mrs McMenamin, 'don't bother me about Leah. You know I don't care and I know you don't mean it.'

'Never mind dear. It's my birthday.'

An angel passed over and then Thomas asked, 'How old are you App?'

'Thirty-nine my dear fellow, but I feel nineteen!'

'Lord give me patience,' said Thomas.

'Keep the bright side up,' said Packy.

'It makes it all the worse marrying your mother,' said Primrose.

'O Nugent,' said Mrs McMenamin, 'you'll be the death of me.'

'And what's more, I'm having a few darlings in for drinks at eight and I want you *all* to come – yes dear, even the little lady who thinks I'm what's-his-name, that Greek boy you know.'

He was gone, clattering his jam-jars, his stolen lilac already wilting on the counter, bells echoing in all their heads. Dr Dargan came up muttering, 'I'll have to get rid of this rubbish,' and bundled up the blossoms for the dust-bin.

'I don't believe it,' said Mrs McMenamin.

'Wonders will never cease,' said Packy.

'I forgot to ask him about the elephants,' said Thomas.

'We're not going,' said Roddy.

'Why,' said Primrose, 'I've never had drinks with a man that married his mother.'

'It'll be cup,' said Mrs McMenamin, 'cup made of cider and meths.'

'It'd drive us all mad,' said Thomas. 'I once knew a fellow who drank meths and he ended up thinking he was a tram, passengers and all. He emigrated to Hong Kong and turned into a rickshaw.'

'What's the address?' said Primrose, and began to sing. But the lark seemed to have a cold and Thomas said, 'For Christ's sake shut up or go up to the Zoo. Roddy there'll run you up.'

III

Of course they went to Nugent App's, but not before Packy had attempted to swing from a chandelier in a high-class restaurant and got them put out. Roddy said that something seemed to have got into Packy that night and Thomas said 'Drink.' Mrs McMenamin said that he certainly did not seem to be himself, and Primrose six times expressed the view that the fellow was not quite right in the head. When she opened her mouth to say this a seventh time, Packy took her hand lovingly and bit it.

She was still moaning, 'He bit my hand,' when they arrived at ten o'clock in Fitzwilliam Square. App flung open the door to them and carilloned, 'Come in, come in, I've a sup taken, and I have a lovely surprise for you all, you sweet crowd of perfect ducks.' There was a greenish glitter in his eyes and Primrose whispered audibly, 'I think he's the Devil.'

The house in Fitzwilliam Square was owned by Nugent App, or jointly by App and Leah, or perhaps only by Leah, no-one knew. Mrs McMenamin rented the top floor, the middle floors were let to girls who went out to business, App and Leah had the ground floor, and in the basement lived two aging young men of reserved disposition referred to by App as Dot and Carry. Occasionally he would go downstairs and harangue them about the decline in the marriage rate, the joys of conjugal love, and their duty to the Nation. App had never squashed the yarn that years ago in Seville he had gotten a gipsy with child and in moments of exceptional sentiment he would sob about his little Juanito.

'Come along my darlings,' screeched App, 'you'll be thrilled.'

The room was littered with very young men and women. There was a sound like the humming of bees as they wooed each other daringly and asexually. Some of them held glasses containing an amberish liquid. In a corner an interesting figure was whisking ferociously and at random in several huge glass jugs. It was Leah. She wore a very low-cut gown that hung perfectly vertical from her large yellow shoulders. Her powderless face was wounded with lipstick, and on her head she carried an enormous blonde wig.

'O God, it's the Cup,' said Mrs McMenamin.

'Let me out of here,' howled Thomas, but App clutched him by the shoulder so powerfully that he froze in motion, one leg lifted, manic horror on his face.

'Silence,' yodelled App. The bees stopped. 'I want you,' App began, 'I want you all to know and love each other – here are Thomas whose divine work you all know, and Rose who is something more in my life than a mere tenant, and Packy who handles all our little legal difficulties, and Roddy who's an Old Faithful, and this bewitching creature who thinks I married my mother, called Violet or Jasmine or something – and these,' he swung his fine white hand around the room, 'these are some of my Past Pupils, grand boys and girls from the Top Schools of Ireland who never forget their Dear Old Teacher who taught them the Art of Noble Speech, and some of them in the theatre themselves now, the dears.'

'In the Name of Suffering –' moaned Thomas.

'You don't have to drink the Cup,' hissed App.

'Over by the window-seat with you all and I'll bring you Jameson Ten and Cork Gin and Pernod. I fecked masses of bottles at darling Birdie Bernstein's the other night. One by one out to Dollie Finch's car. O what a night! And we had champagne at Birdie's!'

'Birdie Bernstein,' said Thomas laying about him to the window-seat, 'Dollie Finch.'

'Dollie Finch,' said Mrs McMenamin, joining him, 'Birdie Bernstein.'

'Birdie Bernstein was once bitten on the behind by a police-dog,' said Packy, taking the last place on the window-seat.

App arranged bottles and glasses on a too-small table. Roddy sat at the feet of Mrs McMenamin and gloomed at her. Primrose squatted against Packy's knee and pretended she didn't feel the deliberate pressure on her spine.

'Dollie Finch,' said Packy, 'once stole a police-car.'

'A very fine woman,' said Thomas.

App had taken up his position by the mantelpiece on which there were signed photographs of Queen Marie of Rumania, Ivor Novello, Mistinguett, and Alfred Byrne, T. D., many times Lord Mayor of Dublin. Already that night App had lost his temper twice explaining to the Past Pupils who these people were.

'Leah,' crooned App, 'you know everybody.'

'I do not,' she growled.

'Of course you do,' he gonged. 'All except Buttercup there who thinks you're my mammy.'

'Let me at her,' Leah said absently. She did not move. Whisking, whisking, staring straight ahead at a photograph of Nugent App in a leopard-skin loin-cloth.

'Tell me App,' said Thomas, above the humming of the Past Pupils, 'where were you born?'

'Now it's funny you should ask me that. I remember Jean Cocteau asking me exactly the same question when I was a very young man in Paris and I said "Why do you ask?" and he said "Because you have a face, not English, but *vraiment celtique*" and after that he took me to see Mistinguett . . .'

'Mistinguett me granny,' said Thomas. 'Where were you born?'

'And she said practically the same thing and I said of course I'm not English but Irish, of Cornish and Manx extraction . . .'

'Where were you born?' said Thomas, minatory.

'As a matter of fact I was born on the Liverpool boat so I could claim to be English if I wanted to, but not after 1916 and all that. I remember Douglas Hyde saying to me – An Chraoibhinn Aoibhinn you know – saying to me in his lovely garden at French Park, "*A Nugent a thaisge*, you have chosen the good portion".'

'Jean Cocteau,' said Thomas, stupefied. 'Mistinguett, Douglas Hyde.'

'Those murals by Cocteau in the French Church at Leicester Square,' said Packy authoritatively, 'are very sound.'

'Birdie Bernstein, Dollie Finch,' said Thomas.

The humming seemed to have grown louder, and it was some time before anyone grasped that a new burden had been struck up, a harsh yap-gulp sound, some animal in labour perhaps, but devastatingly human. For it was Leah struggling with tears such as Titanesses weep, and she advanced like a tank on Nugent App.

'Goats and monkeys,' she pronounced carefully. The bees stopped. 'All the perfumes of Arabia could not sweeten that little soul.'

'She's drunk,' said App amiably.

'App,' she said, 'you are a traitor to your peoples.'

'Go to bed, cream-in-my-coffee,' said App. He had begun to shake.

'App,' he said, 'you are a Jew and you were born in the Ghetto of Warsaw where your poppa and momma died and your brother Jan was shot by the pig-Germans.'

'Aaaaaah,' moaned App. 'What a scene before the Past Pupils.'

'App,' she said, 'it is you that are drunk. You are drunk from lying and cheating and the fear that I'll die and leave you alone for a dirty old man.'

'Stop.'

'I am going to study the Works of Shakespeare,' she said. 'There I will find peace,' and she moved from the room like a mobile pillar.

'A decenter woman never shat,' said Thomas.

She did so decently before entering into her cave for peace. She locked the door and she stuffed a sheep-skin rug into the slit between her and the world of App. She did not have to shut the window. Carefully, with massive movements, she lit her gas-fire. She poured out a tumbler of gin, and with a great sigh-grunt settled herself in her basket-chair. She adjusted herself to pick up the Works of Shakespeare, opened them and read,

> The blind mole casts
> Copp'd hills towards heaven, to tell the earth is throng'd
> By man's oppression; and the poor worm doth die for't.

The mammoth tears began again. 'Man's oppression,' she groaned. She trundled to her desk and took out her bottle of aspirin. Ten, maybe fifteen, she swallowed and drowned them in gin. She turned off the gas-fire, turned it on again, did not light it. She took more gin, and the gathering fumes were mild as Abraham leaned to clasp this child to his bosom. She was dropping off into a muddled dream of Nugent App and he was saying, *Liebchen*, *Liebchen*, love, love, love will conquer all.

'Cross old Leah,' App was saying. 'I'd better go and fetch her.'

'Surely,' said Thomas, 'I'm convinced she'd know far more about elephants than you.'

'You're a renegade,' said Packy sternly.

'She's too good for you,' said Primrose, 'even if she's your mother.'

'It's not quite the same when you lose your mother,' said Mrs McMenamin.

The Past Pupils were in each others arms, boy and girl curled tranquilly together, passionless, silent, out of this world. A skinny archangel shot up and ever-conscious of the Art of Noble Speech, trumpeted, 'Gas'.

App skiltered to the door, and they heard the knocking and the howls of the damned.

'She turned on the gas,' said Thomas. 'She turned on the gas.'

'Get up to bed, Rose,' said Roddy.

'I couldn't possibly appear at an inquest,' said Packy.

'A man that married his mother,' said Primrose.

'It's a black day for me,' said Thomas.

But when the knocking and the howling had ceased and like cattle they bumped out to the hall, it was Leah, puce, mad-eyed, vomiting, who held App in her arms as he fought against dying from the loss of his mother-wife. Perhaps some sliver of memory about Belsen or Buchenwald had gashed Leah's stupor, and on her forehead was an ugly cross where she'd hit herself turning off the gas.

'The poor bastard,' said Thomas.

The phone rang. Roddy answered. It was Dollie Finch and she said she was coming round. He put the phone down and rang for a doctor and a priest, for App, though of no known religion, had been seen on Sundays in the Pro-Cathedral. He remembered to ring for a Gárda only after Birdie Bernstein had rung up to say she was coming round.

An ambulance took away Leah and App. The Gárda took statements. The Past Pupils took taxis home. Thomas, Rose, Packy, Primrose and Roddy, took the remaining drink upstairs.

But the late dawn saw them distributed each to his own

nightmare. Packy took Primrose with him, and at six o'clock she was saying, 'One hour together and you're asleep.'

'Down, Primrose, down,' said Packy. Roddy watched by the bed of Mrs McMenamin and noted greedily the fragments of her sleep-talk. 'It's not quite the same,' she said loudly, and snored. 'Heart love gas,' she mumbled, and whistled. 'I'll sing a hymn to Mary,' she hummed, and snorted. He had never felt nearer to her.

And in his room Thomas had a drink of Scotch and infinitely weary sat down to his typewriter. His head was full of beasts, of drunken elephants, and performing bears, and mice and poodles and goats and monkeys, and poor human trash.

from *Yarns*, 1977

Bank Holiday

JOHN McGAHERN

It had been unusual weather, hot for weeks, and the white morning mist above the river, making ghostly the figures crossing the metal bridge, seemed a certain promise that the good weather was going to last beyond the holiday. All week in the Department he had heard the girls talking of going down the country, of the ocean, and the dances in the carnival marquees. Already, across the river, queues were forming for the buses that went to the sea – Howth, Dollymount, Malahide. He, Patrick McDonough, had no plans for the holiday, other than to walk about the city, or maybe to go out into the mountains later. He felt a certain elation of being loose in the morning, as if in space. The solid sound of his walking shoes on the pavement seemed to belong to someone else, to be going elsewhere.

A year ago he had spent this holiday in the country, among the rooms and fields and stone walls he had grown up with, as he had spent it every year going back many years. His mother was still living, his father had died the previous February. The cruellest thing about that last holiday was to watch her come into the house speaking to his father of something she had noticed in the yard – a big bullfinch feeding on the wild strawberries of the bank, rust spreading in the iron of one of the sheds – and then to see her realize in the midst of speech that her old partner of the guaranteed responses was no longer there. They had been close. His father had continued to indulge her once great good looks long after they had disappeared.

That last holiday he had asked his mother to come and live with him in the city, but she had refused without giving it serious thought. 'I'd be only in the way up there. I could never fit in with their ways now.' He had gone down to see her as often as he was able to after that, which was most weekends, and had paid a local woman to look in on her every day. Soon he saw that his visits no longer excited her. She had even lost interest in most of the things around her, and whenever that interest briefly gleamed she turned not to him but to his dead father. When pneumonia took her in a couple of days just before Christmas, and her body was put down beside her husband's in Aughawillian churchyard, he was almost glad. The natural wind now blew directly on him.

He sold the house and lands. The land had been rich enough to send him away to college, not rich enough to bring him back other than on holiday, and now this holiday was the first such in years that he had nowhere in particular to go, no one special to see, nothing much to do. As well as the dangerous elation this sense of freedom gave, he looked on it with some of the cold apprehension of an experiment.

Instead of continuing on down the quays, he crossed to the low granite wall above the river, and stayed a long time staring down through the vaporous mist at the frenzy and filth of the low tide. He could have stood mindlessly there for most of the morning but he pulled imself away and continued on down the quays until he turned into Webb's Bookshop.

The floor in Webb's had been freshly sprinkled and swept, but it was dark within after the river light. He went from stack to stack among the second-hands until he came on a book that caught his interest, and he began to read. He stood there a long time until he was disturbed by the brown-overalled manager speaking by his side.

'Would you be interested in buying the book, sir? We could do something perhaps about the price. The books in this stack have been here a long time.' He held a duster in his hand, some feathers tied round the tip of a cane.

'I was just looking.'

The manager moved away, flicking the feathers along a row of spines in a gesture of annoyance. The spell was ended, but it was fair enough: the shop had to sell books, and he knew that if he bought the book it was unlikely that he would ever give it the same attention again. He moved to the next stack, not wanting to appear driven from the shop. He pretended to inspect other volumes. He lifted and put down *The Wooing of Elisabeth McCrum*, examining other books cursorily, all the time moving towards the door. It was no longer pleasant to remain. He tried to ignore the manager's stare as he went out, to find himself in blinding sunshine on the pavement. The mist had completely lifted. The day was uncomfortably hot. His early excitement and sense of freedom had disappeared.

Afterwards he was to go over the little incident in the bookshop. If it had not happened would he have just ventured again out into the day, found the city too hot for walking, taken a train to Bray as he thought he might and walked all day in the mountains until he was dog-tired and hungry? Or was this sort of let-down the inescapable end of the kind of elation he had felt walking to the river in the early morning? He would never know. What he did know was that once outside the bookshop he no longer felt like going anywhere and he started to retrace his steps back to where he lived, buying a newspaper on the way. When he opened the door a telegram was lying on the floor of the hallway.

It was signed 'Mary Kelleher', a name he didn't know. It seemed that a very old friend, James White, who worked for the Tourist Board in New York, had given her his name. There was a number to call.

He put it aside to sit and read through the newspaper, but he knew by the continuing awareness of the telegram on the table that he would call. He was now too restless to want to remain alone.

James White and he had met when they were both young civil servants, White slightly the older – though they both seemed the same age now – the better read, the more forthright, the more sociable. They met at eight-thirty on the Friday night of every week for several years, the evening interrupted only by holidays and illnesses, proof against girlfriends, and later wives, ended only by White's transfer abroad. They met in bars, changing only when they became known to the barmen or regulars, and in danger of losing their anonymity. They talked about ideas, books, 'the human situation', and 'reality and consciousness' often surfaced with the second or third pint. Now he could hardly remember a sentence from those hundreds of evenings. What he did remember was a barman's face, white hair drawn over baldness, an avid follower of Christy Ring; a clock, a spiral iron staircase to the

Gents, the cold of marble on the wristbone, footsteps passing outside in summer, the sound of heavy rain falling before closing time. The few times they had met in recent years they had both spoken of nothing but people and happenings, as if those early meetings were some deep embarrassment: that they had leaned on them too heavily once and were now like lost strength.

He rang. The number was that of a small hotel on the quays. Mary Kelleher answered. He invited her to lunch and they arranged to meet in the hotel foyer. He walked to the hotel, and as he walked he felt again the heady, unreal feeling of moving in an unblemished morning, though it was now past midday.

When she rose to meet him in the foyer, he saw that she was as tall as he. A red kerchief with polka dots bound her blonde hair. She was too strong boned to be beautiful but her face and skin glowed. They talked about James White. She had met him at a party in New York. 'He said that I must meet you if I was going to Dublin. I was about to check out of the hotel when you rang.' She had relations in Dundalk that she intended to look up and Trinity College had manuscripts she wanted to see. They walked up Dame Street and round by the Trinity Railings to the restaurant he had picked in Lincoln Place. She was from Mount Vernon, New York, but had been living in Chicago, finishing her doctorate in medieval poetry at the University of Chicago. There were very pale hairs on the brown skin of her legs and her leather sandals slapped as she walked. When she turned her face to his, he could see a silver locket below the line of the cotton dress.

Bernardo's door was open on to the street, and all but two of the tables were empty.

'Everybody's out of town for the holiday. We have the place to ourselves.' They were given a table for four just inside the door. They ordered the same things, melon with Parma ham, veal Milanese, a carafe of chilled white wine. He urged her to have more, to try the raspberries in season, the cream cake, but she ate carefully and would not be persuaded.

'Do you come here often?' she asked.

'Often enough. I work near here, round the corner, in Kildare Street. An old civil servant.'

'You don't look the part at all, but James White did say you worked in the civil service. He said you were quite high up,' she smiled teasingly. 'What do you do?'

'Nothing as exciting as medieval poetry. I deal in law, industrial law in particular.'

'I could imagine that to be quite exciting.'

'Interesting maybe, but mostly it's a job – like any other.'

'Do you live in the city, or outside?'

'Very near here. I can walk most places, even walk to work.' And when he saw her hesitate, as if she wanted to ask something and did not think it right, he added, 'I have a flat. I live by myself there, though I was married once.'

'Are you divorced? Or am I allowed to ask that?'

'Of course you are. Divorce isn't allowed in this country. We are separated. For something like twenty years now we haven't laid eyes on one another. And you? Do you have a husband or friend?' he changed the subject.

'Yes. Someone I met at college, but we have agreed to separate for a time.'

There was no silence or unease. Their interest in one another already far outran their knowledge. She offered to split the bill but he refused.

'Thanks for the lunch, the company,' she said as they faced one another outside the restaurant.

'It was a pleasure,' and then he hesitated and asked, 'What are you doing for the afternoon?' not wanting to see this flow that was between them checked, though he knew to follow it was hardly wise.

'I was going to check tomorrow's trains to Dundalk.'

'We could do that at Westland Row around the corner. I was wondering if you'd be interested in going out to the sea where the world and its mother is in this weather?'

'I'd love to,' she said simply.

It was with a certain relief that he paid the taxi at the Bull Wall. Lately the luxury and convenience of a taxi had become for him the privilege of being no longer young, of being cut off from the people he had come from, and this was exasperated by the glowing young woman by his side, her eager responses to each view he pointed out, including the wired-down palms along the front.

'They look so funny. Why is it done?'

'It's simple. So that they will not be blown away in storms. They are not natural to this climate.'

He took off his tie and jacket as they crossed the planks of the wooden bridge, its legs long and stork-like in the retreated tide. The rocks that sloped down to the sea from the Wall were crowded with people, most of them in bathing costumes, reading, listening to transistors, playing cards, staring out to sea, where three tankers appeared to be nailed down in the milky distance. The caps of the stronger swimmers bobbed far out. Others floated on their backs close to the rocks, crawled in sharp bursts, breast-stroked heavily up and down a parallel line, blowing like walruses as they trod water.

'I used to swim off these rocks once. I liked going in off the rocks because I've always hated getting sand between my toes. Those lower rocks get covered at full tide. You can see the tidal line by the colour.'

'Don't you swim anymore?'

'I haven't in years.'

'If I had a costume I wouldn't mind going in.'

'I think you'd find it cold.'

She told him of how she used to go out to the ocean at the Hamptons with her father, her four brothers, their black sheep Uncle John who had made a fortune in scrap metal and was extremely lecherous. She laughed as she recounted one of Uncle John's adventures with an English lady.

When they reached the end of the Wall, they went down to the Strand, but it was so crowded that they had to pick their way through. They moved out to where there were fewer people along the tide's edge. It was there that she decided to wade in the water, and he offered to hold her sandals. As he walked with her sandals, a phrase came without warning from the book he had been reading in Webb's: 'What is he doing with his life, we say: and our judgement makes up for the failure to realize sympathetically the natural process of living.' He must indeed be atrophied if a casual phrase could have more presence for him than this beautiful young woman, and the sea, and the day. The dark blue mass of Howth faced the motionless ships on the horizon, seemed to be even pushing them back.

'Oh, it's cold,' she shivered as she came out of the water, and reached for her sandals.

'Even in heatwaves the sea is cold in Ireland. That's Howth ahead – where Maud Gonne waited at the station as Pallas Athena.' He reached for his role as tourist guide.

'I know that line,' she said and quoted the verse. 'Has all that gone from Dublin?'

'In what way?'

'Are there . . . poets . . . still?'

'Are there poets?' he laughed out loud. 'They say the standing army of poets never falls below ten thousand in this unfortunate country.'

'Why unfortunate?' she said quickly.

'They create no wealth. They are greedy and demanding. They hold themselves in very high opinion. Ten centuries ago there was a national convocation, an attempt to limit their powers and numbers.'

'Wasn't it called *Drum* something?'

'*Drum Ceat*,' he added, made uneasy by his own attack.

'But don't you feel that they have a function – beyond wealth?' she pursued.

'What function?'

'That they sing the tired rowers to the hidden shore?'

'Not in the numbers we possess here, one singing down the other. But maybe I'm unkind. There are a few.'

'Are these poets to be seen?'

'They can't even be hidden. Tomorrow evening I could show you some of the pubs they frequent. Would you like that?'

'I'd like that very much,' she said, and took his hand. A whole day was secured. The crowds hadn't started to head home yet, and they travelled back to the city on a nearly empty bus.

'What will you do for the rest of the evening?'

'There's some work I may look at. And you? What will you do?'

'I think I'll rest. Unpack, read a bit,' she smiled as she raised her hand.

He walked slowly back, everything changed by the petty confrontation in Webb's, the return to the flat, the telegram in the hallway. If he had not come back, she would be in Dundalk by now, and he would be thinking about finding a hotel for the night somewhere round Rathdrum. In the flat, he went through notes that he had made in preparation for a meeting he had with the Minister the coming week. They concerned an obscure section of the Industries Act. Though they were notes he had made himself he found them extremely tedious, and there came on him a restlessness like that which sometimes heralds illness. He felt like going out to a cinema or bar, but knew that what he really wanted to do was to ring Mary Kelleher. If he had learned anything over the years it was the habit of discipline. Tomorrow would bring itself. He would wait for it if necessary with his mind resolutely fixed on its own blankness, as a person prays after fervour has died.

'Section 13, paragraph 4, states clearly that in the event of confrontation or disagreement . . .' he began to write.

The dress of forest green she was wearing when she came down to the lobby the next evening caught his breath; it was shirtwaisted, belling out. A blue ribbon hung casually from her fair hair behind.

'You look marvellous.'

The Sunday streets were empty, and the stones gave out a dull heat. They walked slowly, loitering at some shop windows. The doors of all the bars were open, O'Neills and the International and the Olde Stand, but they were mostly empty within. There was a sense of a cool dark waiting in Mooney's, a barman arranging ashtrays on the marble. They ordered an assortment of sandwiches. It was pleasant to sit in the comparative darkness, and eat and sip and watch the street, and to hear in the silence footsteps going up and down Grafton Street.

It was into this quiet flow of the evening that the poet came, a large man, agitated, without jacket, the shirt open, his thumbs hooked in braces that held up a pair of sagging trousers, a brown hat pushed far back on his head. Coughing harshly and pushing the chair around, he sat at the next table.

'Don't look around,' McDonough leaned forward to say.

'Why?'

'He'll join us if we catch his eye.'

'Who is he?'

'A poet.'

'He doesn't look like one.'

'That should be in his favour. All the younger clerks that work in my place nowadays look like poets. He is the best we have. He's the star of the place across the road. He's practically resident there. He must have been thrown out.'

The potboy in his short white coat came over to the poet's table and waited impassively for the order.

'A Powers,' the order came in a hoarse, rhythmical voice. 'A large Powers and a pint of Bass.'

There was more sharp coughing, a scraping of feet, a sigh, muttering, a word that could have been a prayer or a curse. His agitated presence had more the sound of a crowd than the single person sitting in a chair. After the potboy brought the drinks and was paid, the poet swung one leg vigorously over the other, and with folded arms faced away towards the empty doorway. Then, as suddenly, he was standing in front of them. He had his hand out. There were coins in the hand.

'McDonough,' he called hoarsely, thrusting his palm forward. 'Will you get me a packet of Ci-tanes from across the road?' he mispronounced the brand of French cigarettes so violently that his meaning was far from clear.

'You mean the cigarettes?'

'*Ci*-tanes,' he called hoarsely again. 'French fags. Twenty. I'm giving you the money.'

'Why don't you get them here?'

'They don't have them here.'

'Why don't you hop across yourself?'

'I'm barred,' he said dramatically. 'They're a crowd of ignorant, bloody apes over there.'

'All right. I'll get them for you.' He took the coins but instead of rising and crossing the road he called the potboy.

'Would you cross the road for twenty Gitanes for me, Jimmy? I'd cross myself but I'm with company,' and he added a large tip of his own to the coins the poet had handed over.

'It's against the rules, sir.'

'I know, but I'd consider it a favour,' and they both looked towards the barman behind the counter, who had been following every word and move of the confrontation. The barman nodded that it was all right, and immediately bent his head down to whatever he was doing beneath the level of the counter, as if to disown his acquiescence.

Jimmy crossed, was back in a moment with the blue packet.

'You're a cute hoar, McDonough. You're a mediocrity. It's no wonder you get on so well in the world,' the poet burst out in a wild fury as he was handed the packet, and he finished his drinks in a few violent gulps, and stalked out, muttering and coughing.

'That's just incredible,' she said.

'Why?'

'You buy the man his cigarettes, and then get blown out of it. I don't understand it.'

'It wasn't the cigarettes he wanted.'

'Well, what did he want?'

'Reassurance, maybe, that he still had power, was loved and wanted after having been turfed out across the way. I slithered round it by getting Jimmy here to go over. That's why I was lambasted. He must have done something outrageous to have been barred. He's a tin god there. Maybe I should have gone over after all.'

'Why didn't you?'

'Vanity. I didn't want to be his messenger boy. He could go and inflate his great mouse of an ego somewhere else. To hell with him. He's always trouble.' She listened in silence as he ended. 'Wouldn't it be pleasant to be able to throw people their bones and forget it?'

'You might have to spend an awful lot of time throwing bones if the word got around,' she smiled as she sipped her glass of cider.

'Now that you've seen the star, do you still wish to cross the road and look in on the other pub?'

'I'm not sure. What else could we do?'

'We could go back to my place.'

'I'd like that. I'd much prefer to see how you live.'

'Why don't we look in across the road, have one drink if it's not too crowded,' and he added some coins to the change still on the table. 'It was very nice of them to cross for the Gitanes. They're not supposed to leave their own premises.'

The door of the bar across the way was not open, and when he pushed it a roar met them like heat. The bar was small and jammed. A red-and-blue tint from a stained glass window at the back mixed weirdly with the white lights of the bar, the light of evening from the high windows. A small fan circled helplessly overhead, its original white or yellow long turned to ochre by cigarette smoke. Hands proffered coins and notes across shoulders to the barmen behind the horeshoe counter. Pints and spirit glasses were some- how eased from hand to hand across the three-deep line of shoulders at the counter the way children that get weak are taken out of a crowd. The three barmen were so busy that they seemed to dance.

'What do you think?' he asked.

'I think we'll forget it.'

'I always feel a bit apprehensive going in there,' he admitted once they were out on the street again.

'I know. Those places are the same everywhere. For a moment I thought I was in New York at the Cedar Bar.'

'What makes them the same?'

'I don't know. Mania, egotism, vanity, aggression . . . people searching madly in a crowd for something that's never to be found in crowds.'

She was so lovely in the evening that he felt himself leaning towards her. He did not like the weakness. 'I find myself falling increasingly into an unattractive puzzlement,' he said, 'mulling over that old, useless chestnut. What *is* life?'

'It's the fact of being alive, I suppose, a duration of time, as the scholars would say,' and she smiled teasingly. 'Puzzling out what it is must be part of it as well.'

'You're too young and beautiful to be so wise.'

'That sounds a bit patronizing.'

'That's the last thing I meant it to be.'

He showed her the rooms, the large living-room with the oak table and worn red carpet, the brass fender, the white marble of the fireplace, the kitchen, the two bedrooms. He watched her go over the place, lift the sea shell off the mantelpiece, replace it differently.

'It's a lovely flat,' she said, 'though Spartan to my taste.'

'I bought the place three years ago. I disliked the idea of owning anything at first, but now I'm glad to have it. Now, would you like a drink, or perhaps some tea?'

'I'd love some tea.'

When he returned he found her thumbing through books in the weakening light.

'Do you have any of the poet's work?'

'You can have a present of this, if you like.' He reached and took a brown volume from the shelf.

'I see it's even signed,' she said as she leafed through the volume. 'For Patrick McDonough, With love', and she began to laugh.

'I helped him with something once. I doubt if he'd sign it with much love this evening.'

'Thanks,' she said as she closed the volume and placed it in her handbag. 'I'll return it. It wouldn't be right to keep it.' After several minutes of silence, she asked, 'When do you have to go back to your office?'

'Not till Tuesday. Tomorrow is a Bank Holiday.'

'And on Tuesday what do you do?'

'Routine. The Department really runs itself, though may of us think of ourselves as indispensable. In the afternoon I have to brief the Minister.'

'On what, may I ask?'

'A section of the Industries Act.'

'What is the Minister like?'

'He's all right. An opportunist, I suppose. He has energy, certainly, and the terrible Irish gift of familiarity. He first came to the fore by putting parallel bars on the back of a lorry. He did handstands and somersaults before and after speeches, to the delight of the small towns and villages. Miss Democracy thought he was wonderful and voted him in top of the poll. He's more statesmanlike now of course.'

'You don't sound as if you like him very much.'

'We're stuck with one another.'

'Were you upset when your marriage failed?' she changed.

'Naturally. In the end, there was no choice. We couldn't be in the same room together for more than a couple of minutes without fighting. I could never figure out how the fights started, but they always did.'

'Did you meet anyone else?'

'Nothing that lasted. I worked. I visited my parents until they died. Those sort of pieties are sometimes substitutes for life in this country – or life itself. We're back to the old subject and I'm talking too much.'

'No. I'm asking too many questions.'

'What'll you do now that you have your doctorate?'

'Teach. Write. Wait on tables. I don't know.'

'And your husband or friend?'

'Husband,' she said. 'We were married but it's finished. We were too young.'

'Would you like more tea, or for me to walk you back to the Clarence? . . . Or would you like to spend the night here?'

She paused for what seemed an age, and yet it could not have been more than a couple of moments.

'I'd like to spend the night here.'

He did not know how tense his waiting had been until he felt the release her words gave. It was as if blank doors had slid back and he was being allowed again into the mystery of a perpetual morning, a morning without blemish. He knew it by now to be an old con trick of nature, and that it never failed, only deepened the irony and the mystery. 'I'll be able to show you the city tomorrow. You can check out of your hotel then if you wish. And there are the two rooms . . .' he was beginning to say when she came into his arms and sealed his lips.

As he waited for her, the poet's sudden angry accusation came back. Such accusations usually came to rankle and remain long after praise had failed, but not this evening. He turned it over as he might a problem that there seemed no way round, and let it drop. If it was true, there was very little that could be done about it now. It was in turn replaced by the phrase that had come to him earlier by the sea's edge; and had he not seen love in the person of his old mother reduced to noticing things about a farmyard?

'I hope you're not puzzling over something like "life" again,' a teasing call came from the bedroom.

'No. Not this time.' He rose to join her.

In the morning they had coffee and toast in the sunlit kitchen with the expectation of the whole day waiting on them. Then they walked in the empty streets of the city, looked through the Green before going to the hotel to bring her things back to the flat.

The following days were so easy that the only anxiety could be its total absence. The days were heightened by the luxury and pleasure of private evenings, the meals she cooked that were perfection, the good wine he bought, the flowers; desire that was never turned aside or exasperated by difficulty.

At the end of the holiday, he had to go back to the office, and she put off the Dundalk visit and began to go to the Trinity Library. Many people were not back in the office, and he was able to work without interruption for the whole of the first morning. What he had to do was to isolate the relevant parts of the section and reduce them to a few simple sentences.

At the afternoon meeting the Minister was the more nervous. He was tall and muscular, small blue eyes and thick red hair, fifteen years the younger man, with a habit of continually touching anybody close to him that told of the large family he grew up in. They went over and over the few sentences he had prepared until the Minister had them by rote. He was appearing on television that night and was extremely apprehensive.

'Good man,' he grasped McDonough's shoulder with relief when they finished. 'One of these evenings before long you must come out and have a bite with us and meet the hen and chickens.'

'I'll be glad to. And good luck on the TV. I'll be watching.'

'I'll need all the luck I can get. That bitch of an interviewer hates my guts.'

They watched the television debate together in the flat that evening. The Minister had reason to be apprehensive. He was under attack from the beginning but bludgeoning his way. As he watched, McDonough wondered if his work had been necessary at all. He could hardly discern his few sentences beneath the weight of the Minister's phrases. 'I emphatically state . . . I categorically deny . . . I say without any equivocation whatsoever . . . Having consulted the best available opinions in the matter,' (which were presumably McDonough's own).

'What did you think?' he asked when he switched off the set.

'He was almost touching,' she said carefully. 'Amateurish maybe. His counterpart in the States might be no better, but he certainly would have to be more polished.'

'He was good at handstands and somersaults once,' he said, surprised at his own sense of disappointment. 'I've become almost fond of him. Sometimes I wish we had better people. They'll all tell him he did powerfully. What'll we do? Would you like to go for a quick walk?'

'Why don't we,' she reached for her cardigan.

Two days later she went to Dundalk, and it wasn't certain how long she intended to remain there. 'I guess I've come so far that they'll expect me to stay over the weekend.'

'You must please yourself. You have a key. I'll not be going anywhere.'

They had come together so easily that the days together seemed like a marriage without any of the apprehension or drama of a ceremony.

When he was young he had desired too much, wanted too much, dreaded and feared too much, and so spread his own fear. Now that he was close to losing everything – was in the direct path of the wind – it was little short of amazing that he should come on this extraordinary breathing space.

Almost in disbelief he went back in reflection to the one love of his life, a love that was pure suffering. In a hotel bedroom in another city, unable to sleep by her side, he had risen and dressed. He had paused before leaving the room to gaze on the even breathing of her sleep. All that breath had to do was frame one word, and a whole world of happiness would be given, but it was forever withheld. He had walked the morning streets until circling back to the hotel he came on a market that was just opening and bought a large bunch of grapes. The grapes were very small and turning yellow and still damp, and were of incredible sweetness. She was just waking when he came back into the room and had not missed him. They ate the grapes on the coverlid and each time she lifted the small bunches to her mouth he remembered the dark of her armpits. He ached to touch her but everything seemed to be so fragile between them that he was afraid to even stir. It seemed that any small movement now could bring calamity. Then, laughing, she blew grape seeds in his face and, reaching out her arms, drew him down. She had wanted their last day together to be pleasant. She was marrying another man. Later he remembered running between airport gates looking for flights that had all departed.

It was eerie to set down those days beside the days that had just gone by, call them by the same name. How slowly those days had moved, as if waiting for something to begin: now all the days were speeding, slipping silently by like air.

Two evenings later, when he let himself into the flat and found Mary Kelleher there, it was as if she had never been away.

'You didn't expect me back so soon?'

'I thought you'd still be in Dundalk, but I'm glad, I'm delighted.' He took her in his arms.

'I had as much of Dundalk as I wanted, and I missed you.'

'How did it go?'

'It was all right. The cousins were nice. They had a small house, crammed with things – religious pictures, furniture, photos. There was hardly place to move. Everything they did was so careful, so measured out. After a while I felt I could hardly breathe. They did everything they possibly could to make me welcome. I read the poems at last,' she put the book with the brown cover on the table. 'I read them again on the train coming back. I loved them.'

'I've long suspected that those very pure love sonnets are all addressed to himself,' McDonough said. 'That was how the "ignorant bloody apes and mediocritics" could be all short-circuited.'

'Some are very funny.'

'I'm so glad you liked them. I've lived with some of them for years. Would you like to go out to eat? Say, to Bernardo's?' he asked.

'I'd much prefer to stay home. I've already looked in the fridge. We can rustle something up.'

That weekend they went together for the long walk in the mountains that he had intended to take the day they met. They stopped for a drink and sandwiches in a pub near Blessington just before two o'clock, and there they decided to press on to Rathdrum and stay the night in the hotel rather than turn back into the city.

It was over dinner in the near empty hotel dining-room that he asked if she would consider marrying him. 'There's much against it. I am fifty. You would have to try to settle here, where you'll be a stranger,' and he went on to say that what he had already was more than he ever expected, that he was content to let it be, but if she wanted more then it was there.

'I thought that you couldn't be married here,' her tone was affectionate.

'I meant it in everything but name, and even that can be arranged if you want it enough.'

'How?'

'With money. An outside divorce. The marriage in some other country. The States, for instance.'

'Can't you see that I already love you? That it doesn't matter? I was half-teasing. You looked so serious.'

'I am serious. I want it to be clear.'

'It is clear and I am glad – and very grateful.'

They agreed that she would spend one week longer here in Dublin than she had planned. At Christmas he would go to New York for a week. She would have obtained her doctorate by then. James White would be surprised. There were no serious complications in sight. They were so tired and happy that it was as if they were already in possession of endless quantities of time and money.

from *High Ground*, 1985